Jimmy Quinn

Jimmy Quinn

Richard VanDeWeghe

Deeds Publishing | Atlanta

Published by Deeds Publishing in Athens, GA
www.deedspublishing.com

Printed in The United States of America

Cover design and text layout by Mark Babcock.
Cover photo courtesy of Special Collections, Traverse Area District Library.

ISBN 978-1-947309-29-6

Books are available in quantity for promotional or premium use. For information, email info@deedspublishing.com.

First Edition, 2018

10 9 8 7 6 5 4 3 2 1

Preface

WRITING HISTORICAL FICTION DEMANDS THAT THE WRITERS
research provide verisimilitude and a credible account of historical fact. It also demands the artistic bent needed to bring a
story to life—the storyteller must infuse characters with goals
and needs, and plot with conflict to be resolved in the arc of the
narrative. But historical fiction contains within its very name
a tension between history and fiction. British historical fiction
writer Hilary Mantel illuminated this uneasy relationship in a
Guardian blog when she asked: Does historical fiction have a
duty to be historically accurate?

> *[I]f we start using words like "duty" and "responsibility"*
> *about historical fiction — or any fiction — we're in danger of*
> *leaching all the vigour out of it with a sense of worthiness.*
> *A novelist has no real duty to anything except the story he or*
> *she is creating, the characters who inhabit it, and whatever*
> *view of the world he or she is offering with the novel's*
> *ending.* [1]

As historical fiction, *Jimmy Quinn* exemplifies this tension
between story and history. On the one hand, it is an imagined
story of a human relationship that develops over a period of

nearly two years. But that story is directly affected by a real historical event that occurs during the same time period—the closing of the farm program at the Traverse City State Hospital in northern Michigan during the 1950's. Readers will recognize familiar places and events in the novel that are historically accurate. They will also encounter elements of that history that are imagined or altered for the sake of the story.

For example, it is true that the farm program at the Traverse City State Hospital existed for decades, was immensely successful, and closed down in the 1950's. In *Jimmy Quinn*, the closing of the farm operation spans only two years, while the actual historical process took eight years by most accounts. This discrepancy underscores the difference between story and history. Historical fiction always leaves room for dispute about 'what actually happened" back then.

The characters are fictitious, with two exceptions. One, there appear references to the historical figure who founded the hospital, Dr. James Decker Munson; two, one patient (her real name has been lost to history), whose condition included swallowing various objects, also appears. The actual objects themselves have been preserved in the historical archives at the Traverse Area District Library (see the Additional Reading).

---

1. https://www.theguardian.com/books/booksblog/2014/mar/19/
how-true-should-historical-fiction-be-mantel-andrew-miller-gregory (accessed December 12, 2017).

CHAPTER ONE

The Artistic & the Despicable

DELIGHT — OR DISQUIET — ALWAYS CAME WITH THE UNEX-
pected, and the unexpected came daily.

So it was that sunny September morning as I left my room
in Cottage 36, my assigned home until other arrangements
would be made. I rounded the corner on Blue Drive and walked
alongside the massive buff-colored brick wing of Building 50
toward Old Central, the main entrance. Somewhere above me, I
heard a male voice on a crackly radio, singing. I looked up to the
third floor, the women's ward in the west wing of that immense
structure. Moving out on the lawn for a better look, I spied the
open window. A female patient — baggy green-and-white polka
dot shirt — stood behind the metal grate. She held a radio, its
black cord dangling. She pressed the radio to the screen and
waved to me as the singer's voice drifted down:

Love's a gentle gen'rous passion.
Source of all sublime delight.

She looked to her right, then disappeared momentarily. The
male singer's voice disappeared too. When she returned, the
radio was gone. She put her hands on the metal window grate,

and, in her screechy, loud voice, she squawked out the lyrics herself:

Two fond hearts in one unite!
Two fond hearts in one unite!

Then she put her thumbs in her ears, stuck out her tongue, and wiggled her fingers at me. I waved back as if to say hello.

Needs voice lessons, I thought.

Back to the sidewalk beneath the building and out of sight of the woman above, I continued on my way. I checked my wristwatch. I would be early for the meeting.

I turned yet another corner, spotted two black and white city police cars parked behind one another on the circle drive in front of the double-door entrance to Old Central.

What's this all about? I thought.

A handful of patients gathered by the police cars. One man in blue overalls paced frantically back and forth from one car to the other, muttering "Oh, Boy, Oh, Boy." He waved his arms above his head as if to warn others to keep their distance. Two women, worn purses lying next to them on the ground and arms around each other, stood stock still, staring in silence. A third poked under one of the police cars with a long tree branch. She stood abruptly when I approached, waved an ominous finger my way.

"Someone's dead, sure," she shouted. "Dead and burned up and the cops are gonna come and take us all to jail, sure."

"Oh, Boy," said the pacer. "Oh, Boy. Oh, Boy. Not me. I didn't killed no one. I swear." He pounded a fist into a hand.

Two attendants swept through the main doors toward the group of patients.

One shouted, "C'mon now, get away from there, you." The other picked up purses and put them in the women's arms. He pulled the tree limb from the woman poking under the police car and tossed it on the lawn.

"Come on, ladies and gentlemen, time to get on your way," he said.

The crowd dispersed. As she walked away, the tree-branch woman looked back toward the attendants standing beside the police cars.

"Dead for sure!" she hissed. "Dead and all burned up!"

I turned my back on the street scene, entered through the wide, ornately carved doors of the main entrance.

Dr. Spencer's office was on the second floor—top of the broad stairs on the right. On either side of the stairs two paintings were perched on art pedestals. In one, a black and white springer spaniel stood in a field of sunflowers. Poised to retrieve. In the other, a green river wound through a forest scene. On a bench next to this one sat a 70-ish-year-old gentleman in a rumpled brown suit. His necktie sported bright red roses on blue silk. I paused before the painting of the dog.

"Good morning, Mister," he said, rising slowly, one hand on his lower back for support.

"This is my own art, Mister," he began. "I did it all. This one is my Uncle Billy and Auntie Mary's dog where they live at. And this other one is where I lived in Alpena before I had to come live here, before the sickness in my head set in."

"Your art is very nice," I said. "The sunflowers remind me of autumn."

He clapped his hands in delight.

"Yes sirree, bob," he beamed. "That's just what they looked

3

like the day I left there. I brought all my art supplies with me to here. Nurse Greenfield lets me put my paintings here where visitors will see them. This is my art show, see."

"I see. You're good."

"Yeah. Nurse Greenfield said I ought to sign my paintings so I put my name on them now. See, right there."

He pointed to the lower-right corner of the forest scene. *William.*

"That's me, Mister. William R. Lowry, William for short."

I extended my hand and he shook it. "Thank you for the art tour, William."

"Okay. Anytime." He returned to his bench as I ascended the stairs. At the top of the stairs, I glanced back down. Hands on his knees, he sat erect, waiting.

I pulled my diary out of my knapsack.

September 6, 1952:

· Female patient singing to the world from a third-floor window.

· Male patient displaying his original water colors in his solo art show.

· N.B.: Look into what role the arts play in patients' care here.

I turned to the large door behind me. Carved images of flower blossoms on wavy stems graced the casing. *Clearly*, I thought, *someone cared about beauty and craftsmanship in designing this part of the building.* But in contrast to the pastoral imagery of the frame, OFFICE OF THE MEDICAL SUPERINTENDENT announced itself in bold block letters on the frosted glass of the door itself.

I peeked through a clear spot in the frost beneath SU-PERINTENDENT. Mrs. Krueger sat at her desk slitting enve-lopes with a letter opener. I had met her two days earlier, the morning I arrived. A sprightly fifty-year-old, her graying hair curled out in odd ways here and there. She attempted to tame them with strategically placed bobby pins, but the curls seemed to defy her intentions as every once in a while a bobby pin fell to her desk or launched itself if she turned her head too quickly. She was nicely dressed in a pastel blue blouse and white sweater.

Mrs. Krueger was the sturdy gatekeeper for Dr. Spencer, the Chief Medical Superintendent. Friendly and matronly, Mrs. Krueger knew as much about the hospital operation as anyone. All information to and from the medical superintendent passed through her. And, I was to learn, she was also Chief Challenger to his ideas more often than he would prefer.

Mrs. Krueger looked up when I knocked and entered.

She put a finger to her mouth to signal quiet. She beckoned me over with her other hand.

She whispered. "Sit down, Henry. He's in there with some officers."

"What's happened?"

"I'm not exactly sure—yet. He was *very* upset when he ar-rived at eight. He said the police called him earlier. At his resi-dence—that never happens. Mrs. Spencer cannot stand to have business conducted from the residence. He told me to hold all calls—the police were on their way. I was in the ladies' room when they got here, so I guess they just went right in there. But when I brought in his morning coffee, I overheard one say 'damage' and the other say something about one of our delivery trucks. They stopped talking until I left the room. Felt like I was in a spy movie."

I sat down. Voices were muffled on the other side of his door. Mrs. Krueger and I looked at one another. She raised her shoulders as if to say, *Who knows?*

"Did you find Nelson? Did he give you the orientation and tour?" she said.

"Yes to both," I said. Nelson Stanley was Assistant to the Medical Superintendent, specialty in accounting. Friendly fellow, not long on words. Limped slightly from a shell fragment in the war. Mrs. Krueger sent me over to see Nelson when I first arrived. He had prepared a welcome packet that included a list of every department at the asylum and their locations and phone numbers; an identification badge that read "Henry Merchartt, Graduate Student"; and a map of the grounds.

"It was a good tour," I told her. "We visited the carpenter's shop, the butcher shop, the furniture shop, bakery, laundry, electrical shop, cannery, men's and women's dining rooms, infirmaries, and at least 15 offices in Building 50."

The administrative and residential heart of the asylum grounds, Building 50 spread out over four acres. It was designed according to the "Kirkbride Plan"—with residential "wings" that allow sunlight to flood every patient's room. I imagined that, from an aerial view, Building 50 would look like the wingspan of an enormous whooping crane.

"According to Nelson," I said, "I could find asylums all over the country with Kirkbride-designed buildings. He said Dr. Thomas Kirkbride was a medical superintendent at a mental hospital on the east coast. He believed sun is therapeutic, so he wanted every patient room to have windows. Since his time, the most popular hospital design was called 'The Kirkbride Plan'. Makes the most of available sunlight in northern climates."

Mrs. Krueger smiled. "I'm familiar with Dr. Kirkbride. One winter in northern Michigan will convince you of the need for sunlight," she said. "Sometimes the sun doesn't come out for weeks. The endless gray days, all the snow and cold, it can really make people depressed."

"Seasonal depression," I said. "One day that may become a bona fide clinical diagnosis."

"Seasonal depression, winter blues. In my opinion," she said, "it doesn't matter *what* you call it. You don't need to give something a fancy name to make it legitimate. Dr. Kirkbride knew it was real. You and I know it's real. That's enough for ... "

She stopped abruptly. "Well, anyway," she said, "back to you. What do you think of the grounds?"

"I can't believe how huge this place is — and how abundant the orchards and fields." Nelson and I had walked through acres of fruit orchards with trees drooping, full of apples and pears. Stood in loam-rich fields brimming with squash, potatoes, greens, cabbage — and more. Absolutely the lushest fields I'd ever seen.

Seven hundred-fifty acres total. Four hundred-fifty devoted to farming, livestock, and orchards. Three thousand patients and 2000 doctors, nurses, and staff. A small city in itself.

I pulled a folded sheet of paper from my diary.

"Nelson gave me a map."

The map was tattered along one edge as if it had been torn from a book or report. It only showed the buildings in the main part of the grounds, so Nelson wrote where other parts of the asylum were located, like the barns, orchards, milk and cow barns, etc., and he circled where my cottage was in a cluster of other patient cottages on the west side of the grounds. He put a large circle around Building 50, so I could orient myself in relation to everything else. The buildings on the map were numbered, but Nelson couldn't find the key, so he said I would need to pencil in the names of buildings when we went on our tour, but I forgot to do that.

I pulled the folded-up map from my shirt pocket and held it out to show her.

She leaned toward the map, turning her head this way and that as she read it. "He's a better accountant than he is a cartographer," she said with a slight laugh, "but this will do. I'll see if I can get you a better one.

"So many of our patients work in the fields and orchards," she said. "Besides the therapeutic value of the sun, we believe that work is therapy. Every day I see firsthand how important that work is to so many who have been committed. It's their lifeline to some degree of health."

"That's wonderful," I said. "And I enjoyed the way Nelson carries historical data around in his head." I opened my diary and read some facts that I had scribbled down.

"For example, here. In 1951, five births, two of which were illegitimate. In the same year, two suicides, one by hanging; one by ingesting roach powder; and one murder by strangulation. Seventeen natural deaths, half from tuberculosis or alcohol poisoning. One hundred sixty-eight patients released; one hundred ninety-two admitted."

I closed the diary.

"He has quite a mind for numbers," she said smiling, "And not only that…"

Before she could say more, Dr. Spencer emerged from his office escorting the two policemen.

"Thank you, officers," he said. "If I learn anything, I'll be in touch with you right away. And I trust you'll do the same?"

"We will," one said before he closed the outer door.

Dr. Spencer stood by his door, his hand on the knob. His white doctor's jacket was buttoned up just far enough to cover the bottom half of his green necktie. A pencil and small spiral notebook stuck out of a side pocket; the stem of a pipe peered out from the other pocket. He squinted at me over wire-rimmed glasses that rested midway down his nose.

"And you are..."

"Henry Mershartt, from Philadelphia. University of Pennsylvania. I'm here on..."

"Of course!" he bellowed. "Mr. Mershartt! The young man here for his field experience." His words gushed forth. "How nice to meet you. Say, I'm sorry I couldn't be more available to greet you personally, but, by golly it gets busy around here, unexpected emergencies, patients this and staff that, and now this...this...well, how *are* you getting on?"

He glanced at my chest. "I see you have your badge."

I fingered the badge. "Yes, Nelson..."

"Ah, Nelson. Walking history book, that man. So he's given you an orientation? What do you think so far?"

"I'm...it's...an amazing hospital. So large, so...different."

We exchanged niceties for a couple of moments—long trip, missed connection in Detroit, tasteless sandwiches at bus depots, glad to be here—until Mrs. Krueger cleared her throat to signal she obviously had something on her mind.

"Well?" she said to him. "What now?"

He feigned ignorance. "What ... *what* now?"

She rolled her eyes. "The police?"

He shook his head from side to side. "Oh, that," he said. "It's, well, it's not good. But you already knew that."

She stretched her neck forward and cocked one ear in his direction. "I'm all ears, Doctor."

He seemed reluctant to talk in front of me. But the look she gave him was what my mother called "the impatient eye."

"Well," he said, "It seems that one of our delivery trucks, full of watermelons, squash, and greens, was ... vandalized. Attendant and two patients came out of a restaurant to find all four tires slashed and produce strewn all over the alley. It happened early this morning, just after dawn; they were making deliveries, in town. No one saw anything."

"Well," said Mrs. Krueger, "Another one. And no witnesses again."

My eyes went from her to him.

"Another?" I said.

"One other, last month," said Dr. Spencer. "But, by gosh, we don't need to go into that."

Mrs. Krueger spoke up again. We *would* go into all that, if she were to have her way. "This one makes four, all told."

"Three," he corrected.

"Four counting that dog," she corrected.

"Well," he said, "that was diff ... okay, then, four. No need to ..."

I felt awkward standing there between his reticence and her outspokenness. But I had to tell them.

"If you mean the dog in the pond," I said, "I saw that myself, yesterday morning."

I explained that on my way to my second day of orientation

with Nelson, two male patients hailed me from where they stood—next to a large pond on "The Great Lawn" in front of Building 50. They called the pond "Willow Lake," but it was more like a big wading pool. I went over to them and saw what they were so excited about: floating in the water was the severed head of a brown dog. Security arrived and fished it out. Said it was a mongrel dog that roamed the hospital grounds and that patients fed and befriended; patients called him Brownie.

I asked Nelson who would do such a thing—a patient? No, he said, patients loved Brownie. Then he said something curious, that he was "not authorized" to talk about "those things."

"I wasn't sure what he meant by 'those things,'" I said.

Dr. Spencer stood there, his mouth slightly open, eyes flitting about the room as if he were looking for something to change the subject. I sensed that I was walking a fine line between genuine curiosity and prying. It was just a feeling I had from his reluctance to reveal much about this topic—in contrast to his secretary's eagerness.

"Well," he cleared his throat. "I regret that you had to be witness to something so brutal when you have just arrived. But staff are advised not to discuss such occurrences—to keep our patient population calm. I suppose Nelson could have been more open with you, but he does tend to…how shall I put it?"

"Overgeneralizes rules, if you ask me," chimed in Mrs. Krueger.

"Last February," she said, turning full to me, "someone got into the chicken barn and put thirty-two chicks out in the snow one night. Workers found the poor little creatures frozen in the snow in the morning. Innocence destroyed by pure evil."

Dr. Spencer cleared his throat. "The police investigated, of course."

"Not much to investigate," she said. "Half the patient population was out there picking up the chicks by the time the police arrived. Putting the poor critters in their warm pockets, trying to breathe life back into their poor souls, stomping all around like their own body heat would bring those little chicks back to life. There was no way they could tell one set of footprints from another by the time the sleepy cops arrived."

"Well, it never happened again, thankfully," he said.

"Oh no," she said, "*That* never happened again. Not since they put locks on the barns *after* that."

"And so, Henry," he started to say, but she talked through him.

"Then a few months later, it was in June, someone threw a rock into a dining room window at Cottage 40. That's a men's cottage. Glass everywhere. At night again. It was fortunate that none of the men were in that room at the time. Later that same night, another rock was thrown through the parlor window at Cottage 29. Woke a lot of the women right up and scared the living daylights out of them. Some of them had to be moved to another cottage after that, they were so frightened."

"No suspects?" I asked.

She beat him to it again. "Not a one. Leave it to our narcoleptic city police to drop their doughnuts long enough to wander by in the morning to quote, investigate, unquote."

"Now, Bettyanne," said Dr. Spencer. "We can't blame them for having other priorities. After all, no one was injured."

"Humph," she said. "The whole thing smells fishy if you ask me. Someone *could* have been hurt."

Dr. Spencer spoke directly to me. "The police think it was kids." Then, to her, "And we just can't go around ..."

Mrs. Krueger spoke right through him, her voice slightly elevated to signal she had the right of way. "There are people in town, in the police department, who, frankly, don't consider asylum residents as much of a priority as city dwellers."

He started to say something. She put up a hand, a wait signal. He obliged.

"I know, I know," she continued before he could get a word in, "that's just *my* opinion. But my first cousin Bernard cleans over at PD headquarters and he tells me how they talk about us. It's not always too nice—or sympathetic. Anyway, lately we seem to be having more troubles like these. I've worked here twenty-eight years, and I've never seen anything like it. Four times in six months? Kids? Kids don't kill chicks. And patients don't behead dogs."

"Well," said Dr. Spencer, "we don't have to go into that either. All we can do is increase our vigilance and trust the police to do their job."

"Do their job, humph," she said. "Some of the ladies who work here are afraid to walk to their cars after dark these days. It's light now, but wait until it gets dark by six o'clock. They'll be heading to the parking lot at five o'clock. They're scared. *I'm* scared."

I thought she had a good point. Women were much more likely to be afraid than men. What would it hurt if he were to change the workday hours until arrests were made?

But Dr. Spencer seemed oblivious to Mrs. Krueger's complaint.

"As you can see, Henry, Mrs. Krueger has some strong beliefs.

And, to be fair, she has good reasons. As for me, I tend to exercise more restraint. For better or worse."

"It's a troubling set of events," was all I could think to say, though it sounded like milquetoast.

"Indeed it is," he said. "And, Henry, I'm afraid I have to defer our meeting a bit. I must alert our senior staff about this latest…event, so to speak. Quell any more fear as best I can. At least the vandalism has moved off the campus."

"For *now*," she added.

"Yes, well," he said, "Bettyanne, can you arrange for Henry and me to…"

"You'll see him this afternoon at four," she said. "You're to meet a new resident. Arriving on the train. You and Nurse Brownell, and what's-her-name, the greeter."

"Ah hah, yes. Very good. Till then, Henry."

He closed the door. I cast a glance toward Mrs. Krueger, whose eyes seemed to drift up into her eyelids as she shook her head and pursed her lips. She tossed her head in his direction, as if to say, *I just don't know.* She reminded me of the way my mother sometimes disapproves of something my father says or does.

I showed myself out. Out on the sidewalk under a sprawling walnut tree, I sat on a bench and opened my diary:

September 6:

What is this rash of vandalism all about? Frozen chicks, rocks in windows, dead dogs, slashed tires! And why does Dr. Spencer try to downplay it all?

I closed my diary, got up from the bench and started back

toward my cottage. I approached the spot where I had been ser-enaded earlier by the woman at the window. This time I heard different music from above. I couldn't quite make out the song or the singer through the static on the radio. I paused, but I didn't look up. As the volume on the radio was turned down, the voice of the woman behind the window grate floated down toward me. This time her voice had a soothing, lullaby quality to it as she sang:

Though we shall never look on her more,
Gone with the love and joy she bore,
Far away she's blooming in a fadeless bower,
Sweet Rosalie, The Garden Flower.

CHAPTER TWO

Welcome to Our Home

AT 4:00, I WAS BACK IN DR. SPENCER'S RECEPTION ROOM, WAIT-
ing quietly on a red couch. Mrs. Krueger sat at her desk, typing
on a gray Smith Corona. We both looked up as the outer door
opened. A woman entered. Tall and dark haired, mid-thirties.
Dressed in nursing whites. Thin. Skin smooth and pale, high
cheekbones, like Rita Hayworth. Statuesque in her height. *Nurse
Brownell,* I thought, *has to be her. Definitely a looker.*

She had an even sureness of movement and determination.
With those legs, I thought, *Nurse Brownell could have been a pinup girl.*

She greeted Mrs. Krueger and introduced herself to me as
Nancy Brownell, Head of Nursing.

"Very good to meet you," I said, rising.

She motioned me to sit, then she sat opposite me, on a cushioned chair. She crossed her legs; I forced my attention away
from her legs.

She looked over to Mrs. Krueger. "How long?" she asked.

"Hard to say. His phone's been ringing off the hook. One
thing after another all afternoon. Now there's some crisis in one
of the women's cottages." She walked over to his door and put
an ear to it.

"He knows you're expecting him, but, well, you know *him.*

16

Sometimes he can't see the forest for the trees." She sat back down at her desk, opened her eyes wide, shrugged her shoulders, and started opening envelopes and scanning letters, half working and half listening to our conversation as she glanced up at us every once in a while.

Nurse Brownell turned her attention to me.

"It seems we have some time to get acquainted, then. It is very good to meet you. I have been looking forward to helping you get adjusted. I regret that I could not have been here when you arrived. At the last moment, I had to substitute for someone at a three-day meeting in Lansing. I just arrived back late last night. Please accept my apologies."

She seemed reserved but not stuffy reserved. More cautious in choosing her words. Polite, very polite.

"I'm fine," I said. "I've taken this time to get adjusted. I went into town to look around. I had to pick up a few things I needed. Now I'm settled in and ready to begin."

"So how do you like our little town by the bays?"

"Very nice. There were sailboats on the water and swimmers at the beach. I love that little train on the tiny train tracks by the water."

"A favorite for tourists," she said.

"It's a nice town. I bought some things I needed at the Wards store. I plan to take in a film at, what was it? The State Theatre."

"Yes, the State. It burned down a few years ago. It was called The Lyric before the fire. They changed the name to The State when it was rebuilt."

"*High Noon.*"

"High Noon?"

"That's what's playing this week. It's a Gary Cooper western."

"I *loved* that movie," commented Mrs. Krueger, her eyes on a letter as she spoke to us.

Nurse Brownell cut to the quick. "Can you tell me about yourself? In your application letter, you described your academic training."

"Sure. I'm a master's degree student in Psychology at Penn. I have just this field experience and my thesis left to complete. One day I hope to become a university professor specializing in institutional patient care. After the Ph.D., that is."

She waved her hand in a stop sign motion. "You said all that in your letter. What about your *life* back home? If I am to share your supervision with Dr. Spencer, then it would be good for us to know more about you as a person. Are you comfortable sharing any of that?"

"Sure. I'm 26. Until a week ago, I lived in an apartment in Philly, near the university. I grew up in Chestnut Hill. That's a neighborhood north of City Center. Dad manages an insurance office; Mother helps children learn to read at the local library and volunteers in the schools. She was a teacher before she married. Dad served overseas but not in a combat role; we were lucky. I was too young to serve, so I just kept going to school.

"I have a good friend, Clara. She's a teacher. High school English. Very smart girl, and very well-read in literature. She thinks this field experience will be a good experience for me, even though it keeps us apart."

"I'm sure that will be hard for you." I sensed empathy in her tone.

I don't know why, maybe it was because Nurse Brownell was *so* attractive, but I downplayed the importance of Clara in my personal life. After all, it's not like I was *engaged*. So I tried to shrug it off with, "Well, we'll see."

That seemed to end discussion of my personal life, because she then said, "In your letter, you said that the thesis you are writing will be a philosophy of patient care. What do you mean by that?"

"Which one? Philosophy or patient care?"

She leaned toward me. "The whole phrase," she said. There was the slightest air of intimidation in her serious look and her no-nonsense tone.

"In a nutshell," I said, "a humanistic philosophy of patient care. My supervising professor, Professor Hilliger, her expertise is in Humanistic Psychology. It's a new academic area in Psychology. The classes I took from her challenged just about everything I believed about patient care from a *behavioral* perspective. I can say more, but..."

Dr. Spencer's door flew open half way. A balding head with eyeglasses parked midway down the nose. White doctor coat with a row of pencils and pens sticking out of both side pockets. White shirt and tie. Black telephone receiver in hand suspended about a foot from his ear. I could see the phone cord stretched horizontally out toward the wall behind him as he looked imploringly at Mrs. Krueger. He put one hand over the speaking end of the receiver.

"Bettyanne, hold all calls after this one. If I don't help them get this patient settled down, then she's certain to go after someone with a chair or something.

"Yes yes, I hear you," he barked into the phone. "Now just listen to what I know about her."

He looked over to where Nurse Brownell and I were sitting. His hand back over the receiver, he said to Nurse Brownell, "Nancy, it'll be just a few minutes. It's Mrs. Gillison in 23. She's loose again and threatening to kill herself and take an attendant with her."

He removed his hand from the receiver. "Good Lord! Yes, I hear you. Now, try to…" His voice trailed off as the door slammed shut.

I was surprised at how calm the nurse and the secretary were. As if whatever was happening with Mrs. Gillison was just a routine thing. But what did I know? Maybe it *was* routine.

"Poor Mrs. Gillison," said the secretary, "she's been having a rough go of it lately. In my opinion, change of life for her means taking a life. She's got that mean streak."

"Please," Nurse Brownell said, her eyes drifting from the closed door, over to Mrs. Krueger, then back to me. "Continue. You were talking about humanistic psychology."

"Okay," I said, trying hard to regain my train of thought.

"In Psychology, master's theses tend to be empirical, you know, based on observation and measurement. My thesis won't follow in that tradition, with Professor Hilliger's permission and guidance. Abraham Maslow published his theory of human motivation almost ten years ago, and it's getting much attention in the academic world."

She smiled and shook her head slowly, knowingly. "Yes, I am familiar with Professor Maslow's work, and his theory of human needs. It *is* very interesting and insightful for those of us working with mental illness. This hospital is a good setting for understanding that theory in practice. Your Professor Hilliger has directed you to the right place, as you will come to learn."

I was surprised she knew Maslow and his theory. I had expected people at this rather remote location to be, well, out of touch with current trends. *Maybe*, I figured, *they aren't so provincial after all.*

"Professor Hilliger," I continued, "believes that what this new field needs is a *philosophy* of patient care. No one has done that—yet. I'm very interested in humanistic psychology and how it challenges behavioral psychology. By and large, mental hospitals today mainly provide care that meets patients' biological and safety needs, but not their needs for love and belonging and self-esteem. Self-actualization, Maslow's fifth domain, may be a stretch for some people to consider in patient care, but I think there's a place for some version of it in a philosophy that encompasses all of Maslow's theory."

She shifted in her chair, tugged at the hemline of her white uniform.

"That is all very interesting—and quite promising for your future."

"I hope so. Anyway, a thesis along humanistic lines seems a perfect fit for me. I hope my thesis will lead to a dissertation, and the dissertation will be published and that will launch my career."

I had only shared it with Clara, but someday I hoped to do something truly remarkable in humanistic psychology. I didn't just want to be famous; I wanted to make a real difference in the world.

"I can see that you set a high mark for yourself," she said.

"I'm sort of an idealist, always have been. Like Doctor Jonas Salk, you know, the man who I think has actually developed a vaccine for polio. That's astonishing! Or that team of doctors at Georgetown who invented an artificial heart valve. Can you imagine how people's lives will be affected by things like these? I just get very excited when I think maybe *I* could be part of a team like that, in my field.

"I admire your youthful energy," she said.

Mrs. Krueger looked up from her work, pen in hand. "And your dreams," she chimed in. "In my opinion, everyone needs to have a dream, especially young people."

Nurse Brownell continued, "So now you have come to the Traverse City State Hospital. Why here?"

"I'm here because Professor Hilliger recommended I get field experience at an asylum—to round off my academic experiences."

"So, it wasn't *your* decision to gain field experience?" Her emphasis on *your* made me a little uncomfortable. I was starting to feel like I was being interrogated. She could make someone feel that way, just a little. But she had hit on a sore spot. Truth is, I was getting tired of going to school and taking a whole year for field experience was, well, not something I would have *chosen* to do.

"Well, yes and no," I said. "I mean, Professor Hilliger made it clear that if she were to supervise my thesis, then I needed direct experience in patient care. I've more or less only been in school all these years, not in any clinical setting. She believes a full year of clinical exposure will give me in-depth experience with patient care. If I can write the thesis, then go on for the Ph.D. *and* get the dissertation published, then I'll be able to land a position on a university faculty. That's my career path, as I see it."

"You have it all figured out, it seems."

She had this air of superiority that was starting to bug me—and it contradicted my physical attraction to her, because she was also sexy. She didn't wear thick makeup and lipstick like so many other nurses. Her face was smooth as silk and she wore only a trace of light red on her lips. She had her dark hair done in large smooth curls back to where her nurse's cap lay, then it flowed down to her shoulders in a few more large curls. Hers was just a natural beauty. Sitting there in all her starched whites — and curves. Seated across from her, I fought the urge to envelope those long lovely legs with my tender eyes. I imagined the two of us doing it all night in a fancy hotel room until we fell asleep from exhaustion.

I squelched that fantasy before my musing look gave me away. Truth is, she made me nervous, the way she said things so directly — a bit of challenge in her tone. Between that tone and my attraction to her, I felt discomfort, so I sat there like some teenager spellbound by his gorgeous but authoritarian seventh-grade teacher.

"Well, that's my plan, anyway." The *anyway* served as a fork in the conversational road, or so I hoped.

She glanced up at Mrs. Krueger and pulled her head toward Dr. Spencer's office, as if to say *what's keeping him?* Mrs. Krueger put up both hands and raised her shoulders as if to say *I have no idea.*

Then Nurse Brownell asked me why I was interested in treating mental illness in the first place. Like I said, she had this knack for cutting right to the core. She asked direct questions that bridged the personal with the professional, whereas I always tried to separate the two domains. She had already implied that what I saw as idealism, she saw as opportunism, and that made me uncomfortable, even though it was true. I *did* see myself advancing through the academic ranks one day as one of the few specialists in humanistic psychology. I knew that she suspected *that* with her *You have it all figured out, it seems.* Professor Hilliger *did* make field experience a requirement, so what could be wrong in saying that I was, in a sense, serving time?

But that's where the personal gets all mixed in with the professional. See, I had this cousin, Ethel—Uncle Tony and Aunt Pat's youngest. She was a regular part of family gatherings when I was growing up. Ethel was six years younger than me. Her brother Jack and I were age mates who got into all kinds of cousin mischief as we were growing up.

Ethel had autism. I describe her as autistic now, but no one in the family knew to call her autistic then. That was not a term familiar to most people; it was only used in clinical settings or research studies. She was just *Cousin Ethel.* That said it all.

She wasn't completely autistic. She had what I would now call *autistic tendencies,* strange habits that you noticed right away. Jack and I would roll our adolescent eyes whenever she insisted she had to have her two glasses of milk *before* eating anything. And she had to have everything on her plate separated; the ham could not touch the potato salad and god forbid if the Jell-O wandered over toward her buttered roll. Those sorts of things.

She did okay in a regular school, mainly because Aunt Pat tutored her after school; she even sat with Ethel in the classroom sometimes to help her out. In some ways, Ethel was pretty smart. She was good in math and she liked to read. She had a terrific memory, too. She had Compton's Encyclopedia at home and she actually read the whole thing. I think that's why she could recite esoteric facts that most people would never learn in their entire life, like the national currency of Samoa or where dragon fruit grows.

Ethel would drop little nuggets of knowledge like these with the least invitation. We could be sitting in the living room listening to a radio show and someone on the show might mention Jamaica and she'd say, "People in Jamaica eat Ackee." Jack and I would desperately avoid looking at one another because we knew we'd crack up and our folks would give us both a private lecture later.

We knew better than to make fun of her or talk cruelly about her. She was *family*—and no one talked ill of family.

But in college, when I became interested in Psychology, Cousin Ethel lingered in the back of my head. I learned about conditions like autism but they were just abstract terms in a textbook, whereas knowing someone with autism made the academic less remote. I learned that people with autism had many strengths. It occurred to me that there may have been things about Ethel that made her more like Jack and me, things that may have made us value her more.

I never knew any of those things—because I never bothered to find out. I regret that.

That's why Nurse Brownell's question hung out there. I couldn't admit to opportunism any more than I could tell her about Ethel without admitting that I came from stock that ignored its own as much as most families do who have mental illness in their ranks. I felt embarrassed on both counts, so I tried to salvage my pride by taking the high, abstract road.

"My study of Abraham Maslow illuminated the broad spectrum of human needs," I said. "I think, as a profession, we have missed opportunities to care for this important segment of society. I wish to do that."

"That is honorable," she said, "though you sound like a text book when you say it like that."

Damn, I thought. *That's a direct quote from a Maslow review I read and memorized! She's sharp.* "I know," I said, "sometimes I do sound like that. Things just come out that way."

"I hope," she continued, "that *we* can help you reach your goal. I do know something about philosophy, so that may be of some help, too."

"Really? How so?"

"My father was a bit of a self-made philosopher. He was a family doctor by profession. Like your friend Clara, he was widely read—in philosophy. He liked Plato, especially the way Plato's Socrates stirred people up, the way he made them think. That's why Socrates was put to death. His ideas threatened those in power. For him, helping people become more critical, less inclined to follow like sheep, that was his ethic. He was as much an ethicist as a philosopher. If you are to write a philosophy of patient care, I'm sure you will discover many such ethical issues."

Maybe she is kind of likable, I thought. *Genuine—and forthright. Smart.*

"I already have. And I'm sure I'll discover more during my time here."

She smiled, but I couldn't decipher if it was a smile of politeness or a smile of knowing something that I was still to learn.

"I suspect you will. But for now, you have barely settled in," she said. "Do you have any immediate questions?"

"I have two," I responded. "First, it seems odd that high-level administrators would greet a new patient arrival. I mean, you're the Head Nurse and Dr. Spencer is the Medical Superintendent. It seems like you would have so many other, more important things to do."

She smiled again. "I — we — do. But we also think we should make a special effort to welcome each new resident, if we can. It's not always possible, but when it is, we go. At least one of us, ideally two. For every new arrival, Dr. Spencer will examine the patient personally. That is the law — a new patient must be personally examined by the medical superintendent."

I never got to my second question, which would have been, *I'm curious to know about the vandalism of the past few months.* But our conversation was interrupted by the hall door pitching open suddenly. A wildly dressed woman in her 20's popped in as if she had been propelled by gale winds. She had a smile broad enough to fill the whole room.

Mrs. Krueger suddenly sat straight up, startled. "Oh, brother," she muttered.

"Ta-da!" the woman boomed and walked right up to me, hand extended for a shake.

"I'm Eunice. I'm the greeter."

Nurse Brownell introduced her more formally as *Miss* Eunice. Miss Eunice wore a worn, fur-trimmed coat popular in the 30's, white ankle socks under black pumps, and a blue wool felt hat with a turned-up brim. A cloth measuring tape dangled from her coat pocket. *Strange outfit for the heat of September,* I thought.

Nurse Brownell invited Eunice to sit. "Miss Eunice works in the hospital fabric shop," she said, "officially called the Fashion Shoppe, spelled s-h-o-p-p-e. She keeps tabs on ladies' and mens' fashions from reading the magazines."

"That's right, I do, you bet your life I do," said Eunice.

"She has a knack for redesigning clothing that local charities give to the hospital."

"You like this outfit, Nurse?"

"Lovely, Eunice, just lovely."

"Made it just for today, I did. Took all morning. Eileen in the shop asked me to make one for her, too. Paulette in the shop says it's my new fashion line. Paulette's fat, but I make dresses for her that make her look pretty, up and down stripes, not hori-hori—"

"Horizontal."

"Yeah, horizontal. What's your name again, mister?"

"Henry."

"Henry?"

"Mr. Henry," Nurse Brownell interjected.

Staff went by formal titles at the hospital—Mr. Harrison, Doctor Spencer, Nurse Brownell. *Patients* were also called Mr._____, Miss _____ or Mrs. _____, first or last names following, though some, like Eunice, preferred their given names.

Eunice turned toward the window. A train whistle.

"We gotta go, Nurse," said Eunice. "It's coming."

Mrs. Krueger opened Dr. Spencer's office door wide enough for us to see in.

"The train is here. You have a new arrival to meet."

He was walking around behind his desk and talking on the phone. "What else have you tried?" he thundered. "No. I said, what else have you tried?"

He cupped a hand over the receiver as he leaned our way, "Bettyanne, it's the phone problem again," and went back to his conversation.

"Always something," she said to us. "He insists on walking around on a call and stretching the cord almost out of the wall. The phone company has to replace the cord every other month." She rolled her eyes and raised her shoulders as if to say, *What's one to do?*

They were an amusing duo, the superintendent and his secretary.

Eunice looked at Nurse Brownell, imploringly. "We gotta go, Nurse."

"I'll be over just as soon as I can," we heard. "No, just as soon as I can. We have a new patient. On the 4:30 train. Try to keep her calm and put on some music or sing to her. What? Doesn't matter if you can't carry a tune. You're not auditioning and she won't care. I'll be along in thirty minutes."

We heard the receiver drop into its cradle. In seconds, he emerged through the paneled door.

"Sorry for all that, " he said. "Let's go."

The hospital had its own rail spur off the main line — mostly for the coal deliveries but also for the occasional arriving patient and patient escort. We hurried to the train platform just south of the fire station and stopped before ascending the steps to the platform just as the locomotive pulled alongside.

Dr. Spencer put out an arm to signal for us to wait. "Let's give him some time," he said. "Let's not overwhelm him with new people."

The passenger car stopped at the platform. A porter got off first, followed by a bulky man in a suit toting a worn greenish suitcase. He stepped down and looked back. A second man emerged, slowly, hesitantly. He was much smaller — and remarkably thin. His worn grey coat hung on him like an oversized hand-me-down. He looked both directions before emerging onto the platform.

"That would be our escort," said Dr. Spencer, "and our newest."

The suitcase was the size of a kitchen breadbox. I would soon learn that it held all this patient's worldly belongings —namely a change of clothes, a nightshirt, a toothbrush, and a comb.

The porter shook the escort's hand and exchanged a few words, then put his hand out to the patient, who stared silently at him, arms at his side. The porter gave him an open-faced wave, nodded to the escort, and got back on the train, leaving the two men and one small suitcase on the platform.

Both men looked toward the rear of the train, where, from the open door of a cargo car, two hospital orderlies unloaded various boxes of supplies, a porcelain toilet, and a straight-backed, blue-cushioned chair that would eventually find its home in the chapel. From the same platform, one of the orderlies tossed an outgoing canvas bag of something back into the open door. Then he waved toward the engineer. At 4:40, the train continued on the spur to the main line into town. The orderlies put their stores in the back of a black Ford pickup and drove off.

The two passengers stood alone on the platform. The thin one in the grey coat waved at the train. The bulky one turned to see the three of us ascend the steps to the platform. Eunice held on to Nurse Brownell for stability as her high pumps forced her to walk on her toes. The thin fellow stood looking in the direction of the train as the last car disappeared into the distance.

Three steps up the platform and the four of us were standing before the escort and his charge, who still stared at the ghost of the train. He seemed oblivious to our presence.

The escort introduced himself as Norman Grabow, from the Kalamazoo State Hospital. He shook the hands of each of us, reported that it had been a quiet trip — "no problems," as he put it. He jerked his head toward the smaller man near him who now stood looking at the red cupolas atop the tall, yellow-brick Building 50 and the smaller Cottage 20.

"Sat in his seat the whole way," he said. "Didn't even use the facilities. Wouldn't eat. Just sat and stared out the window. Never said a word, though I tried to get him to open up, you know, told a few off-color jokes but even those never seemed to spark him.

"Anyway," said Norman, "this here is Mister James Quinn. Goes by Jimmy. Jimmy, this is your new home. Can you say hello to these nice folks?"

That fragile man finally turned toward us. I could see his full face for the first time. "Hollow" was the first word that came to mind. He looked like one of those men in the war movies who've been held in a POW camp. Though Nurse Brownell had said the new patient was in his early thirties, just by looking at him, you'd guess he was in his fifties. Thin features top to bottom, with stubble of black beard here and there on his cheeks. Dark brown eyes, sunken in prominent cheekbones, eyes that spoke of disequilibrium — and distance. His black slacks were held up by a black belt that had another ten notches to go before it would reach its limit. Tan shirt sporting a dull blue necktie beneath the suit coat. Shoes were scuffed and a bit too big for him. I didn't imagine the extra change of clothing in the suitcase would be much different.

After apologies for being late, Dr. Spencer made introductions. First himself. Nurse Brownell was next. She took Jimmy's hand in both of hers and said how happy she was to meet him. Jimmy looked at her, eyes blank, no expression.

Dr. Spencer turned toward me. He had this weird expression. *He can't recall my name!* I realized.

I stepped forward and put out my hand but Jimmy made no complementary gesture, hands at his sides, just the blank look again.

"I'm glad you are here, Mr. Quinn. Sorry, Jimmy?"

He stood before me, eyes on the platform.

"My name is Henry...Mr. Henry. Whatever you need, I'm your man, ok?"

Before anyone had a chance to introduce her, Eunice spun around from behind me and placed herself squarely in front of him.

"Mr. Jimmy," she began, "I am Eunice the Greeter and I have a greeting to give you from the whole place here, from all the people in Michigan who live here, all the people in the world who live here, and all the people on the earth who live here, and all the people from the fabric shop and the milking barns and the infirmaries and the tunnels and even the animals who live in the woods behind the stables and everything like that."

She kicked off her pumps, and took off her coat and hat, only to reveal a red flowered blouse with pedal pusher pants that came down to mid-calf.

Norman took a step back. Smiles crossed the faces of Dr. Spencer and Nurse Brownell as they backed up too, so I followed their lead, pulling Jimmy with me. I sensed that everyone but the new patient and I knew what was coming. I braced myself for who-knows-what. Nurse Brownell leaned toward me and whispered, "Eunice writes her own songs. This will be one of her new welcome songs."

Eunice turned and walked halfway toward the end of the platform, then spun around quickly and came running at us, half speed. But she performed a nearly perfect cartwheel, legs over arms and body, landing with a wobble in front of Jimmy, whose eyes were now wide as oak leaves. She regained her stability, took a deep breath, and sang, in a cheery high-pitched voice.

YooHoo! You Have Arrived!
In One Piece and Alive!
So Welcome to our Home!
You Have No Need To Roam!
You're Home!

When she finished, Eunice made a short bow before Jimmy and then each of us in turn. We applauded. Norman shouted, "Bravo!" Jimmy's demeanor had changed slightly—from listless staring and lifeless arms to something that resembled horror, then a hint of pleasure: lips turned up slightly, hands raised as if to clap, and eyes that moved slowly from one of us to the other, scanning.

Eunice slipped back into her welcoming outfit as we began to move as a group toward the end of the platform. Nurse Brownell stepped forward and put her hand on Jimmy's right arm.

"You've had a long trip, Jimmy Quinn," she said, "how would you like a good hot meal?" Her voice was warm and reassuring, like Ingrid Bergman in *Casablanca*, the kind you want to hear when you come out of surgery.

Silent and staring, he squinted a bit and cocked his head slightly to one side as if to say *who are you?* He didn't react to her touching him, didn't pull back or anything. Not that I expected him to; I didn't know what to expect.

Dr. Spencer spoke. "Would you like to go with Nurse Brownell to the dining hall? She can help you get your dinner. Then Mr. Henry here can help you to your room and get you set up there."

Jimmy glanced at Dr. Spencer, then at Norman.

"It's okay," whispered Norman. "You can trust them. I'll come along if you'd like."

More silence and staring as Nurse Brownell tugged slightly on Jimmy's coat sleeve—a signal that they could walk together. Jimmy moved with her off the platform in short, safe steps.

"Nurse Brownell will take good care of you," called Dr. Spencer. "Nancy, I'll examine him at the men's infirmary. Bring him by after his meal."

I picked up the green suitcase and followed. Eunice departed the platform, heading in the other direction toward one of the women's cottages. Dr. Spencer stayed behind with Norman. I followed close to Nurse Brownell and Jimmy—with new arrivals, it was protocol to have at least one male staff member nearby, just in case, for the first 24 hours.

In the dining hall, Nurse Brownell and I filled our plates in the serving line. She held one for Jimmy, while I scooped food onto it. I put a little of everything on Jimmy's plate—meatloaf, mashed potatoes, green beans, Jell-O with fruit cocktail—not knowing what he liked or would eat. We sat at a table by ourselves. We flanked Jimmy on either side.

At a table across the room, a patient bolted up from his chair.

"Christ!" he yelled as he tore off a sweater and whirled it round his head and slapped it on the table like he was swatting flies.

The three of us looked up. Nurse Brownell put her hand on Jimmy's arm to steady him. I did the same on his other arm. "Spiders!" the man screamed. "Goddamned spiders! Goddamned spiders and bugs!"

He whirled around. His arms flailed. The sweater shot a few feet and landed in someone's bowl of soup. He reached down to his own tray, and flung it on the floor. The plate shattered and the silverware flew in all directions.

"Get 'em. Goddamned buggers! Get 'em outta here!"

An attendant rushed to him. He grabbed the man's arms and tried to hold him. The man struggled with him and then broke free and ran around the table, pushing chairs and disrupting patients as he struggled to elude yet more attendants who by this time had rushed to the scene.

"Sons of bitches!"

When four attendants finally had enough hands on him, he stopped resisting. He shouted, "Goddamned spiders!" over and over as they escorted him out of the dining hall. Other attendants cleaned up the mess on the floor and picked up the broken crockery. As if they had just seen a circus act, patients who had been victimized by their arachnophobic peer turned their chairs upright and marched off to the serving line to refill their plates.

Jimmy looked to Nurse Brownell. Her hand slid down his arm to his hand. She gave it a slight squeeze.

"Don't worry," she said. "It will be all right. You are safe."

We returned to our meal. But Jimmy neither ate nor spoke. He stared at his food, occasionally glancing at either of us, then back to his plate. Cautious. Scanning. Suddenly, he picked up his glass and gulped the apple juice, and followed that with a belch that brought snorts and giggles from two men at the nearest table. For the first time in my life, I had been encouraged by a belch.

Chuckling, Nurse Brownell smiled and said, "As good a place as any to start."

"That was a great belch, Jimmy," I said, "can we hear another one?" My weak attempt at humor brought no reaction—until, a few seconds later, he let out another, weaker one. Wide-eyed, Nurse Brownell and I looked at one another. Jimmy gazed at the plate full of food.

We waited. He gazed.

Dinner over, we took him to the men's infirmary, where Dr. Spencer found him to be in reasonably good physical shape, though terribly underweight for a man his height. Throughout the examination, the patient stared straight ahead, his eyes following the doctor as he moved about the room. He had yet to speak a word.

We walked Jimmy to Cottage 29, where he was assigned a room; there were fourteen other men in the cottage, each in his own room on the two upper floors.

We escorted Jimmy to his room on the second floor. He stood in the open doorway, looking around, still silent. Nurse Brownell hung back while I got Jimmy settled into his room, which amounted to little more than putting his suitcase items in a chest of drawers, his suitcase under the bed, and his personal hygiene items (toothbrush and comb) on top of the dresser.

I explained that he would share a bathroom with others, and after handing him his toothbrush, I guided him down the hall to the facility. I pointed out the sink, faucets, and the toilet, and then gave him a tube of Pepsodent. I said I would wait for him outside the door.

Nurse Brownell joined me, and the two of us stood outside the bathroom door, listening.

A few minutes of silence ensued, but then we heard the water run, the toothbrush at work, and the toilet flush. Jimmy emerged holding his toothbrush and handed the paste back to me. "Yours," I said. "You can keep it in your room. There's also soap for washing, and anything else you need, just let us know, okay?"

His eyes met mine for the second time that day, and I'd like to say that there were thanks in them, but it was getting dark and I couldn't tell. We walked him back to his room. Though it wasn't very late, we had planned to let him have some alone time, with the option of being around others if that was what he wanted.

Nurse Brownell spoke first. "Now Jimmy, you've had a long day. We thought you might like to get to bed early, so we're going to leave you here. But there are other staff right here in the hall if you need anything or if you just want to be with others. If you need to see either of us, just ask for Nurse Brownell or Mr. Henry. Don't be afraid to ask. Are you all right with that plan?"

Jimmy walked over to the bed, pulled down the cover and sheet, sat on the edge, and removed his shoes. Fully clothed, he lay full length on the bed and pulled the sheet over his entire body, covering his head. I switched off the overhead light.

He lay corpse-like. A body in the morgue. He had retreated to the safety of his own breathing in the darkness.

We watched from the door. "Good night, Jimmy," said Nurse

Brownell, "I am glad you are with us finally and I look forward to seeing you in the morning. Sleep well, dear."

"Have a good night," I echoed, "I'll be right upstairs and will check in on you later."

We stepped out. I closed the door half way and went downstairs. The attendant there reported that Dr. Spencer had called and asked us to meet with him at eight the next morning for a review of the new patient's file.

Nurse Brownell and I said our good nights.

Back in my room, I made another diary entry before turning in.

September 6:

Hospital staff personally greet each new patient, and the Chief Medical Superintendent personally examines each one when they arrive! The law dictates that he should examine each one, but still, he could delegate that duty to an assistant. Who would ever know? There is a deep morality in that simple decision to give each patient his personal care.

And then there's Eunice with her colorful costume, her cartwheels, and her welcome song. Somewhat eccentric, but she seems vital to the whole welcoming protocol. Purposeful.

Clothing design? Goes along with artwork on display. And music. What an amazing place!

CHAPTER THREE

A Culture of Idleness

AT 7:59 A.M. SHARP THE NEXT MORNING, I WAS BACK AT DR. Spencer's office. Mrs. Krueger apparently hadn't arrived yet. The door to his office was open. He and Nurse Brownell sat at his large desk full of files and assorted papers neatly stacked. Nurse Brownell glanced in my direction as I entered; she smiled and nodded me toward the empty chair.

We exchanged good mornings.

"How's our new patient?" Dr. Spencer asked.

"Complacent so far," I said. "He was with an attendant when I left, going to breakfast. I said hello but he didn't respond. He's a quiet fellow."

"Give him time, we'll see," he began. "Mr. Quinn will stay put, for the time being, in Cottage 29. We'll have staff monitor him and try to keep him busy as much as he'll allow. He needs space and time to adjust. In the meantime, we'll set up an ITP."

Nurse Brownell interjected, "Initial Treatment Plan. That is standard protocol for new patients."

The doctor continued, "We'd like you to help set up that plan for him. Get your feet wet, so to speak, with the patient care at this institution."

I appreciated this gesture of collegiality. Clinical Diagnosis

39

had been my favorite course in my program. I thanked him for including me.

"Good," he responded. "The three of us will get to that later today. But this morning, Nurse Brownell and I would like to have a little talk with you about your letter of application."

"Oh," I said, "sure." But I thought, *this is worrisome.*

He opened a manila folder and slid my letter of application flat on the desk.

"I regret it's taken this long to actually sit down and have this talk. But, as you can see, this can be Grand Central Station at times, in a manner of speaking."

He put on his reading glasses and glanced through the first page. I looked sideways to Nurse Brownell. She smiled at me.

"Nurse Brownell and I have been discussing plans for your field experience here. And, we have some questions."

"Questions?"

"Yes. Nancy, will you?"

She took over. "In your letter of application, you mentioned your previous field experience, at Harrisville State Hospital. Apparently, that only lasted a few weeks. Why? What happened there?"

That's what I was afraid of. I really did not want to talk about it. But I saw that I had no choice. *Belli?* Strategy?: I would say as little as possible.

I explained that I was supposed to complete the fieldwork portion of my studies at Harrisville State Hospital. I could have applied anywhere, but, at the time, Harrisville seemed as good a choice as any.

They exchanged glances. I knew I could not avoid what they were looking for, so I backed up in the chronology.

"My supervising professor, Dr. Hilliger, advised against my going to the Harrisville Asylum in the first place; she didn't think it would be the kind of experience with patient care *she* thought I should have. Still, it was *my* decision to make, and so she went along with it, reluctantly. I should have heeded her caution. It turned out to be a huge mistake."

"Mistake?"

"I didn't fit in there. What I saw of patient life, that was very troubling. I expressed my opinion, and, well, let's just say, my opinion was not well received."

Dr. Spencer held the bowl of his pipe to his cheek when he said, "I'm afraid we'll have to know more details. Can you elaborate?"

The last thing I wanted to do was go into what led to my termination at Harrisville. There, I had stood my ground. On principle. Still, being told to go home after just a few weeks was a serious blot on my record.

But there sat my supervisors for my *second — and* probably *last —* chance to complete the required field experience. Holding anything back was not a choice.

I explained how, when I was there, I noticed that some patients liked music, which led me to ask why the patients couldn't get some instruments and learn to play, maybe have a little combo or something. I mean, ninety-nine percent of the time, patients just sat around with nothing to do other than play simple card games or listen to the radio. There was no activity to speak of, same old thing day in and day out. That would drive *me* crazy.

"I felt sorry for them," I said. "People, including mental patients, aren't passive by nature. Even those with phobias or retardation, or whatever, they need an active life. But that institution, it was a culture of idleness. So, I came up with the idea of starting a patient band. I asked around who wanted to join the band and before long, there were six or seven patients lined up.

"But staff there said, 'We can't get the instruments. Too expensive. The patients will just destroy them anyway. A waste of time and money.'

"I didn't think it was a *waste* at all. I went around the town, found some instruments in garage sales and resale shops. I found a snare drum and a ukulele, some bongos, an old clarinet, a guitar, and three harmonicas. They were cheap and not in great shape, but the patients loved them. One actually knew how to play the clarinet and another figured out a few chords on the guitar from a book; others blew in and out on the harmonicas until they figured out simple melodies. They tried to play together. It wasn't really music, but so what? They loved just getting together and *thinking* they were a band. They even had a name — *Benny Goodman's Brothers!*"

"And that got you in trouble?"

"It did. It wasn't long before staff and other patients complained about what they called *the noise*. So guess what? One morning the instruments were gone. No one could say where they went. One attendant said they must have been stolen, but I know where they went — off in the trunk of someone's car."

Nurse Brownell leaned toward me. "I'm puzzled," she said. "You were there to gain field experience, not to change their practices. Didn't you see that going against the grain might jeopardize your position there?"

She had a good point. But in order to explain why I persisted with the band, I had to back up again--this time to the Jesuits.

"That's part of another problem," I said. "Well, not exactly a problem. Some would say it's a strength. At Harrisville, though, it *was* a problem."

I explained how I had gone to a Jesuit high school—St. Joseph's—in Philadelphia. How the Jesuits, as most people know, teach you to question.

"They embrace the skeptical tradition in philosophy. They teach you to think. I have my father's curiosity and my mother's verbal skills, so asking questions just comes naturally. You could say that, at St. Joe's, I became an adolescent skeptic."

"Seems an asset," said Dr. Spencer. "For someone who purports to be a scientist."

"Unfortunately, skepticism didn't serve me well in this instance."

He mumbled something like "hmm" and puffed on his pipe at the same time.

"Brother Benedict was my mentor there. He taught Logic and he taught Latin. He said the best students in his classes would be the ones who challenge ideas and opinions, and then he taught us *how* to question, like Protagoras, who was a Sophist in ancient Greece. He was a great teacher, Brother Benedict. More than that, he was a great friend, really. He also taught me how to box, after school. He believed that boxing conditioned the body *and the mind*."

"You are—a boxer?" said Nurse Brownell, head cocked backward, eyebrows raised, surprised eyes settled on me.

"That might be putting it too strongly," I said. "I mean, I can hold my own—if I need to. Brother Benedict taught Latin when I sparred with him. He'd say, '*Leava, Leava, Dextra*' for 'Left, Left, Right!' And he'd bark out '*Punctum*' for a jab, and '*Uncus*' for a hook."

Smiling broadly, Dr. Spencer said, *"Experimentalis doctrina?"* "That's it, exactly! Experiential learning." *She knows Maslow and he knows Latin!* I thought. *This is definitely the place for me.*

I loved Latin, I told them. And then I explained how, in college, I took philosophy courses for electives. My skepticism merged with a strong sense of moral justice that I got from studying philosophy, especially Kant. But I finally majored in Psychology — that just seemed the perfect fit for a curious mind in a field where science and philosophy know so little about the human mind and human emotions.

"I'd like," I said, "to carve out a career for myself as a scientist *and* a philosopher."

I was getting ahead of myself with them, so I looped back to my time at Harrisville.

"Unfortunately," I explained, "that combination of curiosity and skepticism often gets me in trouble. I seem to have this habit of opening my mouth before thinking. That's what happened at Harrisville.

"*'Ecce ante te largiter,'* Brother Benedict used to advise me. *Look before you leap.* That's always been a problem for me. It was my problem at Harrisville. I asked too many questions. I should have kept my mouth shut."

"Apparently you didn't," remarked Dr. Spenser.

"No, I didn't. What I *did* do was to complain to the Assistant Director of Hospital Operations, a Mr. Greenblatt; he was my immediate supervisor. He just sat there expressionless. He was so sold on the culture of idleness that he could not conceive of anything different. Having a patient band was like having aliens visit from Mars. When his authority was challenged, his thick black caterpillar eyebrows started twitching and he would place two palms down on the desk in front of himself. He'd rub the desk until you'd think the varnish would come off. Then he'd glare at me with those singular eyes beneath the vibrating caterpillars. Sorry, I don't mean to be sarcastic."

Nurse Brownell put a fist to her mouth. Stifling a laugh.

"Mr. Greenblatt recommended that I keep my ideas to myself from then on. Which I tried to do. But I couldn't stop wondering why the patients couldn't have a richer life. Why couldn't they have dances? Why couldn't they have field trips, men and women together? What about hobbies? Patients who liked to sing should have a choir. Those sorts of things. I mean, their lives were empty of any purpose. Sit around all day and wait for the next meal? To me, that just seemed wrong.

"Finally," I said, "I just lost it with Mr. Greenblatt. I went to see him again with my complaints. It was another tense meeting with the varnish removal routine and the caterpillars. I told him I thought his whole operation fell unreasonably short on the scale of integrity."

Nurse Brownell looked up to the ceiling, fist over mouth again. Dr. Spencer wrinkled his forehead, opened his eyes a bit wider, and stared over the rim of his glasses at me.

"On the scale of integrity?" he said.

"That was the most civil thing I could say, at the time. But then I lost it.

"I asked Mr. Greenblatt how he could sleep peacefully at night, knowing his residents were miserable (sorry, sometimes I overgeneralize)—and the hospital rules were unreasonable (well, not *all* the rules). I may have said some other things I regretted; I'm sure I did. At any rate, when his hands curled into tight fists on the desk and his face returned to normal, he whispered a creepy *'That's it'* and said my field experience was terminated. I was to leave immediately. I didn't argue. I had had enough. So, I just left."

I just left seemed to hang in the air for a few moments with no other words exchanged between us.

"It's probably too late, but I just don't want you to think I'm a troublemaker," I said. "I won't cause problems here. That's all behind me."

They both had neutral looks, like neither one was about to confirm or deny they had suspicions about who I was or what I might do during my time there. Dr. Spencer just nodded, thinking; Nurse Brownell stared out the window. Both waited patiently.

I couldn't just sit there in silence, so I filled the vacuum: I explained that though I keep in touch with Brother Benedict, I never told him about my Harrisville experience. I didn't know if he would be sorry that I didn't heed the *Look Before You Leap* rule, or proud because I followed the worn path of the impudent skeptic.

"At any rate," I continued, "I returned to the university still needing credits for the field experience.

"I went to see Professor Hilliger, feeling like the prodigal son come home for redemption. She never said I told you so. But this time she insisted I apply to the Traverse City State Hospital. She had heard Dr. Spencer give a talk at a Psychology conference in Chicago a year or so earlier. His talk was about patient care here, and she was very impressed; she said he referenced Maslow's work. She thought I should have come here in the first place, but she was willing to give Harrisville a chance — and me the opportunity to succeed *there*."

Nurse Brownell spoke. "I'd like to know, Henry, if you learned anything about *yourself* from your time at Harrisville?"

I was looking over her shoulder at a wall of books behind her, but my peripheral vision caught a flash of her knee as she uncrossed and crossed her legs. I didn't dare look down at it. I kept my eyes glued on the books.

"Henry," she repeated. "I asked, *what did you learn about your-self?*"

I shook my head as if I had drifted off. "Oh, sorry. Yes, I learned to keep my questions and opinions to myself. Dr. Hilliger suggested I keep a diary and write down my thoughts and observations. She called it a field experience journal, but it's just a diary that I carry with me. I use my diary to pose rough ideas that may become part of my thesis. I've also found that writing is better than, you know, blurting things out half-formed."

Nurse Brownell: "So, you write in your diary instead of speaking your rough thoughts, the ones that get you in trouble?"

"That too, sometimes. I wish I had done a lot of that at Harrisville. But after Harrisville, I swore that I would not push people's buttons in the next internship. Bite my tongue if I have to; but keep my eyes on the prize. Otherwise, I'll never finish the degree."

Her slight, knowing smile again as she spoke: "I hope you will find the right balance between your natural wonder and your new sense of opportune moments to speak your mind."

There was a knock and the door opened. Mrs. Krueger poked her head in.

"Senior staff meeting in the canteen," she said. "Fifteen minutes."

We stood.

Dr. Spencer and Nurse Brownell excused themselves, they

were expected to preside at the meeting. Could I return around eleven to continue our conversation? Which, of course, I could. After all, I still didn't have any schedule of activities. I expected that would be coming in part two of our conversation.

I found a quiet corner with a table and chair in the lobby down the hall from the hospital mailroom. There I wrote a letter to Clara, telling her about my first days at the asylum. I needed an envelope and a stamp, so I walked down to the mailroom. That's where I first met Mrs. Dorman.

Perched on a stool behind the glass window, Mrs. Dorman grinned at me from beneath her jet-black Bettie Page rockabilly bangs cut straight across her forehead. In an earlier life, I imagined, Mrs. Dorman had poured coffee and waited tables in a café full of long-distance truckers.

She gave me an envelope and a stamp, and explained that the envelope comes "au gratin," by which I figured she meant *gratis*, and the stamp was "on the house." I thanked her and went back to my little table to address the envelope.

Back at her window, I handed her the envelope, sealed and stamped.

"I'd like to mail this letter."

Through too-red lips dangling half of a Lucky Strike, she nodded affirmatively. She pulled a long draw on the Lucky and stuck it between two fingers as she leaned over the counter, pulled open a little hole in the side of her mouth and blew smoke out it.

Her "Sure enough, darlin'" was accented by a smack of chewing gum. "Mail goes out twice a day, next time 4:38 p.m. That soon enough?"

"That's soon enough."

CHAPTER FOUR

A Vagrant in Detroit

AT ELEVEN O'CLOCK, THE THREE OF US SAT ONCE AGAIN IN DR. Spencer's office. He announced that we were going to review the file for the expected new arrival, James Quinn. I was invited to apply my clinical psychology background to the review. I felt honored to be included.

Dr. Spencer leaned back in his swivel chair, puffing on his pipe. He scanned the documentation and paraphrased aloud.

James Quinn. Late 20's. He had lived in East Detroit with his grandmother—same family name, Quinn—in a flat she had rented since his grandfather died just before the war. According to a neighbor lady who was friendly with them, Quinn came to live with his grandmother sometime in '43 or '44. She said he looked to be in his twenties but she never learned just how old he was at the time. Where he came from, the neighbor never learned. Mrs. Quinn kept to herself, though she did tell the neighbor "the boy needed a good home" and his "other family" was having hard times.

Dr. Spencer speculated, "It's likely that, at some point, the birth family no longer knew what to do with him. So many families have no idea of what to do with a child with retardation, not to mention when that child becomes an adult. But, other than family, our society doesn't provide for them very well at all."

"Is there any mention of him being a threat to others, or cruelty to animals?" I asked.

"Nothing like that." His finger pointed to a place in the report. "Says here that the neighbor knew Quinn was different just by the way he stared or waved at passersby from the front porch. 'Sometimes,' she said, 'he would shout *Hi. I'm Jimmy. What's your name?* But none of this is much to go on." Dr. Spencer glanced over at Nurse Brownell and said, "Another possibility is that the family sent him to the grandmother after her husband passed away so the two could support one another."

Nurse Brownell: "If that was the case, I wonder how much of that move he actually understood. If he didn't understand, he could have felt abandoned."

"Good point," said Dr. Spencer. "Let's keep that in mind." He continued reading and paraphrasing.

The grandmother died unexpectedly — brain stroke — in June of this year. The neighbor lady told police that she didn't see Mrs. Quinn or the boy for days. When newspapers started piling up on the lawn, she called police. They found the grandmother in her bed. Her covers had been pulled up to her neck and there was a glass of juice and a stale sandwich on a side table. They estimated she had been dead for three days. They found Jimmy Quinn hiding in the basement.

They were able to coax him out of hiding, but when they tried to get him into the patrol car, he ran. They were unable to catch him. He just disappeared.

A distant cousin and his wife came from Toledo to tend to the remains and clear out the premises. They said they didn't know where the boy's family lived, never heard of him before. Mr. Quinn, meanwhile, disappeared into Detroit's east side and apparently lived there through the summer months. Somehow.

"Who knows what his state of mind he must have been during that time," commented Nurse Brownell. "I can't imagine his fear, his confusion, how lost he must have felt. And the skills he'd need to survive while living in the parks and alleys, with vagrants and who knows what. What do you think so far, Henry?"

"It's rough living on the streets," I said. "Dangerous. He would have had to develop survival skills fast. I'm still wondering why he was sent to live with his grandmother in the first place. Did he have a violent streak? Did he hurt animals? Did he hurt someone in his birth family? Is that why he was sent to live with her?"

Dr. Spencer pulled his glasses off and placed them on the papers. He stared at me just a moment too long for my comfort. I was speculating on the basis of no evidence. I had spoken too soon. I felt foolish.

He cleared his throat. "We know nothing about his previous life, one way or another. Let us continue."

Quinn was finally picked up in August when police cleared out Chandler Park after a brawl one night. He was booked for vagrancy and assault. He spent the night locked up. When the police realized he had no ID and was retarded, Social Services got involved, identified him, and secured his release. He was transferred to the Pontiac Asylum for intake and evaluation.

Nurse Brownell spoke. "Nothing must seem stable to him, nothing predictable and no one to trust. He must be terrified not knowing what tomorrow will bring."

I asked, "What is his diagnosis? Can we even justify his being committed to a hospital? The neighbor said he was *different,* and we all know what that means, generally speaking. Not *normal*. A clinical diagnosis would help us make sense of who he was and how staff are to support him."

My curiosity was addressed in the officialese of the Kalamazoo report. Dr. Spencer read it aloud:

> *Multiple violent episodes in first week at Pontiac, to be detailed in full report ... transferred to Kalamazoo State Hospital August 24 ... non-compliant at KSH & more violent episodes ... profoundly non-communicative with staff and peers ... seclusion needed on two occasions ... calm and compliant since September 1 ... erratic and unpredictable behavior consistent with schizophrenia ... overcrowded conditions here ... recommend transfer to the Traverse City State Hospital.*

"I am not comfortable with that diagnosis," said Nurse Brownell. "That seems premature. After all, just consider what his life has been like. How would *any* person react to such trauma?"

"But," I said, "If Quinn *does* suffer from schizophrenia, that would be consistent with his violent outbreaks before he came here — and his flat affect since arriving. Is there anything in the report about hearing voices, or hallucinations?"

Dr. Spencer studied me in a way that made me feel discomfort again. Where he and Nurse Brownell were moving cautiously, I had jumped the gun and accepted the given diagnosis. Had I been too quick to typecast Quinn? Had I been too much the eager clinician? His look suggested I had.

"It *could* explain his behaviors," he said. "Let that be *their* diagnosis. We'll conduct our own evaluation.

"For now, let's withhold judgment. Pontiac could not keep him because they only have non-violent patients. And although Kalamazoo does have a small population of patients with some violent tendencies, it's terribly overcrowded. And, they didn't think Mr. Quinn was serious enough to be sent to Ionia."

"Ionia?" I asked.

"The Ionia Hospital for the Criminally Insane."

Nurse Brownell let out a deep sigh. "Thank God they didn't send him there."

"Yes," said Dr. Spencer. "But let's remember, major traumas like the ones he's suffered can cause many symptoms, including violence. As for diagnosis, I lean toward some form of TAR."

"TAR?" I asked.

"Traumatic Adjustment Reaction. Couple that with his mental deficiency, and a picture may begin to emerge. Still, when someone is mentally slow to begin with, and doesn't have the language ability to express complex emotions, well, he nonetheless has to express those emotions somehow—and violent expressions may be all he can do at times.

"Nancy," he said, "your thoughts?"

Pensive, she was studying her folded hands in her lap. She looked from him to me and then back toward her hands.

"He will teach us about himself, sooner or later. We cannot possibly predict what patients will teach us, but you can be sure, they *will*, although you may not like what you learn. It takes, I believe, a special kind of listening, even when one of them is shouting to get your attention, calling you vile names, or standing naked before you, screaming obscenities. You learn to not take it personally. I'm just preparing you, Henry, for what you might expect to see here."

Dr. Spencer cleared his throat. "In this case, time is on our side. Meanwhile, Henry, we have a proposal for you."

I sat up straighter, "A proposal?"

"We discussed this before you arrived this morning. What would you think of conducting an intense and extended field evaluation of Mr. Quinn? We'd like to move him to your cottage, where you can observe him, come to know him. Given the constraints on our time and manpower here, this is nothing any staff member could do, normally. We never have staff spend so much time with one patient. With 3,000 residents here, it's too costly—in spite of the benefits. But you are not paid staff. You're a...how shall we say, a guest specialist, so to speak. You're different."

I felt uncomfortable being "assigned" to one patient.

"How long would this evaluation take?" I asked.

"That depends on the patient. Perhaps weeks."

I didn't like what I was hearing. It made me uncomfortable—all that time with one patient. "Not to disagree with you, Dr. Spencer, but..." I stopped, hesitant.

"Go ahead. You can talk freely. You're not at Harrisville."

"Okay." I cleared my throat. "I worry that if I spend so much time with just one patient, I could lose...objectivity. Whereas if I could be exposed to so many more in the same time frame...what I mean is, professional distance."

Nurse Brownell interjected, "We all have to maintain distance from the patients. You will need to use your observational skills as you would in a laboratory, to find patterns and form hypotheses. In that sense, this part of your internship would be as objective as observing *large* numbers of our population. But you raise a good point about broad exposure, and we have thought about that, too. We don't want to keep you from experiences with the general population."

I had expected macroscopic exposure, not microscopic evaluation. That feeling must have showed on my face because as I started to object again, she interrupted me, and, in a sloweddown delivery style for emphasis, she said, "You-will-have-to-trust-us-here, Henry."

"Of course," I said. "I do." I wanted to say more, but I had already promised that I would not cause any problems, and here I was doing just that. Anyway, her authoritarian comment hung in the air as the doctor shuffled papers back into the folder. An eerie silence settled in for a few moments, which he then broke.

"How do we proceed?" he asked, not looking up.

"Slowly—and thoughtfully," she said, "I would like to arrange a series of, let's call them *invitations*, for the next week or two—some planned ways to invite Mr. Quinn into the life of the hospital. To help him get oriented and socially connected. Henry, you would be present at these invitations—observing, taking notes.

"At the same time, you would continue to observe elsewhere throughout the campus, so you can keep taking in the overview."

I could see the balance in this plan. I nodded my agreement. "And so," she continued, "Evaluate Mr. Quinn, yes, *and* observe broadly at the various hospital locations. I will prepare a list of those locations and a time schedule for each.

"You will begin your work in the hospital archives. To learn the history of the asylum. You know from your academic training the value of an historical perspective."

"I do. I look forward to that."

"And that knowing the past helps one understand the present. So, as you also know, we are experiencing some problems with vandalism. We have been for some time now. Your research there will likely be illuminating in that regard. In the meantime, as you research in the archives, Mr. Quinn will remain under the care of nurses and attendants. They will orient him to the grounds and provide an initial structure to his days as they make their own observations."

Dr. Spencer: "When you do begin to accompany Mr. Quinn on these invitations, be careful. Remember his profile. If there's any hint of trouble, alert orderlies."

"I'm sure I'll be okay..."

He raised a hand. "Don't be so sure," he continued, "You are to call orderlies in an emergency, that's protocol. If you don't know where all the call boxes on the grounds are located, then put that first on your list. Bring your questions to Nurse Brownell. She meets with me weekly, so I'll be kept informed. If you need to talk with *me* directly, check my schedule with Mrs. Krueger."

We rose as a group, said our goodbyes. I followed Nurse Brownell into the hall. We walked down the long stairwell together. William the painter was gone, though his artwork still stood on the two easels.

At the bottom of the stairs, she paused and turned toward me.

"Henry," she said, looking back up the stairs as if to ensure our privacy, "I have thought about what you said this morning, about keeping your eyes on the prize or you may never complete your degree."

"I didn't mean..." I started to say, but she cut me off.

"I believe I *do* know what you meant. In fact, I reached a

point in my own medical education when all I could think of was getting done and getting on with my career."

"But I didn't mean ..."

She put up a hand for me to stop. "Wait. At one point, I too felt that same student impatience. I shared those same kinds of feelings with my father."

"The philosopher."

"The would-be philosopher. I shared them with him in a letter. A week or so later he wrote back. He quoted a few lines from Lao Tze, a Chinese sage you may have heard of."

An attendant approached us from down the hall. Nurse Brownell pulled on my shirtsleeve to move us away from the stairs. "Here," she said. The attendant nodded a silent greeting toward us and ascended the stairs. Nurse Brownell waited until he disappeared at the top of the stairs.

She continued. "I have never forgotten those lines. They shape my daily life."

"What were they?" I said.

She cleared her throat. "They were taken from the Tao Te Ching."

A good traveler has no fixed plans
and is not intent upon arriving.
A good artist lets his intuition
lead him wherever it wants.
A good scientist has freed himself of concepts
and keeps his mind open to what is.

Silence enveloped the space between us. I pursed my lips and nodded, unsure of what to say.

She spoke again. "Don't confuse this internship with the university classes you have taken. It will be very different. You are no longer meeting course requirements so you can accrue more credits. There are no semesters here. Immerse yourself in the culture. Let the culture guide you. Let it teach you. Let it penetrate you. Become the scientist who has freed himself of concepts. Realize that you are no longer a student."

Those last words echoed in my brain. She said, "In the morning, I will send you instructions for your archives research. Today, please become familiar with the entire campus. Use your map. Find those call boxes and mark them on your map. You will need to know where you are at all times and how to get where you need to quickly."

That was it. No goodbyes, no enjoy your day. All business. She turned and walked down the hallway. She disappeared through the door at the end of the corridor.

I retrieved my map from my room. I wandered the grounds for the rest of the afternoon. I located buildings and call boxes, and I memorized routes. By the end of the day, I had probably walked four or five miles back and forth altogether, until I had a pretty good sense of things. Still, I would need my map on me for the next few weeks, just in case.

That evening, seated at my small desk, I wrote a brief letter to Clara describing the colorful arrival of this recent new patient, my role in the welcome, and Eunice's remarkable skit on the platform. I told her how much I loved her and how much I missed her.

Then I wrote one line in my diary.

September 7, 1952:
You are no longer a student!

I put down my pen, looked out the window and stared at lush, green fields that stretched far to the southern perimeter of the asylum grounds. Closer in, cows grazed leisurely in vast pastures beyond two enormous yellow- and brown-bricked barns. A group of maybe fifty or sixty workers stretched out on a dusty dirt road bending from those same fields. Some carried bushel baskets in both hands, some balanced stacks of baskets on their heads like African traders; others walked with various tools slung over their shoulders. Two horse-drawn carts followed them, other workers standing in the wagon beds holding on to the fenced lattices as the wagons wobbled and jerked their way through the rutted road.

I closed my eyes as my mind drifted to a mound of snow outside a chicken coop at the break of dawn on a frigid February morning. Tiny, feathered corpses litter the snow — grey, brown, cream beige. Some huddle on one another like puppies asleep in a cardboard box. Others lie on their backs, separated; their pink stick legs gathered flat against their round tummies. The wind blows fresh snow over them. Slowly they disappear, until only a few beaks and legs protrude.

Frozen chickens. Slashed tires. A dog's head in the pond: what would research in the hospital archives reveal about all that?

CHAPTER FIVE

Well-Being

THE NEXT MORNING, I DISCOVERED A LETTER FROM NURSE Brownell pinned to my door. I was assigned to the Office of Admissions and Records for the next two days. That is where I would do research in the hospital's archives. Mr. Dziewa's new assistant would get me oriented.

This research, she wrote, *will help you understand better how our philosophy of patient care originated in the work of Dr. James Decker Munson, our first medical superintendent. I expect you will find that our philosophy complements the humanistic framework from Mr. Maslow that guides your research. I suggest you focus on the REPORTS section of the archives.*

Bring your questions to me. Inform me when you have completed your research.

A ham and egg breakfast in the Men's South Commons dining room preceded a hurried walk to Admissions and Records in Building 50.

That office was on the first floor, east wing. I was greeted by Mrs. Dorman from the post office and her double dose of lipstick. Her tabletop centerpiece of a rockabilly hairdo was now done in a set of large curls that piled up on her head like coiled ropes. The ropes bobbed when she talked.

"Cutie patooti!"

"Ah, Mrs. Dorman. I thought you worked in the mailroom."

She beamed. "Hold your horses, dumplin'. Because I got some bad news for you, and I got some good news."

"I suspect the bad news is coming first?"

"Well, as a matter of fact, it is. The bad news is that Mr. Dziewa, our admissions director, is out sick. Strep throat. Gone all week, likely."

"The good news?"

"Good news is that yesterday was my last day in the mailroom. I got promoted! And transferred! No more sticking mail in tiny boxes all by my lonesome. Never liked working alone any hoot and holler. But now, I got majorly responsibilities, *majorly*—and an upgrade in pay!

"I knew it was coming, but I didn't tell anyone until it actually happened. You know how things can go south the minute you tell someone. Didn't even tell Mr. Dorman. He'd just celebrate by drinking up my first pay upgrade with the boys. Sure as sheetrock, I'll tell him eventually, but first I'll put a down payment on that orange couch I been eyeing at the furniture store so he can't weasel any extra bucks for himself."

Mrs. Dorman reminded me of Marie Dressler in that old Tugboat Annie movie—a rough-and-tumble woman whose sentences never seem to end.

"Now," she continued, "before you start to thinking about turning your behind around and scooting back to wherever you started from this fine morning, you need to know that if you're looking for Mr. Dziewa, you ain't gonna find him here. Like I said, he's out sick. But I'm his *personnel* assistant, so I'm all you got. Get. Nurse Brownell sent me a message, well to Mr. Dziewa actually, but I get first crack at his mail."

"Do you mean *personal* assistant?" I interjected.

"That's what I said, blossom! With the boss gone, I already set up an itinerary for you, starting today with showing you intake and dismissal, records, and such. Should take us an hour. Then you can do your work downstairs in the records room or you can work up here, in the boss's room here, and you can close his door for pri…privateness. I got all my own work to do anywhoo, so no one's gonna bother you, least of all me. That's the way it'll be until you say different. Besides, the hourly girls will be here soon to start running errands. They keep me busy keepin' *them* busy!"

She gave me a whirlwind tour of the two-room office, offered me a smallish table off to one side in Mr. Dziewa's office for my research, and then ushered me to the "files" in the anteroom office.

CURRENT files held information on all the patients presently at the hospital. Those were kept in tall cases along the wall, all alphabetized.

"You want to know anything about anyone who's a patient here," she said, "this is where you find it. If *it* ain't here, *they* ain't here. That's my job, keeping track of everyone, alive, dead, and in between. Sorry, deceased. If you want to know about staff, that's over in Personnel. I need another promotion to work there. But I'm real happy here. No reason to move. Now we need to go downstairs, to the archives. This way, apricot."

Her sentences ran together like boxcars.

The basement stored large boxes stacked upon others, all labeled on the sides. One stack had boxes for DISMISSED PATIENTS 1885-1895 and so on up to 1950, one box for each decade; another had DECEASED PATIENTS, fewer boxes but still organized by decades up to the present; another stack held CORRESPONDENCE TO/FROM the hospital, again by decades; and finally, a stack labeled REPORTS—GOV-ERNANCE, CONSTRUCTION, SERVICES.

"This here is where the Nurse Director thought you might do your work," she said, "but you got better lighting and a desk upstairs, so you ought to bring boxes upstairs to read from. I could be your Research Assistant!"

A shudder went through me. I politely declined.

"Whatever you say," she said. "You know where to find me."

For the rest of the morning and early afternoon, I dug into the boxes. I skipped those that had to do with patients dismissed or deceased. I thought the reports on governance would illuminate history the best, so I hauled those boxes one by one back upstairs to read at my little table. I closed the door to Mr. Dziewa's office for privacy. True to her word, Mrs. Dorman went about her work silently, except for whispered instructions to the hourly girls. I never saw them, but I heard them come and go throughout the day.

Mid-afternoon, I opened a box labeled ANNUAL RE-PORTS OF THE BOARD OF THE NORTHERN MICH-IGAN HOSPITAL (1889 - 1911) and two boxes named AN-NUAL REPORTS OF THE TRAVERSE CITY STATE HOSPITAL (1912 -).

I worked my way through the early ANNUAL REPORTS' facts and figures, financial records, demographics, grounds expansion plans and changes, and all sort of charts and graphs. All the early reports contained lengthy passages written by Dr. James Decker Munson, the hospital's first Medical Superintendent, from 1885 to 1924. The longest-serving superintendent, Dr. Munson brought to the hospital a multi-faceted view of patient care. Based on his belief that *beauty is therapy*, he collected trees on his travels that were planted throughout the campus and that gave rise to lovely stands of willow, oak, and walnut trees as well as flower gardens and orchards.

Also, a believer in *work is therapy*, he oversaw the development of a thriving farm operation, where, as one report stated, *crops are planted and harvested in great abundance; dairy cows and pig herds flourish; acres of fruit orchards fill the hillsides; and gardens, parks, an artificial lake (Willow Lake), and lawns proliferate. Barns, livery, root cellars, milk house, greenhouses, and granary with large silos support the huge farm program.* By 1907, the farm had over 400 working acres.

In the BIENNIAL REPORT OF 1908, Dr. Munson himself wrote:

It is with great pleasure that I report that the farming program has become a successful economic asset to the financial well-being of the hospital, as the financial reporting for the year clearly shows. The hospital has not only maintained considerable herds of dairy cattle and pigs, but has also produced fruit and vegetables that have exceeded by a factor of two our expectations.

More importantly, and consistent with past years, the bulk of the farm work has been done by male and female patients voluntarily. Normally separated by gender on the grounds, they work side by side, with supervision, in the fields, barns, and greenhouses.

Deference is not shown to either gender. If a woman can do work normally expected of a man, she does it. And vice versa. Both genders also work in the storehouses, orchards, and on the grounds cultivating flowers and shrubs for the gardens, lawns, and parks. No one is forced to work; some patients are simply unable or unwilling to work. But we have found that those who do work derive significant benefits.

The farming and grounds programs have, from the beginning of their development, functioned as a significant therapeutic treatment approach that affords patients the opportunity to contribute importantly to the overall "family" of the hospital, much as one's children would contribute to the health of their farm family. This sense of contribution brings with it pride in workmanship and the positive self-esteem that accompanies work well done. It boosts morale while it also confirms, for some, their identity as a worker (planter, cultivator, harvester, milker, etc.).

Working on the grounds also exposes patients to a form of beauty--the horticultural beauty of the natural world that has proven to be of immense therapeutic value. Grounds workers will spend hours arranging flowers and greens to adorn the halls of the cottages; and they will tend to the many gardens throughout the campus. Staff photograph their work to send to relatives, and patients create scrapbooks full of photos that they share with one another and visitors, with great pride. The beauty of the natural world is as therapeutically significant as it is for those for whom music is beauty, art is beauty, and so forth.

The annual reports revealed similar accounts by Dr. Munson on the economic impact of farming, dairying, and orcharding. In the 1921 Annual Report, he wrote:

The combined revenue generated by farm, dairy, and orchard operations exceeds the entire cost of the hospital itself. The hospital costs the taxpayers not a penny, in great part because the labor is free and in great part because the produce, milk, and meat is abundant and in great demand in the local market where our surplus is sold.

What an extraordinary legacy! I thought. *What testimony to innovative patient care!*

I thumbed through the annual reports up to 1948. The same themes emerged year after year: agricultural success, economic self-sufficiency, beauty, art, identity, relationships, and pride. Dr. Munson and his successors were most proud of what could be done with *natural* treatments that help *most* human beings to thrive. From a psychological perspective, the Munson approach based treatment of mental illness on *ability*, not *dis*ability. While it did not ignore the fact that some people suffered from illnesses who may *never* be affected by natural treatments, it held promise and hope for many others who well may benefit from such therapies.

I picked up the last Annual Report in the box — 1949. In it, I discovered a list of 24 causes for people committed in that year. Some may be considered legitimate diagnoses — for example, traumatic head injury, sexual violence, manic-depression, schizophrenia. But others simply represented hard times, medical challenges — life as we know it:

- business reverses
- disappointed affections
- domestic infelicity
- grief and anxiety
- overwork

- complications of giving childbirth
- sexual excesses
- excessive discordance
- privation (otherwise known as poverty).

I put down the report and opened my diary:

September 8, 1952:

As recently as three years ago, people could have been committed if they were despondent over a business failure, lonely due to loss of a lover, incompatible with their spouse (surely only a husband's option), or poor. Hell, my "excessive discordance" at Harrisville could have been reason enough to have me committed!

This raises questions about the whole diagnosis enterprise. For example, what makes a diagnosis valid? Do "professionals" really have the ability to accurately diagnosis the mysterious operations of the human mind, especially human emotions? How much is guesswork? How much is science? Is what we call "mental illness" truly mental illness?

I think that if you cast a wide enough semantic net called "mental illness," then what ends up in the net is a range of ill people, some less in need of asylum than others. Which raises more questions: Does every patient belong here? And, for those who have been committed, how much time and human resources are needed to be certain every one of them belongs here?

Is that why I've been assigned to evaluate Quinn? What did Brownell, say? Understanding the past illuminates the present. That would be especially true for understanding

patients, like Quinn. What circumstances in <u>Quinn's</u> life
brought <u>him</u> here? How can we even begin to talk about
treatment until we know his trauma history? But what do
we do when there is no record of that history and he won't
talk? Ah, but if he begins to trust me, then maybe some of
his story (wait, his history!) will come out.

So, my lesson is, that I should exercise caution in
"diagnosing" the others in that big net. But the reality of
the institution is that the sheer numbers and lack of time
normally prevent any deep or comprehensive patient
evaluations. I see their wisdom, Spencer and Brownell, of
giving me this rare gift.

I glanced at my watch. It was getting late in the afternoon.
Mrs. Dorman was nowhere to be seen. I returned the three boxes of annual reports back down to the archives. I was standing
down there surveying the stacks of boxes when sunlight suddenly flooded the dimness. Mrs. Dorman came halfway down. She
squinted, looked around.

"You okay down here, pumpkin?"

"Fine, Mrs. Dorman. I'm fine. I'll be leaving soon."

"Okay then. No hurry. Just checking to see if you're still
breathing. You need any help, you just yell. The door will lock
behind you when you leave." She stomped back up the stairs. I
lingered until Mrs. Dorman and the girls were long gone. Then
I went upstairs.

The late summer sun was ushering in another slow, red-and-
orange dusk as I pulled the office door behind me and heard it
lock.

CHAPTER SIX

Invitations

THE NEXT DAY, THEY MOVED JIMMY TO COTTAGE 34, INTO A SEC-
ond-floor room just below mine. Cottage 34 housed a large number of patients with depression. Many of these men complained
loudly about every little thing—the weather, the food, the mos-
quitos, staff. Some sat on the porch for hours at a time, staring
idly, while others shuffled through the hallways in pajamas.

Jimmy spoke to no one in the cottage. He would pass through
the living room or hall, with no response to greetings—or jeers.
His was a self-imposed protective shell. How I was to break
through that shell—or even if I *should*, given my non-medical,
non-staff status—was my dilemma. My mentors said I was to
observe and report my observations to them, which I understood to mean an objective, clinical approach. But when you're
with someone all day long, day after day, you quickly feel that
apparent objectivity begin to fade.

My "intensive observation" of Jimmy consisted of my chap-
eroning him from wake up to bed at night. Nurse Brownell
had given me a slate of "invitations" for Jimmy to work with
others at a job—she suggested laundry, bakery, and kitchen for
starters. We strolled the grounds, stopping here and there to
observe the work. I pointed things out to him but he remained

a mute observer. Occasionally, when I would talk with staff or patients, Jimmy would politely stand off to one side, watching me or looking about—scanning, I figured—to get a sense of his bearings in that locale. What he actually saw, I had no idea. I felt he was actively constructing his sense of the entire place, location by location.

As the days passed, I became eager to see some progress. Even a simple yes or no to my questions would have been a start. But no, he just stared, at me, or at nothing in particular. Sometimes I would take him gently by the arm and lead him—a frail, speechless man-child.

A few days of evaluating the mysterious Jimmy Quinn left me speculating, with little data to go on, as I wrote in my diary:

September 11, 1952:

Day three of my evaluation of Jimmy Quinn. Docile, withdrawn, uncommunicative. Responds to requests and commands. Follows directions without dispute. Shows no interest in people or activities. Completely inward. A tortoise drawn into his shell.

Mutism. He doesn't talk, but he can hear. Is his social unresponsiveness constant? So far, yes, but social circumstances can change that symptom. Blank expression & staring off: Avoidance? Protection? Fear? Shame?

Note: Kussmaul identified this disorder in the 1880's. He called it something different that I don't recall, but that's what it was symptomatically—self-induced mutism. Could Jimmy's be a form of it, some kind of reaction to being in this strange new environment? Or a reaction to what happened after his grandmother's death?

I heeded Dr. Spencer's advice about being cautious. Wherever we went, I checked for the nearest call box. I had attendants look in on him throughout the night and stand outside the door when he used the bathroom. He and I ate together in the dining hall. He ate his meal, disposed of his dishes and silverware, following my lead. He spoke to no other patients or staff, even when spoken to.

In spite of his passive ways, Jimmy's withdrawal was not like his hall-mate Siederman's — no first name that I knew of — his only clothes as far as I could ascertain were changes of nightshirts. He stationed himself in a rocker in the hall early morning and except for having to go for meals and bathroom, that's where he stayed. He mumbled to himself, nothing that I could make sense of. Staff put him into winter clothes and galoshes in bad weather so he could get to the dining hall without freezing. Once back, he stripped off the outer garments and boots and took up his station for the next few hours. I greeted him regularly: "Mornin'," and "What's buzzin' cuzzin'?" But he just rocked and mumbled.

Siederman was *unable* to participate; Jimmy was *unwilling*. Something told me there was a soul alive in him, a core that, in time, would reveal itself. Over the next few days, my goal was to invite him into a variety of activities. I would explain how he might participate, and he would listen, nodding as if he understood. He would politely watch, for example, Beverly prepare meals in the dining hall kitchen, but then walk away, shaking his head no. The same would be true of the crew sweeping the streets — okay to watch but not to do. At the power plant, at the warehouse, and at the stable, he chose to be a spectator.

One day I took him out to the fields on the other side of

71

the huge cathedral barn. The fall harvest was going full steam by this time as patient-workers tended acres and acres of broccoli, cauliflower, eggplant, and every variety of gourd I could imagine — pumpkins that would grow to the size of enormous beach balls; zucchini and colorful winter squash; and all the root vegetables one could possibly name — potatoes, of course, but also turnips, parsley, beets, carrots, onions.

This harvest struck me as a cornucopia from some mythological tale.

Then there were the patient-workers. I was amazed by their calm deportment as they went about their work with serious intent and deliberate care. Working, for the most part, in silence. When someone did speak, it was in low, measured tones, as if there were a baby asleep somewhere and they didn't want to wake her. It was like an ant farm or a beehive, where the insects, by design, all busily go about their work.

These were not the wide-eyed jokesters or unpredictably high, or low-spirited patients I had encountered elsewhere on the campus. Some may have been the same people, but here they seemed transformed — perhaps, I speculated, by the singular meaningfulness of their work, perhaps by the responsibility they felt toward the living plants they cultivated. I couldn't be certain, but that's how I interpreted what I saw. *Work is therapy,* I had read in my archives research. Here was concrete evidence of it. In time, I would come to understand more fully what this work meant to them, but on this day, what I saw appeared to be contemplative occupation.

We walked rows of vegetables three hundred feet long that had been meticulously weeded and groomed as if they were in a landscape painting. We came upon a group of workers on hands and knees inspecting each individual plant. Carefully turning up leaves and peering underneath, they would daintily pick bugs with one hand and cup them in a closed fist in the other.

Jimmy watched cautiously as one red-bearded old timer rose from his bent position, reached out a closed palm to Jimmy, and then turned it over to reveal a handful of crawling critters. Startled, Jimmy lurched back, stuffing his own hands in his pockets.

"Aw, c'mon buddy," the old guy said, his voice calm and reassuring. "They're just little old cutworms and flea beetles. They won't hurt you. They're out here foraging for their own food, just like God intended. Cute little critters."

Then he squeezed his clenched hand tight, picked up a canvas bag from the ground where he worked and shook the tiny red and black bodies into his bug bag.

He smiled at Jimmy. "Now they'll just be mixed in with the earth to fertilize next year's crop. That's what Mr. Meyer always says. Mr. Meyer says even the tiniest pest has a purpose in this here life. Just like humans, Mr. Meyer says. They just got to figure out what it is, is all."

I don't know what it all meant to Jimmy. He took in the entire scene, as he had every other scene we'd come upon in our circulation of the hospital grounds. When I asked him if he'd like to lend a hand and join in with a crew, he screwed up his face and shook his head side to side.

After I returned him to his cottage later that afternoon, I called over to Nurse Brownell to report that Mr. Quinn would have no part of invitations to work and did she have any other ideas? She said she would arrange for more social invitations and that I should have Quinn out in front of his cottage after lunch tomorrow.

CHAPTER SEVEN

Birders & Dancers

NURSE BROWNELL RANG ME UP THE NEXT MORNING TO SAY that she had arranged for two social invitations—birding and dancing—and I should have Mr. Quinn ready for the first one after lunch. I was to note how organized companionship affected his willingness to participate. Thursdays at the hospital, she explained, always had a birding trip up into the woods west of the campus buildings. A forested area of more than 100 shaded acres provided trails for hiking as well as a small stream for barefoot walks in the creek.

So, on Thursday of the second week since he'd arrived, shortly after Jimmy and I returned to the cottage from lunch, we were sitting on the porch taking in the sun on that unusually warm mid-September afternoon. Eyes closed, Jimmy seemed in some sort of reverie when we heard a merry chorus of singing coming up the walk from the direction of Cottage 15. The tune sounded familiar but I couldn't make it out clearly. The voice, however, I recognized immediately as Mrs. Hillman, another of the Fabric Shoppe workers who, like Eunice, was often to be found singing anywhere on the campus.

Twelve patients—mostly female—and two attendant chaperones marched up the sidewalk to Cottage 34. Mrs. Hillman looked in at us and shouted, "Hey you two, you want to go find some birds? We're going on a bird hike. You want to come?"

"We're going to take a hike up the hills and find birds," shouted Mrs. Hillman. "Come on with us, you two."

The others in the group took out binoculars and monoculars, notebooks and pencils, and bird identification books and flapped them all about while making various bird noises. Mrs. Hillman wore aviator glasses and a deerstalker.

A second woman stepped in front of Mrs. Hillman. She wore dungarees and a blue cotton work shirt. Her belt was too long for her slim waist, so it hung in front of her like a brown snakeskin. Slung over one arm was a plaid cloth bag. She was pretty. She pointed at Jimmy. She had a high-pitched voice full of energy—and challenge.

"You there, you on the porch, you. You ever seen a big black crow caw cawing in the fields? You ever seen those lovebird doves that always go two in two together like two and two lovebirds in love like that? We see those birds all the time. And…and…you ever seen those woodpeckers with the black and white and red and gray colors pecking that tree and getting tree bugs? Huh? Hey! You awake or you sleeping with your eyes open?"

Mrs. Hillman stepped forward once again. "Wait up, there, Bernadine. Maybe this fellow is scared of birds. You afraid of birds?" she asked. "You a scaredy cat?"

Jimmy stood up and squinted at Bernadine. "Nah," he responded, "I'm no scaredy cat."

I whipped my head around at the sound—finally!—of Jimmy Quinn's voice. It was as clear as the familiar bell and calm as could be.

Did she just challenge his masculinity? I wondered.

"Well then," Bernadine waved her arm overhead to beckon him, "You got to come and see those birds and all those other ones we'll see. And…and…you can have my binoculars here, and…and…you can have my bird book so you can see their picture and…and…everything about them in the book here." She dug in her birding bag and pulled out binoculars and book. She held them out to Jimmy.

The two staff attendants stood off to the side, waiting, smiling. I looked to Jimmy, he looked to me. "Go, Jimmy," I said. "You might like it—unless you *are* afraid of birds."

"I'm not afraid of no birds," he said.

He grabbed his coat and joined the group. Bernadine handed him her birding bag, looped the binoculars around his neck, and stuffed the book into his coat pocket. "Now you are a bird man, Mister. What's your name, Mister?"

"Jimmy."

Bernadine let out a howl. "Whoo hoo! We got a Jimmy bird right up there in the woods and you'll see that Jimmy bird. We got to go there and, and…You got the same name as that Jimmy bird."

I had no idea what a Jimmy bird could be.

"All right," Jimmy said. "I never heard of no Jimmy bird."

Mrs. Hillman pulled him over next to her, rustled through her birding bag and pulled out a blue Detroit Tigers baseball cap. She handed it to Jimmy, said all the birders had to wear a hat to keep the black flies off their heads in the woods. Jimmy turned it over a couple of times and then put it on. It was a good fit.

Then Mrs. Hillman asked him if he could sing. Jimmy looked at her with a puzzled expression. He didn't respond. Instead, he pointed toward the woods, said, "Gram like birds." He fell in behind Mrs. Hillman as Bernadine took the spot next to her. She wrapped her arm in the arm of Mrs. Hillman.

The troupe went off, Mrs. Hillman and the others arm in arm, singing something about going off to find the robins. The others followed, as did Jimmy, binoculars hanging from some necks, monoculars dangling from others, books and notebooks and pencils bulging from the pockets of coats and overalls.

I thought of trailing after them but then decided to experiment with Jimmy being on his own with just other patients and the attendants. I wondered if my not being around would help him come out of his shell. *Already they had gotten him to utter his first words, maybe more would follow.*

Progressus. Progress. At last.

The hospital held weekly dances for that small segment of the population that showed interest in dancing. Given the large number of patients altogether, it wasn't possible to have one dance for everyone at one time. Instead, smaller affairs brought 50 to 100 together for two hours after dinner.

So it was, that on the same day that Jimmy went birding, a dance had been planned for the women's dining hall that linked two large cottages. Nurse Brownell assigned me to bring Quinn over for the event, which I did right after dinner. I told Jimmy we were going to hear some music and watch some people dance. His eyes grew wide as if he had some jitters about it all, but he didn't protest in any way. We walked over to the women's dining hall just as things were getting organized there.

Nurses brought a phonograph and a stack of records while

kitchen workers filled a table with Kool-Aid, cider, and cookies and cupcakes made fresh that afternoon. Just before seven, residents were escorted over by staff, some dressed to the nines for a night out on the hospital town. I figured that Eunice and the Fashion Shoppe ladies had been extra busy that week taking orders for colorful ties, bright flowered wraps, and white gloves.

At seven sharp, the music began with a trio of Benny Goodman hits — "Don't Be a Baby, Baby," "Slipped Disc," and "Dizzy Fingers." The crowd around the snack table began to peel off as residents moved around the floor to the beat of the music. Some glided around by themselves when the music floated, and they gyrated when the tempo picked up. Others who had taken the dance lessons offered by staff had partners and, holding one another at a great arm's length (that was the rule, strictly enforced), made their way across the floor. I thought a few couples were really quite smooth.

Then there were the wallflowers, men and women who lined the wall of windows and stared at those on the dance floor. When the music changed to Frank Sinatra singing "All of Me," followed by "The Charm of You," the many wallflowers joined the solos on the floor or, with awkward hesitation, invited others to dance. Men danced with women, women danced with women, men danced with men, and even staff got out there.

I was standing behind the snack table replacing cookies on a tray as residents came by to grab one or two when they paraded around the room, or, in some cases, whizzed by alone. Jimmy hung close by the front of the snack table, munching cookies.

Bernadine from birding approached him. "You there. You're the man who likes those grackle birds, ain't you?"

He took a step back.

"Ain't you going to do some dancing? Ain't you going to be-bop and swing and stuff with all the people? You want to do some with me, Mr. Jimmy Jingletoesman?"

"Nah," he said, "I don't know no dancing."

"Ah, c'mon, Jimmyjingletoes. It's easy to dance with me. You want to dance with me or not? Or you want to stand there eating all the cookies till you get the runs?"

"Nah, I'm not going to get no runs."

"Yeah, you are. You'll be in the poop house for a month you keep eating all those cookies and not dancing with me."

Bernadine pointed down at her brown shoes. "Look. I got these swell dancing shoes on and they need to go dancing with a grackle man, not no robin man and no sparrow man either. So, what about it?"

By now she had positioned herself between Jimmy and the cookie trays and stood firm, facing him, arms on her hips. She would wait him out. She pointed the forefingers of both hands at him and said, "I am not going to wait till all the cookies are gone neither, and I am not going to wait till you get out of the poop house."

Jimmy looked imploringly at me. I just shrugged and nodded toward Bernadine as if to say, *I'm powerless.* Sinatra stopped and a fetching classical piece began — Strauss's "Vienna Waltz" — by a symphony with lovely violins and cellos. The music went down low for a few moments as Nurse MacDonald announced that this was the "waltz" that was in the dance class, so everyone had to remember the steps, the 1-2-3, 1-2-3.

"And move around the whole floor everywhere. Arms and hands in place. Proper distance. Okay. 1-2-3, 1-2-3."

The waltz music came back on and couples and solos began moving in any direction, excusing themselves politely ("Oh, pardon me" and "So sorry") when they bumped into one another, as taught in their class, apparently. Bernadine took Jimmy by the arm and shuttled him out to the middle of the room.

"Watch my feet and don't move till I tell you to—or else."

She turned to the couple behind her and barked, "You there. Move over so me and my date here can cut the rug." The couple backed up a few feet just as a ruckus began behind them.

"No no! Not like that, you idiots!"

The booming voice of a male patient violated the strains of Johann Strauss. Roaming the dance floor by himself, he had singled out a dancing couple and began circling them, arms waving over one another in front of himself, as an umpire would signal the runner was safe at second base.

"It's 1-2-3 and 1-2-3!" he shouted. "That's the rule. You're doing 1-2-3-4 and 1-2-3-4. That's wrong! You have to do it right! 1-2-3 and 1-2-3."

He circled the couple and clapped his hands to the 1-2-3 beat.

"That's the rule! You can't make up no other rules!"

The couple stared at him, bewildered.

The male partner shook a menacing fist at him.

"You want a knuckle sandwich? Get outta here, nutcase!"

"You're crazy!" The female shouted. Then she coughed up a wad of sputum and shot it out of her mouth, hitting him on the forehead.

Solo patients continued around the melee, gliding in smooth metrics as the three of them squared off.

Nurse Greenfield was on the spot almost immediately.

"Nurse Greenfield," he pleaded, "look at those two! They're all wrong and they won't obey the rule. Make them obey the rule, will you? They're doing fours instead of threes. And they won't stop it!"

The nurse took him by the arm and whispered something in his ear. He looked at the odd couple, then back to her, then the couple, then her again. He pleaded.

"But they're not doing a waltz! That's some other dance and it's not right. It doesn't belong to the waltz. They can't break the rule just for themselves! And his arm. It's not even in the right place! You have to make them do it right!"

She took his right hand in her left hand, put his other hand on her lower back, and slowly began to waltz, counting out loud, "1-2-3 and 1-2-3." She guided him to the other side of the room in ¾ time.

The fracas ended, as did the waltzing. Couples broke apart, and everyone stood in place, uncertain, waiting.

Next on the hit parade was Count Basie's famous "One O'Clock Jump," a big band tune that had the floor full of people hopping and jumping, twirling and spinning with helicopter arms. Bernadine had Jimmy out there doing some form of primitive swing dancing.

Was this, finally, the real Jimmy Quinn?

With that final song, the dance ended and everyone—residents, staff, orderlies—all clapped wildly in appreciation. Men bowed before women and women bowed before men, yet another lesson from dance class. Then the parade of orderlies and staff began walking out with their assigned residents. Those who remained began cleaning up and putting the place back in order for breakfast.

One woman remained in the middle of the floor, all dressed in flowing white muslin and a white turbaned hat. She was elegant. Oblivious to other people leaving or cleaning up, she danced to her own internal music in lovely, long steps that magically graced the dance floor. As the tables were put back into place, she glided between them and around chairs in the open spaces.

I watched her from the exit door. Jimmy waited patiently on my left. He pointed at the sole dancer and said, "She's pretty. She's got pretty clothes."

On my other side, Nurse Greenfield leaned close and said, "Agnes Coterie. She was a professional dancer, you know. Famous in Chicago in musicals and dance shows. That was before the accident. She fell on stage in rehearsal, hit her head on a floor light. She suffered a serious brain injury and lost most of her mental functions. It's a miracle that she can still dance."

"That really is a miracle," I said.

"I'm sure it's nothing like what she used to be, but we think it's what keeps her going day to day. It's in her soul. She often gets up in the middle of the night and dances in her hallway. We bring her here sometimes so she has more room than in her cottage. She doesn't need music; it's all in her head. Once in a while, though, I get out the phonograph and put some records on. She will dance for hours."

Agnes dancing with all those soft flowing drapes of gauze struck me as one of the most beautiful things I'd ever seen. And the peace in her face as she danced—absolute heavenly bliss—spoke to the beauty there *is* in dance—and, for Agnes, the undeniable fact that beauty is therapy.

Jimmy tugged on my shirtsleeve. "Why don't someone dance with her?" he said.

"I don't know, Jimmy. Maybe she just likes to dance all alone tonight."

"I would dance with her," he said.

Nurse Greenfield passed out into the night, but Jimmy and I lingered, watching Agnes. Her dancing had evoked some deep feelings in Jimmy. I guessed that, in the grace and charm of her movement, he too saw beauty and felt its immediate presence. Jimmy Quinn, I was starting to realize, had a huge heart and a spirit capable of deep emotions.

I shouted, "Thank you!" to her but I doubt she heard it. I turned and stepped out into the brisk night air, Jimmy close beside me as we made our way to the cottage.

That night, in my room, I wrote to Clara. I wrote about the colorful birding trip and the priceless dance. About Jimmy emerging from his protective shell. About the cute social amenities practiced by the patients at the dance. About Jimmy and Bernadine.

And Agnes.

She once had a beauty, I wrote, *in her body and the way she held that body on the stage. And here, in this hospital, she is encouraged to recapture the beauty that so defines her very existence. I am coming to see the many ways that* beauty is therapy, *dance being just one way. I just wish you could be here to share them with me, right here, right now. I love you.*

Then, in my diary:

September 15, 1952:

My client popped out of his shell today, however briefly. What made that happen? What made today different from all the other days? Was it, as Dr. Spencer said, just a matter of time? Perhaps. But the invitations made the difference.

Birding and dancing. Social life. Beauty. All of it; no one thing.

For other patients, what kinds of activities afford them similar social belonging and purpose? Sewing clothes. Baking cookies. Learning etiquette. Learning to dance. What do they all have in common?

1. All are <u>meaningful</u> things to do.

2. All involve other <u>people, playing or working together</u>.

3. All evolve out of a <u>culture of collaboration, purpose, and meaningful activity.</u>

4. All illustrate attention to patients' needs for love, belonging, and self esteem (Maslow).

This is why Harrisville was so abhorrent to me. Patients were <u>spectators</u> to events, not <u>participants</u> — they watched dancers from town perform <u>for</u> them, whereas they themselves should have been the performers. No birding clubs, no choirs, no jazz bands. A culture of passivity.

It doesn't work for <u>all</u> patients. Some just cannot engage. Some cannot be social. Some are disruptive. It is complicated, BUT:

I <u>have</u> <u>to</u> work through the complications.

NOTE: Cousin Ethel lingers: Never once did I invite her to do anything. Did she yearn to be included? Did she have feelings about not being invited? Of course she did. <u>Does</u>.

CHAPTER EIGHT

Pisshead

THE TINY WINDOW INTO JIMMY'S WORLD CLOSED THE DAY AF-
ter that dance. He retreated back into himself in spite of all my
efforts to talk with him and in spite of other invitations. Sure,
he hesitantly accompanied forty-some patients to the beach on
West Traverse Bay for one last chilly October day at the water,
but there, by himself, he sat and stared while others played with
beach balls in the sand or searched for smooth stones.

Somehow, weeks earlier, Bernadine had found a way for him
to open up, however briefly. There was something in the chemis-
try between the two of them that clicked that day. I even recruit-
ed her to come by his cottage and invite him for more birding,
and then for a bus ride to see the sand dunes on Lake Michigan.
"Nah," was all he seemed to muster.

"Time will tell," Dr. Spencer had said. I was to wait out the
ensuing weeks, to continue my evaluation, however little "data"
Jimmy produced. I was becoming impatient. If nothing changed
by the first of November, I would stop trying.

But that change did come on a cloudy, cool day in mid-October.

I had taken Jimmy over to the cow barn to show him the
milk cows and to introduce him to the workers there. Five pa-

tients milked the cows, while others transferred the milk to the milk house. Tom Stephans supervised the milkers, but they had worked with the animals so long that he was superfluous most days.

We stood inside the double doors of the cow barn listening to the sound of milk shooting into metal buckets as the crew squeezed teats and the cows looked toward their rears at the milkers. Jimmy held onto my arm as we advanced toward the nearest stall, where one of the crew was speaking softly to the cow he milked.

"Good girl, Rosie. You like me to squeeze your titty for milk real nice, squeeze easy not hard, Rosie, and you like me to sing oo-la-la-oo-la-la. You make more milk for my pail, Rosie. Oo-la-la-oo-la-la."

Jimmy and I looked over the top rail of the stall and down at the man seated on the stool milking Rosie. Black rubber knee-high boots, a flannel shirt, and bib overalls. His thick glasses bobbed with the rhythm of milking Rosie. The man looked up and smiled broadly, "Hey, Mr. Henry, who's your buddy?"

"This is Jimmy," I said. "Jimmy, meet Mikey, the best milker in the barn. Every cow here is in love with him, right Mikey?"

"Right you are. These cows, they love my singing. Oo-la-la-oo-la-la and they love my patting their butt and they love me giving them hay. They love Mikey. Right, Rosie?"

Jimmy backed away, turned to look straight at me, and, hands in both pockets, said, "Gram likes milk. Gram likes milk and I like milk with Gram."

To me. He spoke directly to me for the first time! He had opened another window, this time into his history. I decided not to press him.

"I like milk, too," I said.

Mikey reached through the lower rail of the stall door and grabbed my leg.

"Does that man want to milk Rosie?" he asked. "He want to milk this old cow?" His strong grasp held my pant leg.

Jimmy, meanwhile, took one brief look at Mikey and walked out the barn door into the sunny morning light.

I tried to shake loose of Mikey's grip but he held on.

"Come on, Mr. Henry. Stay here and talk with me and Rosie."

The barn door slammed shut; I realized my mistake too late. I finally shook loose from Mikey and ran to the door.

By the time I got outside, he was gone. I looked for a call box, saw none. I ran to the stable next door, raced through the open doors. A few horses stood alert as I made my way through the stalls, calling for him. At the other end of the stable, I left through the tack room door. Once outside, I saw him beside a pile of stacked wooden logs, bent over half way. He was sobbing. When he saw me, he put both hands on the pile of logs and began pounding. The anguished sound he made was nothing human.

Something—I didn't know what—had triggered a memory. Was this grief? Rage? I didn't know. Nor did I know what I would do, there, alone.

Slowly, cautiously, I came up to him. I hovered my hand over his shoulder, did not touch. He placed his hands on the sides of his head and rocked his head from side to side, crying. Then he extended his arms and began pounding the logs again.

Calm voice, I thought. *Reassure him.* "It's okay, Jimmy. It's okay. I can help you. Just…tell me…"

He stood up, wiped his eyes with his sleeve. "Gram like Mr.

Henry. Gram likes all nice men. She hates Mr. Pinkskin. Gram said keep away from Mr. Pinkskin. I promised Gram, I *won't*, Gram. But I...I..."

Jimmy pounded with one fist on his head again. He screamed, "He's mean and he's stupid. He's a pisshead. He's a mean pisshead. He hurts people!"

With that, he picked up a hefty piece of wood and heaved it toward the yellow-bricked barn wall. "Yeah, he's a pisshead," he screamed again. He grabbed a larger log with both hands and hurled it at the wall. Then another. And another, all the while screaming, "Pisshead Mr. Pinkskin!"

In a matter of seconds, logs and skinny tree branches lay scattered in the dirt all around us.

Then, "Don't hit that wife, don't hit that boy!" came out of him in a scream-wail.

There were no call boxes, no attendants. I was on my own with Jimmy and this Mr. Pinkskin. He picked up one very large log with both hands again and swung around toward me so fast that he knocked me to the ground. He held the log over his head with outstretched arms.

I lay flat, looking up at him facing me, the huge log suspended over his head. Over *me*.

I knew I was in trouble.

Had I become Mr. Pinkskin? Would "He's a pisshead" be the last words I would hear?

I knew I could defend myself if I could get to my feet. But when I tried to get up, I lost my footing in the scattering of branches and small logs and went down again. I didn't think. I just rolled over on my stomach, prepared for the worst. I covered my head with my arms and shut my eyes. I expected the blow and the pain to come quickly.

What I heard, though, was a loud grunt of exertion and then the sound of the log hitting the ground somewhere beyond me. I peeked out through my arms. The log rolled through a patch of thistle and stopped about ten feet in front of me. Cautiously, I cupped my arms around my ears and rolled to one side. I looked up. Jimmy was looking down at me, sweat mixed with sawdust pouring down his face. He was still crying. Snot dripped from his nose. He stood there, arms akimbo, his chest heaving as he gasped for air.

I looked past him, scanned everywhere. *Where is the goddanm call box?* I thought.

I figured Jimmy might take off but at least I'd be safe and they'd catch him eventually. But then some other part of me — not sure where — said *no, don't leave him.* I didn't really know what he needed, and I didn't know what I could say that would help calm him down. I just lay there helpless. Praying he wouldn't kill me. Praying someone would show up.

He towered over me, heaving with each breath.

When he finally caught his breath, he stepped back and turned to face the barn. He bent over from the waist to gather his breath. I got to my feet, brushed some dirt from my eyes and spit out some that was stuck to my lips. I stationed myself in front of him, hunkered down so he could see my face from his half-bent position.

In nearly a whisper, I said, "I wish I could have had milk with you and Gram, Jimmy. I wish I could have met her. I bet she was really something."

I talked in the gentle way a parent might talk to an out-of-control child.

"She's really something, Mr. Henry. Some *thing.* Gram likes you, Mr. Henry. Gram hates Mr. Pinkskin." His breath slowed. I prayed he was calming down.

I seized what I figured was the perfect therapeutic moment for truth.

"Why did she hate Mr. Pinkskin?"

He squinted, looked up toward the sky, lost in some tragic memory. "Mr. Pinkskin hit his pretty wife. Gram called her Mrs. Blue and Mrs. Black and then Mrs. BlackBlue. And he hit the boy. With a belt. And the boy cried and Mrs. BlackBlue cried and Mr. Pinkskin was drunk and all the time hitting in that house. We heard them from our porch. Gram took me inside when they started up."

I asked, "Did Mr. Pinkskin ever hit you, Jimmy? Did he ever…touch you?"

He turned and began walking away. "Yeah, he's a pisshead," Jimmy repeated as he walked.

I kept a safe foot or two between us as we walked, in silence.

I sensed an opportunity: "Did Mr. Pinkskin ever hurt Gram?" I said. "Did he hurt any animals? Did the police take him away?" Foolishly, I peppered him with questions and I immediately regretted that. The clinician in me had gotten the better of the therapist.

Jimmy said nothing more. He walked silently, sniffing and wiping his eyes and his nose. Two female patients approached, then stepped off the sidewalk, allowing us to pass. Eyes wide, they stared.

We made our way toward Cottage 34.

I made some tea for us and we sat together silently, on the porch, enjoying the quiet and the tea. A half hour passed, the only sounds were our sipping and rocking in the chairs. Jimmy had nothing more to say, and I didn't know what more to say. I followed his lead: we sat in silence.

The incident had passed.

That night in my room I wrote up my first incident report on what had happened at the barn.

I explained that I had taken Jimmy to the milking barn to see if I could interest him in anything there. I described his escape from the barn, finding him behind the stable, and his rage and violent behavior there. I wrote about him tossing logs at the barn and about his cursing fit. I put in the part about me lying on the ground and fearing for my own life. I speculated that he had had a near-psychotic breakdown, had nearly become the other person in a split personality, the side capable of violence that could pose a danger to others.

I finished the report and I sat there, staring at it. *It's a classic personality disorder,* I thought. *One minute he's standing there with Mikey and me and then something—who knows what?—triggers this crazy behavior, this rage that takes over, and he dissociates.*

He could have killed me. Maybe he *was* trying to but he just missed his mark. Maybe, in his rage he lost muscle control and, lucky for me, he overshot his target. Then who knows whom else he might have attacked until the rage passed? Had I been killed or injured, Jimmy would have been arrested. He would have become yet another member of the prison population suffering from mental illness.

But I had *not* been hurt. I stared at the report. Someone

reading it would surely equate Jimmy with violence and danger, just as they had in Pontiac and Kalamazoo.

I had no doubt that his behavior fit within a medical frame of understanding, but what *was* that frame? Multiple personality? Schizophrenia? Chronic Brain Disorder? I was expected to provide a diagnosis, but I worried that I might misdiagnose, and how would that then make me look—sophomoric?

In truth, I didn't know what to make of him. Or what to put forth as a diagnosis. That really frustrated me.

Reading over the report, I realized that putting all this in writing also jeopardized my residency. What I did behind the stable did not follow the protocol for emergencies. I should have left him there and gone for help. Instead, I put myself in harm's way.

I could see myself sitting with Dr. Spencer and pleading, "It all happened so fast, I didn't have time to think!"

It was the weakest of excuses.

On the envelope I wrote, TO THE ATTENTION OF DR. SPENCER.

"What happened, happened," I said out loud. "And what happens, happens."

I took the report over to the mailroom in Building 50 and slipped it in a slot in the door marked "OUTGOING MAIL."

The next morning, I got a call from Mrs. Krueger while I was in my cottage, just before lunch. Would I come to his office at one?

Fast, I thought. *Not good.*

Just inside the entrance to Building 50, a seated woman wearing brown pants and a pink pullover sweater looked up and grinned at me when I entered. Her grin became a broad smile that revealed only a few remaining teeth, but the paint spots on her dungarees identified her as the display artist of the week. Easels lined the walls between the main door and the stairwell. Weeks earlier, I had met William from Alpena, who beamed when I complimented him on his paintings of dogs and flowers. I didn't have the time to stop to talk with *this* artist, but I lingered before a canvas that depicted an adolescent male face; half was recognizable as normal, but the other half was bloodied and distorted. She volunteered that the child was her brother Frederick who died in the war.

"I'm sorry," I said, "for your loss."

"Thank you kindly," she said. "He's better off now."

I could have stayed longer. I could have heard her story. But "He's better off now" just struck me as the start of a long narrative that, frankly, I didn't want to hear. Not at this time, with Jimmy on my mind.

I stayed the course and went up to the second floor.

Mrs. Krueger was at her desk, as usual. She nodded toward his office door. "He's waiting for you."

He was seated at his desk, the endless piles of folders in stacks, his yellow brick paperweight holding down a stack of papers at the corner. We exchanged pleasant greetings and then he lifted the brick and pulled out my report from the top of the papers.

"I've read your report," he said. "Thanks for getting this to me so fast. You did all the right things, Henry. You know that, don't you?"

"I wouldn't know what else to do, sir. But there is one more thing. It's more about me."

"Go ahead."

"Jimmy Quinn is a very complicated man with mental retardation who suffers from grief and loss. But, in spite of all that, he is a gentle man at his core, a man who has a history of pain and loss—and love and affection. I've been impatient. I wanted my evaluation to result in a diagnosis. It hasn't yet, but I feel it should have by now."

He picked up a pen, twirled it in his fingers.

"Henry, you do realize how far you've come, don't you? You've moved beyond—please excuse my bluntness—what seemed like a desperate search for a diagnosis to describing the patient as a man, first and foremost. A man with special talents *and* special challenges. As powerful as a medical diagnosis can be, it remains a top-down term to describe a real person. You now have arrived at a bottom-up description of Mr. Quinn."

"At one point, I thought his diagnosis was *self-induced mutism.*"

He chuckled.

"Well," he began, "in my book, that's not helpful, even if it *were* a diagnosis. It merely describes the patient's behavior. Understanding his history takes you deeper, and it preserves his unique humanity. That's more important—and helpful—than putting a label on him. Time is on your side, Henry. Keep at it."

The pencil continued to twirl. "As you can see, I'm skeptical of premature diagnoses. Putting a label on a person changes nothing but the people who rely on that label to make judgments."

"Lingua est potestatum," I said. "Language is power, Brother Benedict was fond of saying."

"Then you understand what I'm getting at. It shapes our—and others'—*perception*s of the patient. In doing so, I believe we lose sight of so much else about that person. A better course is to avoid labels when there's doubt, to come to a deeper understanding of the patients first—their history, their talents, their desires, their loves—all that they're able to teach us. Our job is to listen, to watch, to treat them with respect, to see them as vital human beings with the same needs, the same desires, as normal people, if there is such a thing as *normal*."

"You see a fluid boundary between the asylum and the rest of the world, don't you, Dr. Spencer? You would treat the patient as you would someone on the outside?"

"I don't like to think in inside-outside terms. That worldview tends to create an us-them mentality. I prefer to think that the work of the mental hospital is a part of the work of the larger society. It is a simple yet profound shift in perspective. It changes things."

I thought of Professor Hilliger sitting in the audience when Dr. Spencer gave that talk in Chicago. If this was the sort of thing she heard, then I now understood why she insisted I come here. This was fresh insight. This would challenge most people's thinking, including my own.

"But to use your language," he continued, "If some things work *outside*, why shouldn't they work *inside*? Consider just the idea that every person needs a sense of belonging. They belong to a family, a neighborhood, a workplace, a club, and so forth. That is key to the mental health of a society. The same principle applies here. We have to build real relationships with patients, invest in them with love and beauty, and work—especially work—and help them find a place where they feel they belong, where they feel they matter, where others depend on *them* doing their part. We're constantly amazed at how easily patients begin to recover once they believe they have worth. That others depend on them. That they matter. They come to know themselves as part of something bigger than themselves as individuals."

"What do you mean, *bigger*?"

He cleared his throat. "Take work, for instance. For many people on the outside, work is just what you do to earn money to take care of your family or get on in the world. Or move up socially, invest to make more money, save for college, and so forth. For others, those who love their work, they see *who they are* in terms of the work they do. An artist, for instance, a teacher, a farmer. Who they are is what they do. And vice versa. Their work, their art, their music, it's inseparable from who they are."

"I see what you're saying," I said, "So the bakers are, in fact, *bakers*, because that's what they do? The groundskeepers think of themselves as horticulturists? Having an identity increases their stability, Maslow would say."

"That's right. In my view, this profession we call Psychology—and I would include Psychiatry as well—doesn't really understand the minds and emotions of the mentally ill very well at all. One day, perhaps they will. But they'll never *fully* understand; the mind is too complicated—it will always retain its essential mystery, even to science. For some mental health practitioners, all they know to do is to prevent patients from harming themselves or others. I call them 'keepers'—they keep patients in line. Their *job*, so to speak, is to prevent or control undesirable behaviors and to encourage desirable ones. That's a behaviorist worldview, somewhat simplified. But...prevention and encouragement is not treatment. A person is more than a collection of *behaviors*."

I wanted to open my diary and write down every word.

"See," he continued, "when institutions and professionals mainly focus on *behavior,* they miss too much that is essential. Don't get me wrong. I'm not about to criticize good people trying to do the right things in a system that cannot—will not—provide the resources, people, and money needed for authentic, proven treatment. But a sole focus on behavior? Why, that just addresses part of the patient in treatment. To stop there ignores and devalues the whole human being. I believe that how a society treats its most disempowered, its most downtrodden, indicates what it values—and what it does *not* value."

I had heard words to that effect before.

"Do you know of that spiritual leader in India, Mahatma Gandhi, the Indian who led the resistance against British rule?"

"I do," he said.

"Gandhi said, 'We can measure a culture by how well it treats its weakest members.' Or something like that."

Dr. Spencer smiled. "That is your humanistic philosophy in a nutshell, Henry."

I glanced at my wristwatch; I really wanted to end the meeting and get to my diary. But he continued.

"There's no doubt in my mind, that if most patients could just live and work in the right setting with the right opportunities and supports, they could find *some* degree of recovery. But if you take away their work, their contributions to the good of the order, take away what gives them reason to get up in the morning, what feeds their souls, you're left with what some poet called the 'hollow men and women of the cells and almshouses.' And there we are back to the nineteenth century."

"Take away what gives *anyone* reason to get up in the morning," I said, "what feeds *their* souls, and the same thing applies. It's basic human nature."

"That, too, is in your nutshell."

He picked up my report and returned his reading glasses to the bridge of his nose. "I'll go into Mr. Quinn's permanent record to remove the working diagnosis. We'll revise the record, keep mental retardation in there, and we'll add in historical trauma, not otherwise specified. We'll leave it at that, for now."

He stood and reached across the table to shake my hand, a signal that our time was finally up.

Our meeting over, I left. Frederick's sister was no longer on the first floor, where I would have asked her more about her art, if she were so inclined to talk. But she was gone.

I returned to my room. And my diary.

October 18:

"We can measure a culture by how well it treats its weakest members" (Gandhi).

This is where humanistic psychology, ethics, economics, and politics intersect. And it is the tip of an iceberg.

Writing my master's thesis will be just the start of a much bigger inquiry. I need to go on for the Ph.D.

CHAPTER NINE

Ice Caves

THE SNOW BEGAN IN EARLY NOVEMBER. I HAD BEEN WARNED THAT winter would bring three feet of snow on the ground until April, and the temperature would hover around 15 degrees throughout January and February. Except for snow shoveling, November marked that time in the year when the work turned indoors.

Women in the Fashion Shoppe continued to mend clothing and cut and stitch sheets and towels for general use. They also made special items used for work, like planting aprons and hemp bags for root produce; enough would be made to last through the next planting and harvest season. Men would sharpen blades, hoes, and shovels; clean plows; paint farm wagons; and refurbish tack for the horses.

Though the hospital did have its own fleet of cars and trucks, it did not use machinery to work the fields. Because one tractor could do the work of ten people, mechanizing the farm would mean less work for patients. Horses were used to till the fields, remove tree stumps, move produce around, and plow snow. It was the only farm in the tri-county area that had not mechanized. No one valued *that* kind of efficiency.

The hospital ethos was, *why use a tractor when ten men and women who want to work can do the work?*

The wagons were regularly used for hayrides. In fact, it was part of my own hospital education that I learn how to harness a horse and drive the hayride wagon myself—a set of skills taught to me by a stocky Swede who yodeled while he drove and whom patients called Mr. Yodelman. When the snow began falling, the hayride became a sleigh ride.

By mid-December, preparations for Christmas were in full swing. Patients decorated Christmas trees that stood in every cottage; green garlands and red-ribboned wreaths draped from porch railings; and tables in the dining halls featured lovely centerpieces made by the ladies from the Fashion Shoppe. Big plans were under way for Christmas parties, where hand-made or found gifts were to be exchanged among patients and staff, and the annual New Year's Eve events would include dropping a basketball from the top floor of Building 50 to a festive crowd of applauding patients and attendants singing "Auld Lang Syne."

For those patients who could participate in the festivities, there was a constant buzz and chatter of eager anticipation as they scurried here and there preparing presents or decorating trees. Others watched from their rockers with wonder or ignored it all with passive bewilderment.

By the advent of the holiday season, Jimmy had come much farther out of his shell. Now a regular partner with Bernadine at the dances and a frequent attendee at Saturday night movies, that side of him that had preserved his juvenile humor and innocent conviviality became more apparent every day. He had gained twenty pounds since his arrival as his general health slowly returned to normal. In September, he had resembled a fifty-year-old prisoner of war, but by December he had recaptured the hardy look of a healthy man approaching thirty. And the more time he spent with Bernadine, the more I saw a twinkle in his eye and a smile that grew broadly whenever they spotted one another.

I left on the day before the annual staff Christmas parties. There were two parties, so that some people could attend one while others stayed with patients. Patients had their own parties, too, in smaller congregations in the cottages and in the corridors of Building 50 during Christmas week. I rode the bus back to Philadelphia where I was to spend the last week in December at home. My parents had a big dinner party on Christmas Eve with select relatives on my mother's side and two uncles on Dad's side. I brought Clara.

Uncle Tony and Aunt Pat came with Ethel, who had graduated high school in June and had just gotten a job bagging groceries at the A&P. Uncle Tony helped her practice bagging at home before she started work, because she insisted that all cans go into the same bag—like things *must* go together. But Ethel got the hang of it and was very proud of her new job, said Aunt Pat.

At dinner, I sat between Ethel and Clara. While Clara chatted away, charming everyone as usual, I paid closer attention to Ethel than I ever had before. It was time I knew her better, time I made attempts to show I cared about her. I tried a few times to strike up conversation—*You must be proud graduating high school, Ethel. What have you been up to lately?* "Okay" was all she could muster. But *how is your new job?* had her actually look at me with a broad smile and an energetic nodding of her head.

"I am a very good bagger," she said, "and a very good sweeper, and a very good stocker."

I had hoped the conversational floodgates would open, but

that was it from Ethel. She went back to staring at her plate as others passed rolls and butter and other things to one another. I held each bowl for Ethel so she could serve herself.

Ethel formed the usual territorial domains on her plate — turkey, dressing, mashed potatoes, green beans — in their little provinces where one could not touch the other. I had always been amused at this little quirk. But when the gravy tureen came to me and I offered to pour some on her turkey, Aunt Pat across the table nearly had a heart attack. Her arm shot across the turkey platter and grabbed my arm, the tureen hovering between Ethel and me.

"Ethel doesn't like gravy!" she said. I hadn't anticipated that pouring gravy on her plate might make everything run together, and that would have set off Ethel's anxiety. I had seen it happen dozens of times in the men's dining room. I just didn't think.

Dad asked for gravy so I passed the tureen to him.

When I tried to engage with her again, I made my second gaffe.

"Well, Ethel, congratulations on getting your new job. You deserve a big pat on the back."

I turned and patted her on the shoulder. She stiffened up like a corpse. That was when I remembered something Nurse Brownell had said about how to approach certain patients on rounds: "Don't just touch without warning, and even then, be judicious — and don't do anything suddenly." Her words hung in the air between me and the cousin I had never really known. I wanted to make up for a lifetime of indifference to my own flesh and blood.

I still had a lot to learn.

The days flew by. Before I knew it, I was back on the bus to Michigan, and Clara was planning units for the new semester.

Jimmy was elated to see me back. He told me that this had been the first Christmas he'd had without his grandmother and how much he missed her. In my own haste to get back to Philly, I hadn't even considered how sad the holiday season would be for him. But now that his "best friend" was back he felt so much better. We made a plan to have an outing every other week—a movie at the State Theatre, sledding down the hills east of Traverse City—anything fun and inexpensive.

I couldn't just take one patient off the campus anytime I wanted. I had to file a request form for an official Patient Outing, reserve a vehicle if needed, and make it a group affair. The request had to be approved by the Office of Patient Affairs, and it always was.

On January 20th, President Eisenhower took the oath of office. I was glad to see President Truman finish his term. I had to give him credit for ending the war against Japan, although he never should have used atomic bombs. But I was glad when he finally sacked MacArthur before MacArthur had us in an all-out war with China. I hoped Ike would end this war in Korea soon.

Also on January 20, ice covered both the east bay and west bay north of town.

On the last Saturday in January—the snow had fallen every day since the fifteenth of December and the temperature hovered in the low twenties—I took Jimmy, his Mexican friend Francisco, and two other male patients, Wallace and Eddie, out to see the snow caves that had started to form on the western side of the bay. I parked the station wagon on Cass Street and we made our way two blocks to the frozen bay. We walked west along the frozen shoreline a good mile.

The caves there were not nearly as big as those I had heard about on Lake Michigan. There, cavernous coils of snow and ice stood as tall as 25 yards and stretched twice as long. The Traverse Bay ice caves were smaller versions of those, but still large enough for a person to crawl inside one. We would stare in wonder at the blue hues of pure ice, the light greens of air-infused ice, and the whites of crusty snow-covered pressure ridges of ice.

We wore all the winter clothing we could find, including rubber galoshes and wool scarves tied around our faces to ward off the frigid weather. We talked with ice fishermen about the perch and walleye they were pulling from little holes in the ice. We had sliding competitions that ended with the winner plowing into a mound of snow and ice at the shoreline.

But it was so cold. After two hours, tiny icicles hung from the places on our scarves where our breathing spots had been. We could hardly shape words, our lips were so cold. So we trudged back into town.

I treated them all to hot chocolate and brownies at Dill's Café. We sat shoulder to shoulder in a booth. I had Jimmy on one side of me and Francisco on the other. Our fingers were red from the cold. As our noses continued to drip, we wiped them on our sleeves. We cupped our hands around our mugs of cocoa and breathed the aromatic steam deep into our frozen lungs.

The men laughed as they recounted the fun we'd had on the ice, jabbing one another in the ribs like schoolboys in the lunchroom.

Francisco had only rudimentary English, so most of what he said was in Spanish, most of which I understood. Especially when he asked me to buy him some whiskey.

"Senior Henry, por favor. Need booze. For the *enfermedad.*"
Sickness. "*No me siento bien.*" I don't feel well.

I knew about his alcoholism. And I knew I would not buy
for him.

I looked at Jimmy. A worried expression crossed his face.

"Whiskey," Francisco repeated. "For the seekness."

Jimmy leaned into me. "Don't, Mr. Henry."

"Time to go, boys," I announced. We slid out of the booth
and started putting on clothing again.

I put my arm around Francisco and walked with him toward
the cashier. Jimmy stayed on my heels.

"Sorry, Francisco," I said, low voice. "No can buy. Booze no
good for you."

Francisco's head dropped in disappointment, but he said
nothing. He looked at Jimmy with pleading eyes. Jimmy gave
his head a firm shake to indicate no.

I was proud of him.

I bought them each a Milky Way and then we cashed out
and left. Once outside, Francisco walked apart from the rest of
us for a while, until Jimmy hit him in the back of the head with
a snowball. Francisco turned to see where it had come from;
smiling, Jimmy pointed at an old woman crossing the street behind us.

"She did it," he said playfully.

"*Mentiroso!*" Liar! Francisco shouted and ran a half block
ahead of us; he disappeared behind a large tree trunk. Jimmy
and I continued walking, arms over shoulders like two chums;
Eddie and Wallace paired up, too, following our lead. We could
hear Francisco holding down his laughter as we approached the
tree. Then he sprang out with a loud "*Sopressa,*" Surprise! and

pelted us all with icy snowballs. We, of course, returned the volley until Francisco escaped and ran ahead to plan the next attack.

Jimmy and I survived six such attacks from the Spanish Armada before we got to the car. Jimmy sat up front with me while Francisco, Eddie, and Wallace crammed into the back seat. We giggled and snorted our way back to the hospital grounds.

"Es muy bueno!" Francisco shouted as my cargo piled out of the station wagon and I escorted each man back to his cottage. Jimmy and I ate dinner and then retired early. Before I turned my own light off, I had just enough energy left to write an important entry in my diary:

January 17:
A memorable day. Jimmy really has become a friend.
The way he supported me in resisting Francisco's addiction
showed me part of his moral code. The huge hug he gave me
once we got back to our own cottage merely confirmed the
immense breadth of his appreciative heart.

CHAPTER TEN

Brady's

CLARA AND I TALKED ON THE PHONE EVERY OTHER SUNDAY
evening. I used a pay phone in the chapel building because that
area was always private on Sunday evenings. Long-distance
calls were a little expensive, but she'd pay one week and I'd pay
the other with saved-up dimes, so it worked out. On one of our
calls two weeks after I got back from the holidays, she brought
up the topic of our social lives away from one another.

Our being apart for such long stretches was hard on her,
she said. After teaching all day, preparing classes and grading
papers nearly every evening, she needed to get out more, even
if that included being with a guy. She had girlfriends, and she
did go places with them and that was good. But when guys
asked her out, she always declined, because of me. She especially wanted to go dancing and she couldn't do that with her
girlfriends.

At first, I didn't think it was a good idea. I was a little jealous
of some guy being with her when I couldn't be. At the same
time, I felt bad that she felt so isolated, so I had mixed feelings
about the whole thing. The letters and phone calls helped, but
there was nothing either of us could do about our being physi-
cally separated. In the end, we agreed to go out with others if we

wanted. She said our relationship was strong enough, and if it turned out that it wasn't, well, we'd find out, wouldn't we?

A date, in other words, with no guilt attached and no need to hide anything from one another. If something happened to weaken our relationship to one another, well, then, maybe it wasn't meant to be. She didn't think it would weaken anything, and neither did I. It seemed the right thing to do.

There were a few male teachers at her school, one in particular whom she often ate lunch with because they were on the same schedule. He was a math teacher named Cyril something or other. I remembered meeting Cyril before I left that summer. He was a little overweight and he wore thick glasses that he kept pushing up on the bridge of his nose. He was also one of the funniest people I'd ever met. He constantly cracked jokes and he was a master of the double entendre. He could imitate voices too, Ed Sullivan or Peter Lorre, for instance. For Clara, he loved to do Ethel Merman or Lucille Ball teaching English to tenth graders. She just ate it up.

Clara saw a couple of plays with Cyril, and they went to this dance hall in City Center. She wrote me that he danced like he was wearing cement shoes but she loved it anyway. I was happy for her, not the least because I knew Cyril was no competition for me.

I had friends too; it wasn't *all* work. Sometimes I joined a poker game with night-duty attendants, but I didn't really care for cards. It was just something to do. A lot of times, I would stop by the canteen in Building 50 and have a pop with staff, so I had plenty of opportunity to strike up a conversation with nurses. I especially liked Nurse Greenfield. Her first name was Ruth and she was originally from Canada. She was about my age and she liked the same movies I did. When she was off duty, she put her hair in a ponytail and wore black-and-white saddle shoes. Her favorite things to do were to go down to the State Theatre to see a movie and go bowling with the ladies' bowling team at the hospital.

You could call those times we went out *dates*, I suppose, but we never kissed or anything. I was always the gentleman. Besides, she was engaged to a fellow who was stationed in Korea, not near the fighting, thank goodness. They planned to get married once he got out of the service. Sometimes we went out with a bunch of nurses and their husbands or boyfriends or by themselves; at other times, we went alone. I say sometimes but it was really only three or four times that winter and spring.

The first time we went out was at the end of January, just the two of us. We saw a terrific musical at the State called *Singing in the Rain*. That song stuck in my head for days. The evening was real cold and it had snowed while we were in the movie, so afterward Ruth suggested Brady's Tavern; it was just a few blocks over, up Union to Lake Street.

I thought about calling a cab, but Brady's was on our route back to the hospital anyway, so we hoofed it down Front Street, and over to Union Street. Ruth wore fur-topped leather boots, and I had on my galoshes all buckled up over my dress shoes. Knowing we might be walking that night, we were all bundled up in thick coats, scarves, pull-down hats, and gloves. Ruth wore wool slacks tucked in her boots and I wore extra socks because my feet were the first things to feel the cold. She slipped on the ice in front of Oleson's Grocery but I caught the bulky arm of her coat in time before she fell. Ten steps later I slipped myself and went down in a pile of snow. We laughed about that for the next two blocks.

Brady's was a beacon of warmth and light when we finally walked in. The place was half full of people sitting at tables and a line of men at the bar, their backs hunched over glasses of beer or highballs.

It was an okay place, nothing special, I thought, *just a typical bar.* But it had colorful neon signs advertising beer, small tables with plastic tablecloths, an L-shaped bar that stretched the length of one wall, and a pool table in a back room. All this gave the tavern a down-home atmosphere that made you feel like you could be in any bar in any town in the country.

We sat at a table between the end of the bar and the poolroom. A group of fellows stood around in there chalking up cue sticks and sitting on chairs waiting their turn. Ruth said she was dying for a bowl of chili and French fries, and *she* was paying because I bought the movie tickets. She had a taste for French fries with beef gravy poured on top.

I thought that was strange.

"It's Canadian," she said. "Add some cheese curd and ketchup and those fries would be perfect. It's called *poutine.*"

Ketchup was right there on our table, but cheese curd was a long way from Traverse City, so she would have to settle for imperfect French fries. I went over to the bartender and ordered a Falstaff for both of us, along with her chili, two hamburgers for me, and fries smothered in beef gravy.

The bartender gave me a strange look.

"Gravy?"

"Very good," I said. "You should try it. If you could toss some cheese curd on the gravy, those fries would be perfect."

"Uh-huh. Sure, buddy," he said, nodding. Then, with a smile, "And how would you like your cheese curds?"

I figured we'd be lucky just to get the gravy.

Our food had just arrived when we heard some loud laughter erupt from the poolroom. One male voice boomed out over the howling and snorting of other men.

"So this one bitch covers her head with a raggedy-assed piece of baby blanket or something and—wait, wait, get this. The other bitch starts whacking her in the butt with a badminton racket and telling her to get on home!"

They all roared once again. "Jesus, Daryl. Cut it out! No more! My gut can't take it."

Then the loudest one again, "So I say to her, you get your own little twat on home or I'm gonna whack you with *my* racket. You know what I mean boys?"

Ruth and I exchanged glances. She rolled her eyes.

"I know that voice," she said.

"Who is it?"

Before she could answer, a man emerged from the poolroom carrying a beer bottle, a broad smile stretched across his face. He stumbled a bit and bumped into a chair, then recovered his balance. He looked in our direction; Ruth put her head down and covered her face by reaching up to adjust her ponytail.

"Daryl. He works at the hospital," she muttered.

In his dungarees and tight black t-shirt, Daryl was lean and muscular. I figured him for a guy who lifts weights. He had biceps the size of baseballs and a chest that stretched the limits of his t-shirt.

He went over to an empty table and smashed a lit cigarette into an ashtray. Then he gulped down the remainder of the beer, put the bottle on the table, and headed down the hall to the john. I heard a loud belch as the bathroom door opened.

"He's such a chirp," she said. "Always trying to impress the nurses and asking them out. But *no one* would go out with him. He's just full of himself, and so crude."

"Where does he …"

"Work? Recreation. I don't know how he ever got a job at the hospital. And in Recreation, of all places. Where he's supposed to help patients have fun. Can you imagine *him* helping patients have fun?"

"I don't know," I said, "I don't know him."

"Well, who wears a t-shirt in the middle of winter, eh? What does that tell you?"

"Warm-blooded?"

She glared at me. It was no time for smart-assed jokes.

"Try *show off*, Henry. The muscles and all."

She caught sight of Daryl coming back down the hall, so her arm shot up to her face again. "Jesus Murphy," she muttered. He went right past us on up to the bar where two guys were sitting catty-corner from one another at the short end of the L.

He slapped one on the shoulder and, loud enough for us to hear, said, "Well, if it ain't my old pal Cisco. And his sidekick Pancho! How you doin' boys?"

The two men swung around on their stools, wide grins galore, and returned the greeting with slap-you-in-the-palm handshakes.

"How're things over in your neck of the woods?" said Daryl. "You still all pissed off about things in my neck of the woods?"

Cisco pulled his hand back and made a fist. "Yeah, we're all still pissed as hell," he said.

Daryl made as if he was sparring with Cisco. "What're you up to now, then? You got any extra dog heads lying around the farm?"

My eyes shot to Ruth's. "Did I hear right?" I said. "Did he say dog heads?"

"I couldn't make it out."

"I think he *did*."

"Piss off," I heard Cisco say as he turned back to the bar and sat on his stool.

The Pancho guy spoke up. "We have it *our* way?" he said, "that funny farm is gonna be an ex-farm, you wait and see. We're not gonna have another year of your fruitcakes selling their vegetables in the bargain basement around here. No sir. We got slowed down, but come spring, look out. We've got numbers now, and we've got the big shots with us now."

"Yeah," said Cisco, "big shots. We got big plans, too."

"Shee-it," Daryl shouted, "plans, Shmams. You boys are all talk."

"You wait," said Pancho, "you just wait. You'll see some walk."

Ruth put two dollars on the table. "Let's go," she said, "they scare me."

I wanted to stay and hear more, but she already had her coat on and was pulling her scarf over her face so she wouldn't be recognized. I'd never seen this Daryl before, so I didn't care if *he* saw me. But I got dressed too and grabbed her elbow as we walked to the front door of the place.

I asked Ruth to wait by the door so I could call a taxi, which I did at the pay phone. We stood looking out the door; the taxi showed up in just a few minutes.

I turned to get one more look. Daryl and the other two fellows were sitting elbow to elbow at the bar now. As I pulled the door shut, they were toasting one another with raised beer bottles.

It was a quiet taxi ride. We were both lost in thought, I guess. Ruth's only comment was, "He's such an ass."

"Yeah," I said, "you can say that again."

The taxi stopped in front of the Men's Infirmary. Ruth's room was on the third floor. Most of her duties were in the infirmary, so it made sense for her to live upstairs there. She paid the driver for the ride and said good night, but I wanted to talk some more about what happened so we went inside and she pointed me to the tiny kitchen on the first floor.

I sat on a chair at a small table in the kitchen while she boiled water in a kettle and put tea bags in two cups. We sat in silence opposite one another swirling the tea bags. I asked if she thought Daryl was the one who killed that dog and left its head floating in the pond last summer.

"I didn't hear what he said about a dog, but if he did, then he's just...I can't even say what he is."

"Maybe he's the one behind all the vandalism that's happened here."

"Oh, I don't know," she said. "I don't even want to think about it. He's pompous--and vain, but...I don't know. He works here, for god's sake. That just doesn't make sense." She had tears in her eyes.

"You're right. He didn't imply *he* did it. He only implied the other two had something to do with it. I think he asked them if *they* had any dog heads."

She put her hands out as if to stop the conversation. "No. No more of this. I just...I just can't bear to think about that poor dog and what happened to him. The patients loved him. We all did. I fed him scraps from our kitchen here when he came around. He was the hospital mascot. Whoever killed him, he had to know how we all loved that poor mutt."

"Or," I said, "he had to have known someone here who knew, someone on the inside."

"And you think that someone is Daryl, eh?"

"Makes sense to me."

"I just don't know. It all just makes me sick."

She drank the remainder of her tea, stood up, and placed her cup in the sink.

"It's late and I'm on first shift. Thank you for the evening, Henry. I'm sorry it turned out the way it did, but I enjoyed being with you. You remind me a lot of my fiancé."

It didn't ask how I reminded her of him. It *was* late and I was tired, too. We would go out again in the coming months, but we would steer clear of Brady's Tavern. I went home that night with more questions about the rash of vandalism and animal slaughter that had plagued the place last year. What did they mean by "the big shots"? And "the numbers"? Numbers of what? Sure, things had quieted down on the asylum grounds, but if the warnings that came from those two guys in the bar had any truth to them, things were going to start up before long.

CHAPTER ELEVEN

Bad Apples

I THOUGHT OF GOING TO DR. SPENCER TO GAIN MORE INSIGHT into the problems at the hospital. But then I recalled how he always pooh-poohs discussion of acts of vandalism on or off the hospital grounds, how he changes the subject whenever the topic comes up.

I figured I might get more out of Nurse Brownell.

The next morning, I was lucky. Her secretary, a prim Miss Beaconsfield with very pursed lips and a black comb stuck in her hair waved me toward Nurse Brownell's office door. I knocked and poked in my head. From her tidy desk, she looked up and smiled.

"Hello, Henry. What brings you here?"

"Am I interrupting? I can come back if I am."

She put down her pen. "No, of course, come in. I was just finishing up before rounds."

She had a large office compared with others I'd been in. There was an antique wooden desk large enough to stretch out on. A bright red sofa with comfortable side chairs surrounding a small coffee table took up what space the desk didn't. Bookshelves floor-to-ceiling housed manuals, medical books, stacks of folders and bound reports, and sprinkled among the stacks and manuals were a number of brightly painted flower pots that sprouted colorful paper flowers—I had seen patients making others in the art building.

I sat opposite her desk. I said I had something on my mind and it would only take a few minutes. I described what Ruth and I had witnessed the night before, though I didn't share Ruth's opinion of Daryl; I didn't want to get her in any trouble with the Head Nurse. When I got to the part about the *big shots* and *the big plans*, she shook her head disapprovingly.

"I'm not surprised," she said. "It was just a matter of time before you had *this* kind of experience. That kind of animosity does exist, unfortunately. It is a sign of the times."

"Sign of the times?"

She leaned her elbows on the desk, and cupped both hands before her, resting her chin on them. She looked directly in my eyes, didn't speak for a long moment.

I waited, but she just stared at me, obviously thinking.

My impatience and my reserve were at odds. I thought I shouldn't be going where I wasn't invited, I shouldn't complain or press too much, that was what got me into trouble at Harrisville.

But I had to know.

"Please, Nurse, tell me if it's none of my business, and I'll butt out."

She shook her head as if to indicate no.

"It is and it isn't," she said. "That is to say, you are here, and you are present when these things happen, so yes, in that sense, it is your business. But you are also a guest here and, frankly, Dr. Spencer and I think you should not be drawn into the sordid business that has beset us."

"Oh, I think I see. In other words, I'm being protected from bad things?"

"In a sense, yes. But it's more complicated than that, Henry."

"I understand complications."

She thought a moment, then nodded affirmatively.

"Perhaps you are right. Well, then, the truth is, that these acts of vandalism and these destructive things people say, they're all part of an attitude, for lack of a better term, that some people in the community hold. Some of it has to do with the local economy, which is a whole story in itself. And some has to do with a general insensitivity toward mental illness of any sort. The latter is not unique to Traverse City; as you know, you'll find that everywhere. That's one reason why asylums were founded in the first place — to keep people with mental illness off the streets."

"Out of sight, out of mind."

"Something like that. On the other hand, there are many good, kind people who have genuine desire, and means, to help those who suffer from mental and intellectual disorders. Right here in tiny Traverse City."

"But, killing animals, and scaring the bejesus out of patients?"

"That is extreme, and relatively recent."

"Okay, but I don't understand why ... "

She waved me off. "We must all be patient. Before you arrived last year, following another incident, Dr. Spencer directed that staff not talk openly about any menace or destruction happening on the hospital grounds. He thought it best for our patient population. Staff thought it best too. Patients overhear things. But they don't understand. They panic. Why contribute even more to patients' instability? Why talk about things that frighten them?"

"But why the veil of secrecy toward *me?*"

"Dr. Spencer and I thought you didn't need to be distracted from your studies here by what amounts to local tensions."

I told her that I came here to learn everything I could about the hospital, as part of my research. I stopped short of saying I had a *right* to know more, but she got the idea. She invited me to bring any questions directly to her, and she would talk with Dr. Spencer about giving me more insight from his perspective. I said I would like that very much, thank you.

"You're welcome. Now then, I will continue to assign you for the remainder of the winter. When the weather changes to spring, we'd like you to engage with some more outdoor locations."

She paused suddenly. Her eyes widened.

"Nurse?"

"Oh my, I'm sorry, but one of those locations is the Recreation Department."

Good lord, I thought. *Him.*

Without skipping a beat, I started again: "How can a man like that continue to work here? What's wrong with him anyway?"

She sighed.

"We are not a perfect place," she said. "In an institution this size, we have a few bad apples. Mr. Forrest is one of them, possibly the worst. They bring that attitude with them; they disguise it just to get a job. But it comes out."

"Why don't you just fire him?"

"That is where it gets complicated. Attendants are Civil Service workers, and the Civil Service has its own rules, its codes. Like the rules in a union, the codes guarantee workers fair treatment and due process. A good thing in theory, but in practice the codes can be used to protect workers who are ill suited to a job. Basically, a person cannot be fired without verifiable evidence of blatant misconduct, criminal activity, immoral acts, and so forth. And so, someone like Mr. Forrest may be rude and he may have significant anger problems, but he cannot be fired for character. He has not hurt anyone, nor has he been derelict in his duties such that he could be fired."

"But he said things..."

"You *think* you heard him say something. Miss Greenfield wasn't sure either. And even if he did say that, he would just deny it. I'm afraid our hands are tied."

"This is just outrageous! I can't believe *this* hospital of all places can allow the likes of this person to be employed here. It's immoral."

I realized I was starting to rant and where that could lead me if I weren't careful. I counted to five.

"I'm sorry, nurse, I didn't mean to raise my voice. But I just can't..."

"Accept. I know, Henry. We *have* tried. On another occasion, the hospital tried to discharge him, but a lawyer intervened and...well...it didn't go our way."

"Lawyers!" I said. "Evidence!" My disgust was apparent.

"Henry, wait. I don't have to schedule you for that department. That can easily be changed."

"No, no. "I'll be fine. Maybe there *will* be more evidence. Maybe I'll be the one to discover your verifiable evidence."

She smiled and stood. "Well then, so be it. I will be eager to learn how it goes for you there, Henry. At the very least, you will learn how vital it is for a hospital like ours to have an equipped recreation department. Recreation is as important to the patients here as recreation is to people in any community."

"Don't tell me," I said, "Recreation is therapy. *That* I understand."

CHAPTER TWELVE

Talent

ON GROUNDHOG DAY, THE TEMPERATURE DIPPED BELOW ZERO and never went above seven for five days. To make matters worse, the heater in the basement of Cottage 32 began to malfunction. The heat would come and go, mostly go. The maintenance crew supervisor himself, Mr. Harrison, came twice that week. From the main floor, we could hear him in the basement, working and cursing about something that had to do with hot water reaching pipes and radiators throughout the building.

But this day, too cold to venture outside except to jaunt over to the dining hall or to the barns and shops to do chores, kept most of the residents and staff indoors playing checkers or putting together endless jigsaw puzzles. All of which became the more challenging when everyone had to wear thick gloves to keep their hands warm.

We wore our winter coats, hats, and gloves indoors and complained constantly about the cold. I checked the thermometer on the first floor: it read 48 degrees — not cold enough to freeze human tissue, but more than enough to exacerbate eccentricities.

We could see our breath. Some of the men had been relocated to the dining hall in Building 50 where the heat was just fine.

The rest of us stayed put because Mr. Harrison had promised for the third time to have everything up and running by 11 AM.

In his rocker, Siederman wore his red-checked winter jacket and a bright yellow wool stocking hat under a Russian ushanka whose fur ear flaps swooped down over the sides of his head and secured themselves beneath his chin. His gloved hands stayed safely in his pockets, and his wool socks stretched up over the tops of his rubber buckle boots. He rocked a little faster than usual to keep the blood flowing. In the five months I had known him, he had yet to utter a word.

Then there was Mr. Jessup, who insisted we call him *Captain* Jessup so we wouldn't confuse him with, in his words, "General Jeremiah Jessup from the Fourth Infantry Battalion, currently stationed on the western front in Canton, Ohio, and out of harm's way at last—since they took a shellacking from the redcoats at the Battle of Kemp's Landing."

Captain Jessup came rushing out of the bathroom and announced that the wireless was reporting that war in the Crimea was all but certain and the troop trains would be leaving in the morning so if anyone wanted to get married, today was the day "'cause it was certain that we'd all be sent to the front where most of us would die in agony or be maimed for life and God Save the King."

Before the war, he had been a high school history teacher. When the war broke out, he was drafted and deployed to the South Pacific. He was captured by the Japanese and became a prisoner of war. That was in 1944, I think. Before the war ended, he and 300 other soldiers had been rescued.

But by then he had lost his mind.

In his current mental state, there appeared to be no boundaries between any historical era, any military battle, or present circumstance. What historical facts he did retain from being a teacher were always lost in a conflation of people, events, and eras.

Captain Jessup had his winter gear on too as he marched up and down the hall in a quickened pace, as if on sentry duty, flapping his arms around his sides to keep warm. Every so often he would exclaim, "Throw more wood on the fires, boys, and keep your spirits up! God willing, we'll prevail. Those krauts will never freeze us out of here, no siree, bob."

Also bundled to the hilt, Jimmy leaned against a wall near the piano; he chewed bubble gum to keep his teeth from chattering. Next to him, Francisco sat on the piano bench rubbing his legs to keep circulation going. During the long winter days inside, Francisco had begun teaching Jimmy Spanish, beginning with curse words mixed with common phrases. "Buenos Dias Bastardo" was his favorite.

"Mierda" was another, which means *shit*. "Mr. Henry," Jimmy would say, a wink in his eye, "Francisco says you're full of mierda." The two of them would giggle and snort when I played the game and thanked him for the compliment.

Mr. Harrison had been working down in the basement since early morning. Every so often he'd surface to have a cup of tea or use the bathroom. Each time, he would assure us that "it was almost done," whatever "it" was. He explained to me that water gets heated in the boiler in the powerhouse and that hot water is conducted through a labyrinth of tunnels to every building on the grounds. But because of the distance the hot water has to travel, it cools. So each cottage and other buildings had to have a heater booster in the basement that works off electricity.

The booster not only reheated the water and circulated it in the building, but it also controlled the temperature.

He disappeared again down the ladder, and again we heard a hammer banging, wrenches being tossed, and the frequent "godammit!"

Jimmy moved to a spot next to Siederman, who had stationed himself next to the ladder to the basement. Jimmy seemed very interested in the goings on of Mr. Harrison. With each curse from the basement, Jimmy peered down the ladder into the dimly lit work area.

"Mr. Henry," he said to me across the room, "When Gram's furnace went out, I fixed it real good. Never gone out again."

"You fixed the furnace in Gram's house?"

"Yeah, I fixed everything in Gram's house. The toilet, and the lights, and the toaster, and the stove, and the icebox and everything. Gram called me Jimmy Fixerup."

Peterson, the orderly, heard this and came over right away. "Jimmy, do you know how to fix the boiler downstairs?"

"Maybe yes. Maybe no. Can't tell from here. You think Mr. Harrison wants help?"

"Jimmy," said Peterson, "If you fix the boiler, I'll buy you the biggest damn steak dinner and the biggest damn piece of chocolate cake you can imagine. I'm so damn cold, I'd buy you the whole damn cake!"

"Okay. I love steak. Me and Gram like the Loretta Young movies. Can I see a Loretta Young movie, too, Peterson?"

"Jimmy, I'm so cold, I'd buy you a night with Loretta Young if I could. You fix the boiler, I'll keep my promise, okay?"

"Okay, Peterson." Jimmy rose and poked his head down the basement entry, hand on the ladder.

I tugged on Jimmy's coat. "Wait a second, Jimmy. There's no furnace down there like the kind your Gram had. It's some other kind of heater thing you've probably never seen before."

"Nah, Mr. Henry. That don't matter. Gramp taught me how to study up what's wrong with what's broke. Gramp said study up a long time and look at it and tinker with it and study up some more. Do this and do that. Then try it out."

"Gramp? You never told me about Gramp."

"He died."

I did a double take: It had never occurred to me to ask about a grandfather. *Just like with Cousin Ethel,* I thought, *how many times would I say, "It never occurred to me..."?*

He pulled his sleeve away from me.

"Can I go, Mr. Henry?"

"Sure," I said. "Go ahead." I was skeptical, but what harm could he do?

Two other attendants chuckled. One poked Peterson in the ribs. "Oh Peterson, you'll be eating the big steak all by your lonely. And you'll be sitting with Henry here in the Loretta Young movie."

"Maybe yes," said Peterson. "Maybe no."

Jimmy shouted down the ladder. "Hey, Mr. Harrison, way down there. Here comes Jimmy Fixerup. I'm coming to help you down there. Okay? Here I come."

The puzzlers and checker players went back to their sports; I got another kettle boiling for tea.

Jimmy and Mr. Harrison were down there a good hour. Mr. Harrison emerged first, pulled his toolbox up to floor level and slid it out of the way of the ladder so he could get himself out. Jimmy followed. The two of them stood there looking at us, Mr.

Harrison sporting the widest grin I'd ever seen on that otherwise dour face, and Jimmy scraping black grease from his fingers.

"Goddamndest thing," began Mr. Harrison. "This man is a genius, I mean a gee-*nee*-us. I been down there for hours trying to figure out what the hell is wrong with the reheater. I tried everything. No luck. Then this gee-*nee*-us comes along, sits down on a stool for 20 minutes, says not a word while I'm ready to dismantle the whole damned kit and kaboodle down there and close down this cottage until summer. Then he … wait … you tell 'em, gee-*nee*-us. Go on, tell 'em."

Head down, foot kicking at the edge of Siederman's rocker, Jimmy said, in a barely audible voice, "Valve stuck in the back. Hard to see it in the dark. Just stuck."

"Exactly! So I got back there and sure enough that was it. Loosened that valve with my wrench and whoosh the water came through like the falls over Niagara. I got no idea how this man knew there was a valve way back there but he did and that's all it took. Why … what's your name, buddy?"

"Jimmy. Jimmy Fixerup."

"What the … how the blazes did you get named *that*? Well, Jimmy Fixerup, I'm going to get you on my maintenance crew. Lord knows we got plenty of muscle and stamina, but we're real short on brains. And you, you're as handy as a pocket on a shirt. You want to come work with me on maintenance?"

Jimmy looked at me. His eyes widened with delight as a broad smile stretched across his face.

"He's real smart, I'm telling you. *My* kind of smart. I'll see about getting him authorized to work with my boys."

"I'm sure Jimmy would like that," I said. Jimmy was pounding gloved fist into gloved hand, he was so excited.

Mr. Harrison picked up his toolbox. He turned back to Jimmy and put his hand out to shake. "I'll be seeing more of you, young man. How'd you ever get a name like Fixerup anyway? That's the goddamndest true name I ever heard, son."

The two men shook hands.

Mr. Harrison pulled on his overcoat and hat, glanced around the room for any remaining tools and walked out the front door, pausing only to look back and say, with a smile, "You're all going to be so toasty now you're going to think you're in Florida. If you have any questions, please direct them to my assistant foreman there." He pointed to Jimmy, winked at me, and left.

The clapping started with Peterson and then spread to the other men gathered in the room. The scarves began to unravel from necks, gloves found their way to coat pockets as the heat returned.

Jimmy danced about the room shouting, "Holy Moly!" He pulled Jessup's stocking cap down over his eyes and he stuck an elbow in Francisco's side.

Francisco shouted, "Viva!" and then, "Tres vivas para mi amigo, Jimmy." The others just stared at him; some scratched their heads. No one understood that he wanted us all to cheer for Jimmy.

Siederman began rocking wildly back and forth.

Then Captain Jessup himself got into it. He called for three cheers for Jimmy, which we all did. Then Jessup announced that there was talk of an armistice, but that was unconfirmed. He was in direct contact with HQ, however, so we should not stray very far from the trench.

Back in my room, I wrote to Clara—a three-page letter detailing what had happened that evening in the cottage. I wrote with all the detail I could muster; that's the kind of thick writing she liked to read. I worked especially hard on the metaphors — *It was colder than the ice caves on the bay*, I wrote. Then, *I miss you more than ever.*

I propped myself on two pillows and pulled up the covers. There was no shortage of ideas as I wrote up the day's notes.

February 2:

Talent-in-action is therapy. How do caregivers discover their patients' talents? Jimmy's until-now hidden mechanical talent. Had the heater <u>not</u> gone out, would anyone <u>ever</u> know of his talent for maintenance?

In the six months I've been here, I've seen so many talents among the patients. And how many have I missed? If you don't know to look for it, you likely won't see it.**

Farming talent from all those skills they learned on family farms.

Artistic talent, like the dancer Agnes, whose dancing intelligence she never lost, in spite of her brain injury. The painters with their work on the easels in Building 50 and gracing the dining room walls.

The fiber arts talents I saw in the women in the Fashion Shoppe, the ones who could do amazing things with fabric, ribbons, and thread.

Bernadine and Mrs. Hillman: Ornithology.

Patients with talent for being empathic to others. Social talents.

Granted, not <u>all</u> patients have talents. But why shouldn't caregivers find ways to nurture and develop *talents? I think of patients like Siederman. Does he have hidden talents?*

If caregivers ignore or blind themselves to patients' talents do they dehumanize those patients? A genuinely humanistic philosophy would, by definition, value patients' unique, typically unknown, talents.

***N.B.: Cousin Ethel. She may lack social talents, but what talents did—does—she have? When I was showing off my boxing skills and Jack was imitating voices from the Jack Benny Show, how must Ethel have felt when the spotlight was never on her?*

She had extraordinary encyclopedic knowledge, but the family never turned on the radio to Quiz Kids or even College Bowl Quiz. Cousin Ethel could have outshined everyone!

CHAPTER THIRTEEN

Tiny Miss

WITH THREE THOUSAND RESIDENTS AND STAFF, THIRTY-TWO buildings, and 750 acres of land, the hospital had no shortage of maintenance chores. Mr. Harrison had three general maintenance crews that looked after everything from plumbing to carpentry and masonry. There were other crews for electrical, snow removal, and automotive, each headed by a supervisor, and each comprised of qualified mechanics or electricians from town, and patients who served as apprentices or helpers, depending on what they could contribute.

Jimmy's crew did repairs and general maintenance throughout the grounds — a broken door hinge here, a window replacement there, the frequent plugged-up toilet. In summer, they would also become paint crews. Three thousand residents, and staff, meant regular wear and tear on the infrastructure.

It was such a pleasure to see Jimmy riding around the campus with his crew. He wore blue bib overalls like others on maintenance and rode in the back of a pickup that scooted from one end of the grounds to the other.

Jimmy would beam a broad smile and wave.

"Hey, Mr. Henry! It's me, Jimmy Fixerup!"

"Hey, Jimmy," I would shout back, "Where you headed today?"

"Don't know, don't care!" I would hear as the truck would fade into the landscape. The broad smile that used to emerge only when he spotted Bernadine now seemed permanently etched in his features. Jimmyfixerup had found his calling.

As had so many other patients in so many other ways.

Back in the fall, I had watched patient-workers harvest melons, pumpkins, squash, and all varieties of root vegetables. Other workers sold the seasonal produce directly to the townspeople at the open market in Traverse City or directly to restaurants and groceries. For the hospital's winter stores, patients filled burlap bags with root vegetables and apples and hauled them into storage cellars under Building 50. That produce would last through the winter and into the spring.

Orchard workers who had picked fruit from the apple and pear trees now joined cannery crews to put up fruits in jars to make sauces, jellies, and jams, and enough preserved fruit for the long winter months. Cannery workers would combine the fall fruits with fruits picked earlier and candied—blueberries and cherries—to make specialty jams and spreads. Other patients decorated the jars with colorful ribbons to be donated to local churches for their annual holiday sales.

The fact that nearly half of the patients contributed in one way or another to the hospital's sustainability was the direct result of the view that *work is therapy*. Professor Hilliger had mentioned the role of work here, but at the time I hadn't given it much thought. But seeing that principle in action, witnessing the collaborative spirit it engendered—why, that just knocked me over. In spite of their hallucinations, their depression, their mental confusion, their retardation—year after year, with guidance, they were able to plan a full-year growing cycle; plant and harvest nearly 400 acres of rich farmland and orchards; and compete successfully with local farmers and growers on the open market. It all seemed to me a smashing success for the hospital's financial viability and for patient care. Especially for the latter.

By early April, my duties shifted to the three greenhouses and the new one under construction on the near west side of the grounds. The greenhouses were vital to the agricultural mission of the hospital. All work in the greenhouses was supervised by Mr. Meyer, a horticulturist from the Michigan State Ag Program who'd been at the hospital since the mid-30's, when the first greenhouse was built.

In Greenhouse 1, workers were busy starting up the head lettuce, kale, and spinach crops that would feed the hospital population come May and the summer months. Greenhouse 2 was devoted to raising parsnips, radishes, and fava beans. Patients in Greenhouse 3 cultivated seedlings that would become the greens and flowers that would eventually fill the vases (painted, of course, by patients) indoors as well as the decorative urns and pots to be found everywhere on the grounds. Construction on Greenhouse 4 resumed from where it had left off in late fall; there, two carpenters supervised patients who built planting tables and bins, and constructed plank walkways between aisles that would, by summer, be full of seedlings ready for planting in anticipation of the fall harvest.

The greenhouses allowed me a fascinating first-hand look into the *work-is-therapy* philosophy of the hospital. As many as thirty patients worked in each greenhouse every day, a three-hour shift in the morning and a two-hour shift in the afternoon. Those who, for mental or physical health reasons, couldn't work a full shift spent whatever time they could. At this time of the year, the main work consisted of preparing thousands of seedlings in small cartons for eventual planting in the cultivated farmland on the south and west acreage.

I was struck by the quiet busyness that pervaded the place. Patients tended to work alone or in pairs—women with women, men with men. What talk there was seemed mere murmurs or an occasional burst of quiet laughter. Patients focused intently on their individual tasks. Mr. Meyer, the supervisor, and his two assistant supervisors passed among the patients, offering corrective advice or changing patients' jobs for variety as the day's work ensued.

For some patients, it truly was a place to *work*. Deliberative in their systematic handling of earth, cartons, seeds, and water, they went about their daily chores seemingly determined to get each seed planted perfectly in the center of each carton; watered in the exact measured amount; and placed gingerly on the transport trays that lined the wooden walkways. When one cart was full, the designated transport person would move it to the rear of the greenhouse, park it with the other carts, and return with an empty cart to be loaded. He would then be praised for his effort with, "Thanks, bub," and "Atta boy," or just a nod of acknowledgement and a smile. This rhythm went on for hours and was only broken by a trip to the outhouse or lunch break.

For some patients, *work* seemed to take on a deeper meaning. Their labor progressed at a slower but no less deliberative pace. Some chatted privately with their plantings. "I love you, little feller," one patient said as he placed his carton on the transport cart. "You have a safe journey with your momma and daddy. Bye now."

One of the women took to naming each seedling as she

carefully placed it in a carton of soil and watered it. "This here is Tiny Miss. She's on her way to Iowa to spend Fourth of July with her cousins on the farm there."

One rainy day, I stopped by Greenhouse 1 and sat adjacent to the planters, observing. I introduced myself as a visitor and they each introduced themselves in return, except for the silent grey-haired woman sitting across from me. Her hair was tied back in a red bandana, her fingers caked brown with soil.

"That's Gladys from Port Huron," said someone down the row. "She don't talk."

Gladys worked slower than the rest, head down most of the time. When she finished one carton, she placed it on the table and her partner next to her put it on the cart for her. Then she would start on another carton. After thirty or so minutes, I noticed that her hands had stopped and she was sitting there, staring at the carton in her palm, turning it from angle to angle and stroking the paper sides with her index finger.

Tears streamed down her cheeks. The others noticed too, but kept on working: a respectful silence enveloped the group. Before long, the bell sounded for quitting time. Workers rose and stretched as they began to leave. Gladys remained until an attendant came to her side and gently removed the carton from her hands.

"Come, Gladys," he said in a near whisper, "It's time to go. This one will be here tomorrow. Don't you worry."

She rose, wiped snot from her upper lip with her sleeve, took the arm of the attendant, and left. When they got to the door, they paused. She turned and looked back to the lone carton sitting on the table at her station across from me. She wiped her nose again, turned and walked out the door.

I sat, astonished by what I had just witnessed. Mr. Meyer began talking as he approached.

"That happens sometimes, we never know when. She'll come back tomorrow and get back to work as if nothing had happened."

"But why?" I said, "What?"

"Well, what I know," he began, "is she lost her husband and four children in a fire, must be four or five years now. Horrible thing. Them all inside the house screaming, and no one able to save them. Firemen got her out just before the roof collapsed but she heard those little ones crying and then they were silent. Folks say she went silent then, too. Hasn't spoken since. Lost her mind over that fire. Something comes back to her here, sometimes. Saddest thing, too. The doctors say this is all good for her. Keeps her active and involved. Otherwise she'd just sit and stare all day long, catatonic, like she was when she first came here. My view is, those seedlings? She's taking care of the babies she lost."

Mr. Meyer glanced at his wristwatch and then stretched his arms overhead. "It's time," he said. "Come, walk outside with me. I have more to tell you."

We stepped outside. The skies were parting and some blue peeped through, though it was still sputtering rain. We walked a brisk pace to a massive old white oak between the greenhouses.

He leaned one shoulder against the broad gray bark of the antique tree. I stuffed my hands in my pockets and leaned against the side of the greenhouse, waiting.

"Maybe you've noticed," he began. "Maybe not. These patients here, so many are wounded souls. Like Gladys. Some have no homes any more, others have homes that they're not welcome to any more. For some, this hospital is the only home they've ever known. They're pieces of china. They fall and they break easily."

"Fall?"

"Just a way of speaking. What I mean is, you spend any amount of time here with them in the greenhouses or in the fields or barns, you come to understand that this work is not *work* for them as it might be for others. It's their lifeline to whatever they still have left in their world. Like that woman and her babies. Lost in that fire but not lost in how she remembers them, how she loved them."

"I saw how she cradled the seedlings. I was … moved."

"What I'm saying is they're not the same as people on the outside working at jobs. This is not a job. It's their *work*. There's a difference. Their cares melt when they kneel in the fields or the gardens. You know what I'm saying?"

"I think so."

He leaned forward and picked up a rock nestled under some tiny broken branches. Then he took two steps and tossed it high in the air across the plain of weeds and dirt. He looked around for more rocks.

"If you don't come in the greenhouse and sit there, and look, and listen, you'd never know how vital their work is to them. Take away that work and you cut out the ground from under them."

He turned and faced me. From his clenched palm, two rocks dropped to the ground.

"In case you're wondering why I'm telling you all this," he said, "Nurse Brownell asked me to guide you while you're over here in our part of the grounds. I just want to be sure you see what's really going on here. Most folks on the outside never get that chance. You're lucky to have it, in my opinion."

He picked up another rock and walked to the shady perimeter of the front of the greenhouse. "I'm sure we'll see more of each other, young man. Watch closely, listen well."

"I'll be sure to do that."

He stretched, pulled one arm back into a pitching stance, and let a rock fly. It hit another walnut tree thirty yards from us.

He turned to me with a broad smile. "Every day, I expect a call from the Brooklyn Dodgers." Then, with a wink, "It's time to go home for the day. I may still get that call this evening."

In my room that night, I recorded thoughts this day had generated:

April 4:

Work is therapy. Many patients here grew up on farms. Many are right at home with livestock or planting and harvesting. Once a purposeful member of a family community, here they find similar purpose. For some, their history is their work, their identity. Through their work, they make their own contributions to the hospital community. Their work is as vital to them as it is to normal people who love their work.

CHAPTER FOURTEEN

Mr. Pinkskin

EVERY EVENING IN THE COTTAGE I WOULD SEE JIMMY AS HE RE-
turned from dinner and prepared himself for early bed. "Working men need sleep," he would say with pride, "We get up early
and fix the broken stuff." Hardly the cowering silent man who'd
arrived on the train just last fall, each day he struck out with
purpose. "Mr. Jimmyfixerup"—that resourceful man who lost
himself when his grandmother died—had returned supremely
happy and full of life.

Until that miserably cold Saturday in April.

The weather shifted back and forth from rain to snow and
sleet all day as the temperatures hovered around 38 degrees, not
unusual for northern Michigan in April. Only those patients
who worked in food prep and dining halls needed to go to work.
Except for fast treks to the dining halls under large umbrellas and bundled up against the weather, the men in Cottage 32
stayed warm and dry indoors. So it was that Saturday afternoon
that the men lounged about in the cozy living room of the cottage or dozed on their beds for extended naps.

Crazy eights was the card game of choice for many. Others
played a form of poker that didn't appear to have any consistent
rules except that jacks were always wild, players would draw and

discard, kept four to nine cards in their hand at one time, and, although no score was kept, eventually someone would declare himself the winner. Losers would ritually slap their cards back onto the table and utter some variation of holy something or other — *Holy Cow! Holy Smokes! Holy Shit!* and the ever-popular *Holy Underwear!*

Siederman was rocking away, as always, a broad smile on his face. On the other side of the room, Jimmy leafed through an old copy of *Popular Mechanics.* I sat nearby reading one of my psychology textbooks. Captain Jessup came down from upstairs, surveyed the scene for a moment, then approached Jimmy.

"How about some checkers, soldier?"

For Captain Jessup, a checker game was a singular battle between the French and the Germans, the French and the English, or the French and the Michiganders. He would announce before each match just what battle was about to ensue, though he seldom remembered which countries were fighting which or whether the army, navy, or marines were involved.

"Well, all right," said Jimmy, putting his magazine on the floor. "I can play checkers with you. I'm tired of looking at pictures anyways."

They set up the little checker table between them and placed their pieces in position. Jimmy chose the red checkers. Captain Jessup stood behind his chair opposite Jimmy and spoke like an announcer in a news reel: "Here we have the bloody British lining up with their red coats blazing in the sun for all of Eisenhower's regulars to see from their perches in the trees and behind fences and mounds in the fields. They march to the drum and fife, but little do they know what the fickle hand of fate is about to … to … hand them."

The two attendants had gone upstairs for bed check, leaving me with the fellows downstairs. I needed to use the toilet, and everything seemed okay, so I stepped into the bathroom toward the rear of the living room and locked the door for privacy. *Jessup was just plain amusing*, I chuckled to myself as I sat and listened as he framed the next epic battle of the checkerboard.

"They got their red uniforms on 'cause they're all Communists, all red commies. And they ran the czar out of town with the queen, and ... and ..."

"Ah c'mon Jessup, get the game going," Jimmy whined, "or I won't play."

Captain Jessup's voice rose. "Don't you give me orders, private! You need to learn your place in this man's army."

Then he exploded.

"Don't you forget who's in charge, you son of a bitch!"

Fast as I could, I stood, flushed, and banged open the bathroom door. Siederman was snoring away in his rocker, and the poker players held their held cards close as they looked over from their tables.

Jimmy sat back, a startled look on his face.

Captain Jessup continued. "Don't look at me like that, soldier. Hell, you probably aren't even one of us. You must be one of those pinko commie spies. Yea, pinko commie spies come here to kill us. Why ... why ... I'll cut off your wiener, you pinko, with this here saber I got on my belt."

I reached the two of them just as Jimmy upended the checkerboard and wrapped his fingers around Jessup's throat. He pushed Jessup back full force a few steps, screaming, "I'm no pink face! You don't touch me!"

Jessup let out the anguished guttural sound of a man choking.

"'Cause I'll kill you! And I'll spread your guts all over!" His voice was shrill; I hardly recognized it.

I was between them then, one hand on Jimmy's breast and the other trying to pry his hands off Jessup's throat.

Jessup was choking for air and slapping his arms toward Jimmy, over my shoulder. When Jimmy did release his grip, Jessup fell to the floor, coughing and spitting.

An attendant burst through the stairwell door.

"What the hell?" he shouted. He pulled Jimmy back. Jessup rolled to his stomach, still coughing and gasping for air. I went to Jimmy and bear-hugged him. The attendant freed his grip on Jimmy and went over to kneel beside Jessup, his hand patting Jessup's back.

"Easy, Jessup. Stay down."

Jimmy was all tensed up. Tears streamed down his cheeks, snot dripped from his nostrils. I held him close in my arms. I moved with him to the other side of the room, almost as if we were dancing partners. As Captain Jessup's breathing became regular again, the attendant helped him to stand. Jessup brushed off the dust on his sleeves and the front of his pants.

"I say," he said, in a mock English accent, "you've a strong grip for a radioman. We could use you in the infantry."

"Let's go, Jessup," said the attendant, who grabbed him by the elbow and escorted him to the stairwell door. "Let's get some distance now, Captain," I heard him say as the door closed. "You can look in on the other troops."

I eased up on my hold of Jimmy and suggested we get some fresh air — in spite of the weather.

"Okay," he said. "I don't like that Jessup man no more. He's nuts."

We put on our wet weather clothes, grabbed two umbrellas, and sloshed over to the chapel, where I knew we could find a quiet place to talk. We left our umbrellas and wet coats in the vestibule.

The chapel was silent, empty. One dim light shone at the front, over the chancel. Jimmy and I sat in the back row of chairs. I had some Black Jack gum with me. I offered him a stick. He ignored me. He was breathing evenly now, but his fingers twitched and formed momentary fists, then opened up again. He was still agitated.

We sat in silence. I waited to see how the calm of the chapel would affect him. Before long, his hands relaxed.

"I can have your gum now, Mr. Henry, if you still want to share."

I fished the pack back out of my pocket. He took a stick.

"Would you like to talk with me about what happened back there, Jimmy?"

"Naw," he returned. "That man is nuts. He better not come by me no more."

"Were you afraid he was going to hurt you?"

"Naw. I'm not afraid of him. He don't ever hurt nobody. He just talks. About war and stuff. He just made me mad when he called me pinko and said he would touch my ... you know."

"Your personal part?"

"Yeah, that." He was staring straight ahead. I stared ahead, too. Before long, the stillness and comfort worked their restorative magic.

"I like this gum," he said. "It's real good."

"I do, too," I said, "it's my favorite. What I'm wondering,

though, is if what Captain Jessup said made you think about Mr. Pinkskin?"

It was a gamble, I knew, but the time seemed ripe.

Jimmy stared in silence for four or five seconds before he spoke.

"Yeah."

"Can you tell me more about Mr. Pinkskin, Jimmy? Can you tell me more about who he was and why you didn't like him?

"Yeah, I can. I don't like to think about him, but I can tell you."

"Good. I'd really like to know. Maybe I can help you with that.

"All right."

"Why do you call him Mr. Pinkskin anyway?"

Jimmy looked up at the high ceiling, at the crystalline lights suspended on long cables. His eyes moved across the ceiling when he spoke, as if a movie of his life were playing up there.

"That's what Gram called him. 'Cause his face was real pink and sweaty. Most of the time. He was always running around his house calling his wife and the boy names. And drinking beer. Always drinking beer. Gram said Mr. Pinkskin is mean and don't go around by him."

"He was your neighbor in Detroit?"

"Yeah."

"And he was mean to his wife and little boy?"

"Yeah, he lived across the street. He hit that boy with a belt and that boy screamed and we heard them in that house yelling and then it got real quiet for a long time."

"And you kept away from him, right? That's what Gram said to do."

Jimmy's fingers started twitching again and curling into fists and then uncurling again. My question had struck a nerve. This time I didn't wait for calm to return. I took the chance that seemed right.

"Maybe you didn't stay away, Jimmy? Maybe you made a mistake?" I watched his hands as they stayed clenched in fists. His gaze shifted from the ceiling to the large stained-glass windows that lined the walls.

"Yeah," he said, "I made a big mistake. Gram was at the store and I went over to the alley behind Mr. Pinkskin's house. I was looking for the flowers that stick out of the fences behind the houses over there. I wanted to surprise Gram with flowers when she got home. Mr. Pinkskin came out by his fence and ask me do I want to see real big pretty red flowers in his garage."

"Flowers in his garage?"

"Yeah. He was nice to me. I said sure I do, they're for Gram. So he takes me in his garage but there's no flowers there. Then he locks the door. He has a big hammer and he tells me take off my pants now or else. So I do and he touches me on my…you know…and he pulls his pants down and he says I need to touch him on his—or else. So I do and I'm crying and he's making all kinds of oohs and ahhs and his you-know gets real big and I'm scared he'll hit me with that hammer so I keep touching him."

Fists tight. Eyes straight ahead. Crying again.

The movie reel was spinning.

"Then his dog comes round from the house. He's barking and that man says, 'Damn dog' and he pulls up his pants and tells me pull up mine and get out of his garage. I tell anyone and he's going to bash in my head and cut me up with his saw."

Tears streamed down Jimmy's face. His hands relaxed again and he turned to me, looked directly into my eyes.

145

I took both his hands in mine. Softly, I said, "Have you ever told anyone about this, Jimmy? Did you tell Gram?"

"No. Oh no. Not Gram, not no one. Gram told me stay away from Mr. Pinkskin but I broke the rule. And I don't want him to hurt me for telling so I don't tell no one. But now she's dead and I can't never tell her anyway. Maybe someday in heaven I can tell her I'm sorry and she'll forgive me for breaking the rule."

"I'm sure Gram forgives you right now," I said, rubbing his hands.

Rain battering the roof, wind driving strong raindrops into the windows. We sat for a long time before I spoke again.

"Jimmy, Captain Jessup wasn't trying to scare you the way Mr. Pinkskin did. He didn't mean to hurt you, you know."

"That Jessup, he's crazy is all. He just made me remember Mr. Pinkskin from what he said back there. And I got mad. I'm sorry, Mr. Henry."

He leaned his head on my chest. I stretched my arm around his shoulder, and patted him on the side of his head. He was a child in my arms.

"You don't have to be sorry, Jimmy. It's all over. He just chose the wrong words. He did not mean to hurt you."

"Yeah."

"But look, Jimmy," I said. "Look how well you handled yourself. You stopped before you hurt him. You listened to me when I asked you to back up. And you never said anything more once Captain Jessup calmed down. You should be very proud of yourself. I know I am. Very proud of you."

Jimmy sat up. A smile broke. He leaned against my shoulder again, and let out a long sigh.

"You're my best friend, Mr. Henry. You take care of me. I love you."

"I love you, too."

"You're all right, Jimmy. All right. You did the right thing telling me about what happened to you in Detroit. I think your Gram would be very proud of you, too. You are a very brave man. I am proud to be your friend."

I gave him a gentle squeeze and said, "So let's go over to the dining hall and see if we can get something special to celebrate your brave day. Okay?"

He stood and yanked me out of my own seat.

"Okay, Mr. Henry. Maybe we can have some cookies too, from Miss Mabel. She's my kitchen cook friend. Some people call her Mama Mabel, but I call her Miss Mabel cause she's not my mama. She's like a mama though."

"Well," I said, "Let's go see if we can get Miss Mama Mabel to help us find some cookies."

Miss Mabel did have cookies, and she even made hot chocolate for us. Then I took Jimmy back to the cottage. The other patients had dispersed by that time, except for Siederman — rocking away — and Captain Jessup, who glanced up from a magazine when we entered.

"Welcome back, soldier," was all he said.

Jimmy said nothing back as the two of us went up to his room. Exhausted, he turned in for the night.

In my room, I wrote up an incident report. I described what happened with Captain Jessup as a fairly normal argument between two patients that unfortunately became physical. "*No one was hurt; staff intervened; both parties recovered*," I wrote. Then I reported what Jimmy had revealed to me — the sexual abuse; the neighbor man who threatened him if he told; guilt for breaking his beloved grandmother's rule; his secret hidden all these years; my therapeutic support for Jimmy in the chapel.

I struggled to make my account as objective as possible, but it was all I could do to keep from saying I wanted to drive straight to east Detroit, find this Mr. Pinkskin, and report him to the police—after I beat the shit out of him. Of course, the better side of me prevailed and I said that more elegantly, but I did ask if the authorities could be contacted anyway.

"Who knows whom else the man may have victimized?" I wrote. "And what about the abusive ways he treated his own family? He should be arrested and thrown in jail."

Two days later, when I finally did speak with Dr. Spencer about the incident, he agreed that the authorities in Detroit would be contacted, but he doubted that anything would be done about what he did to Jimmy.

"They may be able to investigate the family situation," he said, "but as for Mr. Quinn, it'll turn into denial and accusations that he is mentally ill, etcetera, etcetera, etcetera, and making everything up. That's what happens much too often. So many of our patients have been victimized by sexual predators. At least, the ones we know of."

I didn't mention my thoughts about beating up Mr. Pinkskin in revenge. But, in truth, if the guy lived in Traverse City, I would have beaten the crap out of him last night when my blood was boiling. Good thing for me Detroit was 250 miles away.

By the time I wrote in my dairy that evening, I could be more reflective.

April 21:

"*Come to a deeper understanding of the patient,*" *Dr. Spencer said.* "*Time will tell.*"

Back in September, I worried—would spending so much time with one patient threaten my objectivity? Would I become too close? Did I lose objectivity today when I crossed the line from therapist to friend? When I told him I loved him? When he became more like the brother I never had? Yes, I did *lose objectivity, but look at what I gained.*

Now I question whether he even belongs here. If he had a home, and a family, a job, and a genuine community—isn't that where he belongs?

CHAPTER FIFTEEN

Proof

April 27:

As my father often said, success breeds contempt, and, apparently, this is true of the hospital's farming success, too. Nelson Stanley, the hospital accountant who keeps track of market sales, and the man whom I first met when I arrived, told me yesterday that he gets occasional phone calls — anonymous — from men who complain that the hospital produce drives down prices for everyone else. One caller told him, "The nut house ain't supposed to be in the business of putting the rest of us out of business. May be time someone put you out of business."

That sounds like what Ruth and I heard at Brady's Tavern back in January.

Yesterday in the canteen I found a copy of the Traverse City Sentinel. Whoever left it on the counter there had folded it to the editorial page. One letter to the editor caught my eye when I saw the word "Hospital" in the header. The writer called the hospital the "loony bin." Claimed that a member of the writer's family had gotten food poisoning from some tainted hospital potatoes. I seldom read the local paper, but friends tell me that ugly letters like that show up all the time.

Such animosity and venom has to be connected to the
animal killings and vandalism. These are not random acts.
They must be connected.

The business with this Daryl fellow really rankled me, but not as much as the bigger business of threats to the hospital. I suspected that Daryl was connected somehow to bigger things, that it was more than just wise-guy boasting. But about that business, I couldn't just stand by and do nothing. Scaring patients, destroying property, killing innocent animals, threats — all that was illegal and just flat wrong.

I knew I couldn't create a stir that could be traced to me, as that *could* harm my tenure at the hospital. But maybe someone *else* could — like a reporter doing an investigative report. The *Philadelphia Inquirer* regularly ran such stories, to expose truth and to champion justice. I wondered if the *Traverse City Sentinel* might just be that gutsy.

It was worth a try. I had to do *something*.

At noon, I walked down to the *Sentinel* office on Front Street. At the reception desk, I was stopped by a prim fiftyish woman with a squeaky voice, tiny eyes behind cat-eye glasses, and pursed lips. Her hair was pulled back so tight I wondered if she could even close her eyes. I asked who was in charge of approving letters to the editor and could I speak with him.

"That would be Mr. Remington, our editor," she squeaked, lips creased as if they were knitted together. "He's very busy, *very* busy. Is he expecting you?"

I explained that I didn't have an appointment but that I just wanted to take five minutes of his time to ask a couple of questions.

"From one journalist to another," I said, "professional matters of the highest concern. I promise he'll appreciate very much this opportunity and will thank you for your help." I neglected to say that my journalism experience amounted to one summer job where I wrote a feature story on noteworthy Psychology Department alums for the Penn alumni magazine. Fortunately, she didn't strike me as one to seek out details.

She pulled her eyeglasses down her nose and stared at me over the top of the rims. *Testing my credulity*, I figured, *with the old stare down*. Unflinchingly, I held my lying ground.

"Upstairs, first door on the right," she said finally.

I knocked and entered in one fell swoop. He sat at a cluttered desk, a glass half full of something yellow on his right. He pulled open a desk drawer and put the glass in there and then sat back in the reclining swivel chair, arms behind his neck.

I introduced myself as a graduate student from the University of Pennsylvania completing a field experience at the State Hospital. Could I have five minutes?

He motioned me to sit in a chair opposite his desk. Mr. Remington lit one cigarette with the remainder of another.

My five minutes with Mr. Remington stretched to ten as I explained that I often read letters to the editor that were critical of the state hospital and that maligned patients with fabrications and lies. I cited the damage to trucks and buildings, animal cruelty, and harassment of patients. It's ironic, I said, that his paper was publishing falsehoods while real damage was being done to people and property on hospital grounds.

He sprung forward in the swivel chair. "First of all," he said, "What makes you think you can come in here and accuse this paper of something so serious as calumny?"

I realized I should have used a less direct approach.

"I'm sorry," I said, "I didn't mean to accuse. I just wanted to set the record straight. Those letters critical of the hospital are full of falsehoods and exaggerations. What they claim has no truth whatsoever." I wanted to say *and you, you nitwit, should be ashamed of yourself for allowing them to appear in print.*

"Where'd you say you were from?"

"The University of Pennsylvania, but I have been here at the state hospital since last August, and I've been a witness to much of the vandalism and violence. I think there is a developing conspiracy against the hospital."

He perked up a little then, and he asked me if I had any proof.

"I'm sure a good reporter could conduct a few interviews," I said. "He could discover some alarming facts. He could expose the truth in an investigative story."

He stared at me for a moment in silence.

"Do you have any actual proof of this alleged conspiracy?"

"I overheard some men talking in a bar," I said. "And there have been these incidents on the grounds."

"I asked you about *proof, not hearsay.* Of a *conspiracy.*"

"I know what I heard. And the woman with me heard it, too. I'm not alone; others who work at the hospital agree. We think there are people in the community who want to make the hospital look bad. They want it to stop farming. I'm not sure why they've targeted the farming operation—yet—but I have a well-grounded theory. There is a story waiting to be written here."

He mashed a cigarette in a glass ashtray, stood up, and came around to my side of his desk. He hit the edge with his thigh when he cut the corner too sharp. I stood immediately. He came up close enough for me to smell alcohol on his breath.

He told me, in few words, that without any proof, there would be no story. He wasn't about to stir up a hornet's nest based on one person's zany theory, even if others believed it, too. And if I thought to write a letter to the editor claiming there was such a conspiracy, it would not see the light of day. Not under his watch anyway, and certainly not a letter from an out-of-towner and based on mere speculation. But thank you very much anyway and close the door on your way out.

Provincial, I said to myself in the hall. *Safer to report drain commission meetings and PTA cupcake sales. He was not in the business of ruffling feathers.*

I went back to the hospital, discouraged but not defeated. I was determined to find a way to get other voices to speak for the integrity of the state hospital, even if my own voice were to be excluded.

I had an idea. He wouldn't publish letters from *me*, but what about letters from others? Letters that suggested a conspiracy without ever actually saying that. Letters that accurately represented the good work done here and the important role farming plays in the mission of the hospital and the lives of patients? More importantly, letters that exposed the unjust torment the hospital had been suffering. The first two people I thought of were Nelson Stanley, the accountant who gave me a tour of the asylum grounds when I first arrived and whom rumor had it was a closet writer, and Nurse Ruth Greenfield.

Back on the hospital grounds, I stopped by Nelson's office. I had imagined an accountant's office to be a sterile place where accounting books lined the shelves and an adding machine and ledger books filled all available space. And that *is* what I found, except for one corner where a black Smith Corona typewriter sat on a small desk, an open dictionary on one side and a stack of typewritten pages on the other.

As it turned out, Nelson had been writing and sending such letters for years. His was a frequent voice that told stories of patients helping clean up the beaches, bringing urns of flowers for the National Cherry Festival Banquet, that sort of thing. He tried to keep the community aware of the ways the hospital supported the town, always keeping to the light side of events. They were nice letters, I surmised, not the kind I would urge him to write.

He pointed toward his Smith Corona in the corner.

"I write stories about the patients here," he said. "It's what I do when the numbers crowd my head too much. I'm an accountant by trade, and, you could say, a writer by avocation. I fancy myself a chronicler of life at the hospital, even if my stories never see the light of day. It's just a hobby. But I like it."

It didn't take much to convince him to write letters telling how the violence against the hospital affected patients here.

"Well now," he said, "that's much different than my little stories."

"But your *stories*," I interrupted, appealing to his vanity, "they're journalism." I mentioned Howard K. Smith and Edward R. Murrow, famous reporters during and after the war.

"No one out there knows about the hospital mascot being killed, or about rocks through windows that scared the hell out of patients and staff alike. Investigative journalism, that's what it would be. Why, it's a start. Who knows where that might lead?" I was grasping at straws.

He stared at his typewriter a few moments, then looked back at me. "I could *do* that," he said. His voice got a little louder: "I could do that very well."

He said he would describe those things and how they affected patients and staff. He would also write about the role of farming in the mental health of so many patients. He would bring out the emotional toll of those threatening incidents and he would focus on the emotional recovery of those people who worked the farms and orchards. He was glowing with anticipation. I couldn't have asked for more.

Nelson lived in Garfield Township, so he had a legitimate claim to being a local resident. That would be important when he had to put his name and address on the letter for the paper to check on its legitimacy. He suggested I get letters coming from nurses, too, because they knew the patients better than anyone. He told me to try Nurse Greenfield.

"She cared for a patient whose family lives in Kalkaska," he said, "and they might be willing to post letters from that address."

Which is exactly how it turned out. Ruth had many opportunities to listen to patients' stories in the men's infirmary. She was eager to share them and even more eager to write letters. She thought she could convince the Kalkaska family to send them in under their own name.

Ruth would also talk with other nurses she thought would join our efforts. It was my hope that within weeks, the *Sentinel* would regularly be receiving letters to the editor that shined a positive light on the hospital as *we* knew it. Would Mr. Remington publish them? I was keen to find out.

CHAPTER SIXTEEN

Degrees Of Evil

"THE RECREATIONAL DEPARTMENT," THE NOTE FROM NURSE
Brownell read, "provides opportunities for our residents to engage in on-campus programs such as lawn games, bat-and-ball
games, net games, and the like—as well as off-campus trips to
public beaches, basketball courts, swimming pools, etc."

I should report to Mr. Schultz, the Recreation Manager, to
get my week's itinerary.

Brady's Tavern still fresh in my mind, I was nervous about
my stint with Daryl. Brother Benedict once said that when I get
anxious, I should think in Latin.

"It will calm you down before you say or do something rash,"
he said, "*tranquillus.*"

Latin was his antidote for everything.

Bonum cogicatones, I thought. *Think good thoughts.*

The Recreation Department was housed in the north-
ern-most wing of Building 50. Photographs of professional
sports figures—Babe Ruth, Johnny Weissmuller, Agnes Ke-
leti—adorned the walls. It had two offices. The largest one
housed lockers and benches for attendants; padlocked cages
full of balls, bats, rackets, and other athletic trappings; and a
long table with folding chairs. The smaller office belonged to

Mr. Schultz, a tall, angular man with a black pencil mustache and the kind of wire eyeglasses that Edward G. Robinson wore in *House of Strangers.*

I spent a half hour or so with Mr. Schultz, getting the lay of the recreational land. He explained that the three attendants in his department were gone to a training session for working with polio victims. He showed me the lockers and the equipment cages, and he explained how I could sign out equipment. He gave me a pair of white pants and a white long-sleeved shirt.

"You'll need to wear these," he said. "Recreation Department rules for all staff, which, for this week, you are. There's an empty locker for you over there." He jerked a thumb over one shoulder.

He also handed me a thick black binder.

"Read this," he said. "It'll get you familiar. Daryl will be back tomorrow. He's in charge of daily activities here."

He pointed to the long table.

"Have a seat, " he said.

Then he disappeared back into his office. No one was in the room, so I tried on my rec whites — a bit loose in the waist and long on the sleeves, but I would make the most of it.

I sat at the table and opened the notebook. It had rules and regulations for competitive sports and social lawn games. I skipped those. There was a section on procedures for keeping patients from unruly behavior while engaged in activities: "gain control over the individual and isolate him from peers quickly," for example, and "do not permit cursing, audible references to body parts, and malicious interpersonal comments intended to intimidate or harass." I never once came across the word *fun.*

After twenty minutes, I closed the notebook. Mr. Schultz

was holed up in his office; no one else was around. I figured that was it, so I changed again and left for the day.

When I returned the next morning, shortly after nine, Daryl was waiting for me in the big room. He wasn't wearing the regulation shirt, just a white t-shirt. Beneath his ever-so-tight t-shirt, biceps bulged. His waist was as trim as the rest of his athletic body, like a boxer's. He wore long sideburns, his hair slicked back into a ducktail. I hadn't noticed that the night I saw him at the tavern. In the rush of events that evening, I suppose I didn't notice very much about him other than his voice and what he said.

I walked over to the long table he stood behind. I nodded, said, "Good morning."

He reached across the table that separated us. "Daryl Forrest," he announced.

His handshake was tighter than it should have been. Stubby fingers wrapped around my hand like a vise.

"Shultz said for me to orient you," he announced. "So that makes me your orienter, ha ha."

I smiled. "I'm Henry. Merchartt. Mr. Schultz said I'd meet you today. I'm eager to get started."

He pointed to a blackboard behind me. "Those're the activities for the day. Schultz puts 'em up in the A.M. before we all get here. We all know what to do, so it's pretty simple. Doesn't take many brains to get this set up for the brainless, ha ha."

I could see where this day was going. I stared past him as if I were looking around for the first time, orienting myself to the room.

Tace. Hold your tongue.

"All right, then," he continued. "First we set up croquet on the Great Lawn. We got thirty ladies coming at ten for lawn games. Them as can follow any damned rules in the first place. Them as has got any wits left about them."

It was going to be a long morning.

This was an unusually warm April day—cloudless, with brilliant sun pouring through the giant elms and maples out on the Great Lawn. We set up the croquet hoops and stakes, measured out the approximate distances by foot, and then hauled out the mallets and balls from storage. By 9:45, female patients began arriving in clusters of five and six until about thirty had gathered, one male and two female attendants supervising.

"Here come the goonies," Daryl announced with a wink.

The ladies stood off to one side, milling around the equipment. Some picked up balls and tossed them toward the colored croquet stakes.

Daryl captured their attention with, "Now hold on there, ladies. I'm gonna show you how to play this game first, so just hold on with tossing them balls."

Most of the women stood stark still. A few giggled and pointed to the ones who had thrown the balls around. One large woman wearing a lime-green dress, a red ball still in her grasp, stepped forward. Shrill voice, screechy. Croquet ball was slowly lobbed from one hand to the other, like she was warming up.

"Look here, mister. They're just having some fun. You got no cause to yell at those ladies. You do that again and I'm gonna bust you in the chops."

The male attendant rushed to her side and pulled her toward the rear of the pack.

"Come with me, Wilma. Over here. Take a break."

He moved her toward a bench where the two of them sat down. She shouted back toward us, "In the chops, mind you!" The attendant pried the red ball from her grasp.

Daryl winked at me again with a look of benign superiority.

"So, as I was saying…" he continued to the group. He proceeded to instruct in *all* the rules at once—one after the other as if he were reciting a grocery list. He "covered" wickets and stakes, colors on the stakes, points, rover ball, turn taking, correct position—two hands on the mallet, legs straddling the ball. The patients stood there, polite but bewildered. He could have been reading a dictionary to them. It wasn't long before some of the women sat down on the grass and fanned their legs on the ground, while others picked up mallets and pounded them on the grass.

One patient, whose arm only went as far as the elbow, raised her stump. "Mister, I have a question," she said. "How am *I* supposed to hit the ball?"

"Yeah," came a voice behind her, "how's Joycey supposed to play?"

"Hell," answered Daryl, "I don't know. Maybe you can just watch."

"But…but…I want to play. I want to play, too!"

Daryl looked over to a female attendant. "Can you do something with her?" he asked. "Take her home or something?"

The attendant pulled Joycey aside and whispered in her ear.

I walked over to him. "Daryl," I said, just loud enough for only him to hear, "I'm not sure they're going to be able to remember all this. It's a lot of information at one time."

He turned toward me, gave a silent glare and said, "I, sir, am the orienter. And you, sir, are the intern. I teach. You learn. Get it?"

Before I could respond, a blue croquet ball hit him in his back. His head shot forward from the blow and his arms went up to clutch the back of his neck. Then he spun around to find the offender. Wilma had rejoined the group; she held a second ball in one hand, raised the other ball next to her ear, ready to launch.

Daryl stood still. For just a second, it was a standoff.

Then he let loose.

"Get that bitch out of here!" he screamed. Wilma held her ground but the male attendant removed her from the group, blue croquet ball notwithstanding. She was escorted back to her bench for detention.

"As for the rest of you, " he said, "here are the mallets and there are the balls. You figure it out." Under his breath but loud enough for me to hear, "Bitches," he muttered.

"Whoopee" went up simultaneously from the crowd as the ladies picked up mallets and began knocking balls every which way. Daryl turned back toward me.

"Okay, smart aleck," he said. "You think you're so smart, you teach 'em." With that, he kicked over a case of upright mallets and headed toward the equipment room.

I stood there as the balls flew around me and across the grass. A female attendant approached. Petite, with jet black hair pulled back in a ponytail, a serious look stretched across her face as she rolled her eyes upward and pulled a thumb toward Daryl's back.

"Don't take it personally," she said. "He's like that a lot."

"I don't understand how he keeps a job here," I said.

"His boss protects him."

"Mr. Schultz?"

"Daryl is his nephew. I hear that he's drifted from job to job because he gets fired so much. He has anger problems. Schultz got him the job and Schultz makes sure he keeps this job. All in the family, as they say."

"I get the picture. Obviously he hates his job."

"No one likes him, not patients, not staff. But they're all afraid of him."

"Afraid? Why?"

"He's such a bully. Most of us hate to bring our patients over here when he's directing activities. But we never know until we get here."

Two ladies started fencing with their croquet mallets.

The attendant pulled on my sleeve. "Could you ... try to help them? They just need some simple rules."

"I'll try," I said.

I clapped to get everyone's attention. The fencers disengaged, put down their wooden rapiers. In a loud voice, I said there were only three rules.

Number one: balls must stay on the grass, no throwing.

Number two: two players on a team share one mallet and one ball; they take turns hitting the ball.

Number three: hit the balls through the hoops, in any direction.

"Have fun!" I shouted.

The mayhem began, balls sailing through the grass, women chasing one another as much as they chased the balls, laughing and shouting. When they tired, they rested and watched, then got up and went at it again. At the end of their scheduled time, the mallets and balls were put back in two piles by where I stood and the women were escorted toward Silver Drive in the direction of the women's cottages.

"Thank you, mister!" one shouted. "I like your game."

I waved back.

When I entered the equipment room, Daryl was leaning against a locker, talking with another attendant. He eyed me silently as I approached. I stopped a few feet away. The other fellow nodded a generic greeting to me, walked silently past me, across the room, and out the front door, leaving the two of us alone.

"Well," said Daryl, "here comes Mr. Know-It-All. What expert advice do you have for me now?"

I looked down and counted to three before I looked him square in the face.

"Look here," I said. "We've gotten off on the wrong foot today, and ...I regret that."

"No shit, Sherlock. You show me up like that again and I'm gonna break your balls. You hear me?"

"Look, I'm sure you can hurt me. Let's just try to start over."

"So, Mister Fancy College Boy HAS got some sense!"

He moved directly in front of me. He towered. Saliva curled in the corner of his mouth. A rabid dog. His fists were clenched. I steeled myself.

Brother Benedict's voice echoed in my head.

Ictos! Averto! Defendere! Dodge! Parry! Defend!

I was not afraid of Daryl. I was sorry for him, but I was not afraid. I knew how to defend myself—and I would if necessary; I could go on the offensive, in fact, in a split second.

I also knew that getting into a fistfight would have me on the next bus to Philadelphia.

Tene Linguam. Hold thy tongue.

At the same time, I knew I had to defend myself, so I moved into a defensive high guard.

Before any swinging began, Mr. Schultz burst through his office door. He shouted. "Hold on there! Just hold on there! What's going on here? You two break it up!"

Daryl took a step back. "Nothin' can't be fixed," he said, the voice now normal. He looked straight at me when he said, "Nothin' can't be fixed later."

Mr. Schultz stepped between the two of us and faced me. "Look here, uh, uh, Harvey..."

"Henry."

"You better take the rest of the day off. I don't know what happened here, but you two need some distance. Go change your clothes and leave. Go on now."

I said nothing. I was relieved it was over.

When I reached the locker, I glanced behind me in their direction. Their backs to me, Mr. Schultz walked next to Daryl. His hand held the scruff of Daryl's t-shirt at the neck as he guided his nephew toward his personal office. They entered and the door closed behind them.

Once changed and outside, I took in deep breaths of fresh air. I found a bench under a huge willow tree and pulled out my diary:

April 30:

This is wrong, plain and simple. This man treating patients like that. And his uncle-boss protecting him. Twice wrong. How can a place that prides itself on its humanistic

integrity allow someone like this to continue working here?
I don't get it.

I went in search of Nurse Brownell.

"Try Women's Infirmary," her secretary said.

Nurse Brownell was descending the wide front steps to Cottage 12 when I arrived. Two nurses with clipboards full of papers followed her. She saw me, waved. I waved back.

At the bottom of the stairs, she turned to the nurses trailing behind her; she told them to continue rounds, she would catch up. She came over to me, out of earshot of the others.

"What is it, Henry? You look distressed. Has something happened?"

I explained to her in general terms my experience with Daryl and Schultz and the Recreation Department. I quoted some of the things Daryl said to residents, and I told her what the female attendants told me.

She looked behind and around us, checking on our privacy.

"It didn't take long, did it?"

"I just think it's wrong that he is allowed to talk that way and bully others." I blurted it out.

"I agree. It is not right at all. I can see how upset you are. I am so sorry."

"He's just…cruel. And abusive."

"I will look into this. But as I told you before, too often our hands are tied by civil service."

I just stood there staring at her, my incredulity apparent.

"What…how can your hands be tied?"

"I am sorry, Henry. But terminating the employment of a civil servant is difficult, if not impossible, especially for character flaws. It was a mistake to hire him in the first place. But that is water under the bridge now. Until we have more evidence than his manners, as abhorrent as they are, there really is not much we can do."

"Well, what counts as evidence, then?"

"Assaulting a co-worker, drinking on the job, theft. He's not done anything like that, as far as anyone knows."

I shook my head in disbelief. "He's protected by his uncle, Mr. Schultz."

"That may be true, too. It would take an attorney to sort all of this out," she said, "and, well, that would be something Dr. Spencer would have to initiate. So far, he has not felt compelled to do that, again."

"But why? Daryl is such an ..." I caught myself before "asshole" came out.

She had this troubled look.

"I know," she said, "But the fact is that everyone, once in a while, says things to patients they later regret. It's just human nature in a place where this many people have this many issues, these immense needs. It happens to all of us. It will happen to you. Daryl is just an extreme example of what many others exhibit from time to time. That is not an excuse for him. Just an explanation of what the legal argument will be if we go down that road. We have to have *more* to go on."

I pursed my lips and looked up to the ceiling.

"Goddammit," came out too quickly.

"Take some time, Henry. Take a walk, clear your head. I think you can safely avoid the Recreation Department for now. Please, come by in the morning and I'll have a different assignment ready for you."

I took her advice about clearing my head. I went for a walk along a stretch of cottages in the direction of the barns. *Something* has *to be done,* I thought. *Someone has to do something.* Just beyond the ancient black willow trees, my thoughts were interrupted by a pair of male patients running across a fallow field of upturned earth, toward me. Both were mongoloids, struggling to make their way through mounds of dirt and clumps of roots and dried leaves. They ran one behind the other, but then the shorter of the two fell face-first into an ankle-high mound.

He screamed, "Samuel. Help! Help me!"

The other circled back to help him up.

"C-c'mon, c-c-c'mon, Rudy," the taller one stuttered. He brushed dried weeds from his fallen friend's head, helped him to his feet, and took his hand as he jerked his partner off to a slow run, again in my direction.

I raised my hands as if to say stop. Twenty feet before they reached me, they slowed to a walk. They were out of breath.

"Fellas," I said. "Slow down, you'll hurt yourself. What's your hurry?"

Rudy bent over double as he gasped for air. Samuel pointed behind himself toward the pasture.

"O-o-o-over there, Doctor."

"In the cow field."

"Th-th-th-there." He pointed toward the barns. "B-b-behind th-th-th-them barns. R-r-r-r-Rosie, she's dead. She's awful d-d-d-d..."

"Dead." Rudy finished Samuel's sentence, grabbed his hand and pulled.

"We got to go tell Mikey," Samuel shouted. "Rosie's his milk cow. Mikey, he's our friend. Doctor, you got to go help Rosie. Maybe she's just hurt. Maybe she's not dead, I don't know."

They took off again, this time in the direction of Cottage 40. I jogged toward the barns, keeping to the walks, not the fields. Past the great barn. Then to the cow pasture behind. I squinted toward the tree line, where I spotted two men standing. I recognized Mr. Meyer from the greenhouses.

As I approached I saw a third man kneeling beside a black and white cow lying in the dirt in the middle of the group, its legs extended straight out. The man on his knees stroked her hip. The fur on the white part of her neck was red; the few square feet of soil beneath her head were darkened.

Mr. Meyer turned toward me. He wiped at his eyes when he spoke. "Some goddamned fool cut her throat," was all he said. Then he turned back to the cow. His companion ground a heel into the dirt; the other continued to stroke Rosie's fur.

"She was my favorite," he said. "Mikey's favorite. His love."

"Some son of a bitch will pay for this," said Mr. Meyer. "Some low-down son of a bitch will pay."

I approached slowly. I knelt next to Rosie's head and rubbed her long nose. Her eyes were open. "Who? What?" I mumbled, looking up to Mr. Meyer.

"I called the police," he said. "They're on their way." He was shaking his head in disgust. "Gibbs here," he said, nodding toward the kneeling man, "found her this morning, early. Gibbs is in charge of livestock. For him, this is personal."

"She was put out to pasture at dawn, as usual, and this is how I found her," Gibbs said, rubbing the cow's rear. "She was all bled out by that time."

Gently stroking the cow's tail, Gibbs finished his thought.

"And before we knew it, patients were coming over to see for themselves. Word gets out pretty fast around here. Scared the hell out of them. I couldn't keep them away. Damned awful thing for them. I just don't know…I just don't know."

The third man, silent until now, said, "This is the same work as the ones who killed those baby chickens."

He pulled a red handkerchief from the back pocket of his britches and blew his nose. "Damned shame, it is. Just a damned shame."

Gibbs stood up, dusted dirt from his knees. "We need to get her out of here. I've got a tow truck coming from town to lift her. Jake, why don't you go over and get the big pickup so they can lift her into the truck? I'll find a spot to bury her."

"Right," Jake said. He folded his handkerchief into even quarters and returned it to his pocket. He took one more look at Rosie, kicked a mound of dirt, and then started across the field toward the barns. From what I could tell, Jake was one of the paid farm hands who supervised patients in the farm program.

My eyes wide, my hands outstretched, I looked inquisitively to Mr. Meyer.

"I have to find this patient, Mikey," he said, staring at Rosie, "and break the news to him. That won't be easy."

Mikey, I thought, *of course, the jolly man who invited Jimmy to milk back in September, the day Jimmy had that breakdown, with the log.*

"Why, I know Mikey," I said. "He's the one who milked this cow."

Mr. Meyer nodded. "He'll be heartbroken. I don't know how he'll handle it. But I need to get to him before others do."

"Wait a minute," I said. "Mikey! There were two patients I ran into who were rushing to tell him about this. Five, maybe ten minutes ago. You better get a move on if you're going to get to him before they do!"

Mr. Meyer turned and began running toward the barns. I was left alone with Gibbs and Rosie.

"Livestock die all the time here," Gibbs said. "It's a part of life and these patients have come to know that. But this…this is different."

I looked down at Rosie again, her eyes permanently fixed toward the sky. It was the saddest thing I'd ever seen. The innocence in the face of that cow. The ground saturated with blood. It was just unspeakable.

Gibbs and I stood in silence. He wiped his eyes with the scruff of his jacket sleeve and turned and walked toward the cow barn. As he walked away, a black-and-white city police car was making its way up Red Drive toward where I stood.

They would survey the crime scene, take pictures, and then question Mr. Meyer and Jake when they came back. They would write a report and they would send extra patrol cars around the hospital for the next few days. Patient life would return to normal for those who knew about this tragedy. Except for Mikey. It would take him a very long time.

In my room that evening, I could hardly bring myself to write. I was still haunted by what I had been through that day:

April 30:

In one day, I have seen the vile spectrum of inhumanity—from mean-spirited to evil-hearted.

I could try to understand people like Daryl; I could

even tolerate him to some extent, if I thought he had some redeeming qualities.

But killing Rosie? Who could do such a thing? Like the dog and the chicks: this was unadulterated wickedness.

I felt powerless to do anything about the rash of vandalism and animal killings. Those were outright criminal acts, and the police were handling those, however inept or disinterested the police may have been.

But I could do something about Daryl. At least I could *try* something. I could lodge a complaint with the Michigan Civil Service Commission. I wrote it by hand that night. I left the inside address blank until the next morning when a clerk in the Mailroom could help me find the address. I explained who I was and said that what I had seen that day, in my opinion, amounted to unprofessional conduct bordering on harassment.

"He may be better suited to a position that does not involve daily interactions with patients," I wrote. I didn't ask that he be disciplined or even fired, only that he be transferred to another Civil Service job more akin to his "unique talents." I tried to give the impression that I was being kind, not retaliatory. I didn't want to sound like this was a personal vendetta.

The letter went out in the next day's mail.

CHAPTER SEVENTEEN

Counting Votes

STORIES ABOUT WHAT HAPPENED TO ROSIE THE COW GREW
more hideous and alarming as word spread quickly through the
patient grapevine. Within three days, anxiety became visible. In
the more extreme forms, patient attempts to flee the grounds
had staff regularly rounding up individuals and pairs carrying
bundles of belongings and heading toward the woody trails on
the west side of the grounds or toward town on the east side.

For Mikey, Rosie's personal milker, it would be months before he would even set foot in the milk barn. Time heals all
wounds, I've heard it said, but the scars remain forever.

If the perpetrators' intent was to scare the dickens out of the
patients, they were supremely successful. If their intent was to
show that they had the run of the campus if they so chose, that
too worked.

Cutting Rosie's throat could not have been more intimidat-
ing.

The police investigated but there simply was no hard evidence and no leads. They increased nightly patrols on the hospital grounds, and for the next week they stationed a patrol car at
the entrance to the hospital proper on Eleventh Street. None of
that would deter the criminal minded from entering the campus

on foot through the fields or the woods, day *or* night, and hiding when the patrol car came around. But I really didn't know what else the police could have done: vandals are clever at not getting caught.

On the last day of April I had my monthly appointment with Dr. Spencer. It was my scheduled time to report on how my field experience had been going for the previous thirty days. Her ear in a telephone, Mrs. Krueger waved me into his office.

I stood before his door, gathering my thoughts. I wondered how he would view this latest incident. Would he whitewash it—as did the others? Would he put more pressure on the police to do something about the threats to hospital security? I knew I had to temper my curiosity with caution, had to remember my place in the scheme of things here. Lots of counting to three—and Latin rehearsals.

I sat down. A copy of the *Traverse City Sentinel* lay on his desk between us.

He pointed to the newspaper. "There is a very nice letter to the editor in today's *Sentinel* from a family in Kalkaska. Their son has been here since '48 and they sing our praises for helping him. He suffered brain damage from a motorcycle accident. Terrible tragedy."

Ruth's letter, I thought.

"There was another one last week," he continued, "written by Mr. Stanley, one of our own hospital accountants. I think you know him. He made quite a case for the mental health benefits of patients who work on the farm here."

I had seen Nelson's wonderful letter the day it appeared, but I feigned ignorance in that moment with, "Oh, I'd like to read that."

"It's always comforting to see people who appreciate our work here," he said, smiling. "As you may know, we often see letters to the opposite effect in the paper."

I said I hoped there would be more people who would share their stories as the Kalkaska people had. (In my mind's eye, I was winking.) He turned the paper over and asked me how my past month had gone. I talked for five minutes or so in a sort of litany of how I had been spending my time at my various locations on the grounds.

I kept Daryl out of the conversation. Bringing up Daryl would distract from the story of my role in discovering the slaughter of Rosie, which I did in great detail. This sad, bewildered look came over him. Then that look turned into a scowl when I went on to mention a rumor I had heard about a fire near the piggery.

Dr. Spencer folded his hands on his desk. He sighed. His eyes narrowed. He looked up, stared past me, to the bay window and the grounds outside. I turned and looked out, too. In the distance, on a sidewalk, a man with an opened umbrella stretched over his head paced back and forth. The bright sun cast a shadow that followed him.

"Oh," he said. "That. Yes, it's true. A small fire, but night security put it out before it did any real damage."

"How did it start?" I said, turning back toward him.

He sighed again, ignored my question.

"These are uncertain times for us, Henry." He continued to study the man outside as he spoke.

"Sir?"

"Most of our staff know this. Nurse Brownell and I think it's time you should, too. You got an inkling of our troubles on the day when Mr. Quinn arrived. Do you recall the slashed tires?" His eyes fell on mine finally.

"Yes," I said, "And the dog's head, the baby chickens, the milk cow. Have there been more?"

"The fire, most recently.

"I've tried to keep these incidents quiet, for the patients' sake. I'm not certain that's been the right thing to do. At least, not any more. These awful things...they seem to be increasing. I...uh, I'm not..."

He stopped in mid-sentence. He was distressed by something, I couldn't figure out what.

"You see," he continued, "there are forces at work outside of our hospital who would like to see us as a very different place."

"Different? How so?"

"More like the hospital you were at before coming here."

"Harrisville? That would be awful."

"It would indeed. But these are people who believe our hospital threatens their economic well-being."

"I've heard about the letters to the editor in the paper. I've read some. They can get pretty cruel, the way some people talk about the patients and the hospital."

"Yes, well...If some of these people had their way, we would become just another underfunded state hospital isolated from the community."

I remembered what Nurse Brownell said about how the vandalism was related to the local economy. "Which is a whole story in itself," she said. But she never did tell me.

I was about to learn the story.

"There's talk among the legislators, and there are rumors that they envision changes for us. Just what those changes will be, I can't say, but I'm frankly worried. I would like to think it's all political posturing and speculation right now, and some vandalism — which, if related, is intended to intimidate us. Why? I'm not sure. Most likely, it's some people's crude way of expressing their hostility."

"But can't you just …?

He waved his hand as if to say hold on.

Sanctus. Comes. Slow. Count.

"There's little we can do," he continued. "The police, as you know, have investigated but turned up no leads. For my part, I have tried a political approach by representing ourselves to our local legislators. I went to both Representative Nickols' office and Senator Merker's office. Met with both of them personally. I told them about the rumors, and I described attempts to intimidate us. I asked for their help."

"I'm sorry, but I don't know these officials. How did they react?"

"Like the polite but savvy politicians they are. A lot of affirmative nodding of heads and comments like 'I appreciate knowing that,' and 'you have a lot to be proud of.' In the end, I think it was the senator who said, 'You know, Dr. Spencer, we have a lot of voters here in this part of the state, and I have to be responsible to them, too. If they come to me with complaints, then I'm sworn to pay attention. You are one of those voters, and I intend to pay attention to you, too, just as I would anyone else.' "

"That seems odd," I said. "Of course, he pays attention. That's just common sense."

He shook his head no.

"Oh, Henry. You're young. You'll come to understand politics. With politicians, one has to read between the lines, one has to consider all that they could possibly mean when they talk with people. On the surface, they're saying, 'I'm a fair man. I listen to everyone.' But below the surface, by God, they're counting votes. The hospital may have three thousand residents, but none of them votes. Whereas in the community, loud voices speak for themselves as well as for the quieter voices, and *those* voices, combined, cast votes."

I squirmed in my seat. Something about him made me uncomfortable. I was sure he spoke truth, but his tone was whiney, his words defeatist. I hadn't heard him talk this way before.

"Sir," I said, respectfully, "I may be naive about politics, but isn't there any way you could get out there and convince others that...that...I don't know, just...beat a loud drum? What's happening here is outrageous. It's criminal!"

I was raising my voice, probably getting a little out of control, when he waved his hand again.

"Well, Henry. That may be how *some* superintendents see their work, but I'm not one to go to Lansing and make a row. I've been here a long time, and these sorts of things come and go. We can wait this one out."

It was all I could do to keep my mouth shut. I felt the urge to scream that this was an ethical, or, at least, a moral issue. There was injustice and that was intolerable! I had to let off some steam without offending him. It was a fine line to walk.

"With all due respect, sir. I just wonder if a brash voice should not be heard down there in the capitol. *Make* them listen. I mean, what does anyone from 200 miles away know about what goes on here? What does it take to get their attention? Why don't you just..."

He looked taken aback as he sat upright in his chair. He folded his arms across his chest.

I stopped in mid-sentence. I could hear my own words bouncing off the leather covers of old books on the shelves and spilling onto the carpeted floor.

Shades of Harrisville all over again: I was out of order.

Apparently, I had struck a nerve. And a sensitive one. *But, damn it,* I thought, *he has a responsibility — to the hospital, to the patients and staff. He's shirking that responsibility!*

Mitescere. Calm down. Count.

He rose and walked to the window, stared out at the expanse of lawn, mused as he spoke, slowly, his back to me. I could hardly hear him, so I turned around from my chair to face his back.

"Much of what you say is true. Perhaps someone *should* be shouting. Perhaps someone *should* make them listen. You know, some *have* tried. I've gone to our Board of Trustees and asked for their help. I specifically asked if any of them would speak on our behalf to people they know in the governor's office, if not the governor himself."

Of course, I thought, *the trustees. I had read some of their reports in the archives.* Trustees ought to stand up for the institution! Or were *they* a bunch of chickenshits?

He went on to explain how certain of the trustees spoke with their contacts in Lansing — to alert them that we were being subject to some hostile acts and awful rumors. I asked what trustees actually do *as trustees,* and he said they establish broad policies, approve annual budgets, and review the institution and the medical superintendent. He also said they have a vested interest in the integrity of the hospital, and so the ones that spoke to their contacts felt that that integrity was being tested. But

179

they were assured by the people they spoke with that nothing ill would befall the hospital. They were told that the hospital would continue to operate as it always has.

"They reported all this to me with a great deal of confidence in the powers that be."

"Well, that should give you some comfort," I said.

He said it should, but I had to realize that what those in charge say and what they do are not always aligned. Dr. Spencer didn't think intervention by the trustees would make much of a difference because they can't change policy or deflect actions coming directly from those in the governor's office. He asked, did I realize that trustees are appointed by the governor, not elected?

I said I didn't, but I could see how that very fact changed things. He said that if a trustee became too critical, too outspoken, he ran the risk of being replaced. Dr. Spencer, a governor appointee himself, ran that same risk.

He returned to his chair and pulled his pipe from a drawer. He put it in his mouth, no tobacco. Like a pacifier.

"In the current political climate," he said, "that is a real possibility. No, my work is right here, at the hospital. When it comes to politicking, well, I've tried. But the truth is, well, I'm just not cut out for that sort of thing. Never have been. I've been superintendent for more than two decades now, and that's just not how I've served these many years, and I've always had my contract renewed. Besides, all this will pass."

There are idealists who challenge the world because they believe in their cause. There are idealists who lead others because they believe they have right on their side. And there are idealists who have visions of a better world but who, unfortunately, lack the will or skill to do the hard work that would create that world. Dr. Spencer, I realized, was an idealist of the latter type.

I was disappointed. *All this will pass* wasn't viable. Clearly, all this wasn't going to pass. His was a Pollyanna strategy that I found hard to swallow. I sat there, torn between speaking my mind and holding my tongue. I opted for the held tongue.

But I saw the connection between the legislators' indifference and the fact that Dr. Spencer's appointment as Medical Superintendent was subject to periodic renewal.

"Did you say 'renewed'? I thought medical superintendents were …just… "

"Permanent?" He laughed. "That would be nice, but no, not permanent. A hospital superintendent is appointed by the governor, and he serves a three-year term. Renewable at the discretion of the governor. My current contract expires in August of this year."

"Of course you'll be renewed. Why wouldn't you? I mean, you've done such good work here. You must have statistics. How many patients have recovered, how many have returned to their families, how many nurses have been trained? There must be so many ways of showing progress and success!"

His brow furled again. He mused, in silence. I waited.

"Yes," he said, "there *are* many ways, but what if you show those statistics, and share those facts, but those in your audience are not the least bit interested? What if, for them, the facts do not matter?"

Coming from the academic world, where facts — *truth* — matter more than anything, I was stunned by his comment. My expression must have betrayed my dismay.

"I can see how that shocks you," he said. "It is hard for me to believe, too, but one learns to live with those things over which one has no control."

I recovered from my shock enough to say, "How can anyone not appreciate what this hospital accomplishes? How can anyone not see that?"

"Let me put it this way," he continued. "Because we are a state institution, we are, by default, subject to political fortunes, as any government entity is. Fortunately, we have some degree of financial security because of our farming program. It feeds us and it brings in additional resources so that we can care for our population as necessary, not as others *think* we should care for them. Other, less sustainable institutions depend on the government for *everything*. We, fortunately, have not had to. Yet. And that has given us a measure of independence.

"In any case, the sad part of this story is that those in power on the *outside* are not concerned with how patients are on the *inside*. Unless they themselves have a relative who has been institutionalized. Unless they themselves have had direct experience in caring for the mentally ill—why, they just don't understand. Patient care of any kind is merely an *abstraction* to them, nothing they can see or feel or know first-hand."

"All right, then," I said, "has that congressman or senator ever spent any time at this hospital? Have they ever been with patients in the greenhouses, or seen them in the fields? Have they ever come to one of the social events?" I was shooting one question after another at him.

"Neither of them have ever set foot on these grounds, nor has our other senator. No legislator has, as long as I've been superintendent. We've invited them, more times than I can remember, but they've always begged off with some excuse. You get the picture."

"I just thought, if they, if they could see first hand ..."

A dark look came over him. "As I said," he measured his words slowly: "Never. Set. Foot."

The mood changed as he settled back comfortably into his high-backed chair, then stretched to look at something in the window behind me. I turned to look. A pigeon landed on the sill outside the window. It looked in at us, his grey and purple head moving sideways in little jerks and stops.

"The truth is, Henry, I'm getting tired. I have put my all into this hospital, but my all may no longer be enough. It may be time for me to make room for someone else."

In my mind, he looked small—and worn out. He seemed to have lost his resilience. The institution faced a threat, and its leader had lost faith in his ability to lead. I wanted to say something like, *Yes, it may very well be time to make room for someone else. But...*

Oculum ad praemium. Eyes on the prize.

His gaze shifted back to us in the room. Suddenly more upbeat, he changed the subject. Predictably. It was clear to me that that subject would not come up again this morning.

"But more of this at another time. I just wanted you to be aware. And you yourself will understand more, first hand, now that the planting and growing season is beginning. Out there in the barns and in the fields is where the most significant therapy goes on. Along, of course, with the kitchen, the fashion shop, the laundry, the greenhouses ..."

"The maintenance shops?" I interjected.

"Indeed. You get the picture. Well then, for now, I'll update Mr. Quinn's record. As for you, Henry, we have your next two assignments.

"First, Nurse Brownell will direct you to the Office of Patient Rights; there you will learn how we view patient privileges and restrictions. You will go on what we call *rights rounds*. I think you will find that rather thought provoking, given your interests in ethics.

"I would be *very* interested in that."

"She thought you would. Next, she would like you to work some more with Mr. Meyer. I know you've already visited with him in the greenhouses, but as we move closer to the spring harvest, we think you can learn more about the farm operation as it pertains to the local market. You've expressed special interest in how our patients interact with the community, and the market would be a good place to see our patients doing just that. I think that kind of experience will further illuminate for you our *work-is-therapy* philosophy."

I said I would like that very much. I said I found Mr. Meyer to be a wealth of knowledge.

"Good," he said. "Around the beginning of June, then, you will go with a group of patients to the market where we sell surplus produce. That's one of the main places where patients interface with town residents, so you can have the experience of what I call 'patient life on the boundary.'"

In my May 15 diary entry, I let loose on Dr. Spencer as if I were talking directly to him:

> *You've outlived your time, sir. You were the right man for other times, other challenges, but not these. Your "story" seems a good lesson for me if ever I were in such a position of leadership—I ought to know when it's time to step aside; know that I shouldn't hang on just because I once was the right man for the job.*

But then I softened:

I can imagine how hard this is for him, though. How hard it must have been to be that honest with me, of all people. But, maybe, because I am an outsider of sorts, he felt he could be honest. No, he could not be so candid with his staff. In his guise as medical superintendent, he must remain the staid leader. But why in the world doesn't he summon the troops and make a huge collaborative effort to protect the asylum? Is he too much the isolationist? Too much mired in the myth of the solitary man? In that sense, he seems an enigma, to me at least.

Nero fiddled—and we saw how that turned out.

I find his comments about abstraction intriguing. How distancing oneself from "otherness" insulates oneself. How it isn't until mental or physical disability becomes personal that these things matter. That caring for all our citizens in the best possible ways is our moral responsibility. That they too have a right to as much health as they are capable of having.

CHAPTER EIGHTEEN

Rights And Privileges

DAY AFTER DAY OF DREARY LIGHT RAIN WAS INTERRUPTED OC-
casionally by thunderstorms rolling in from the west. Umbrellas
and rubber galoshes were in great demand among patients as
they began bartering with one another, offering cigarettes for
rain ponchos, hoarded cookies for plastic rain hats, as much as
a buck for a slicker. The sodden grass sagged two inches when
you walked on it, and the mud ran in brown rivers down the
sidewalks. One patient who claimed to be God went around
warning patients that it was time to start boarding the ark.

Thus began the third week of May. Nurse Brownell called to
say that, given the weather, I should go to the "Office of Patient
Rights and Privileges."

Ever since my most recent meeting with Dr. Spencer, I had
been thinking about patient rights to quality mental health care.
But I hadn't considered other "rights" they may have. One tends
not to think that those with mental illness have *any* rights other
than those most fundamental to living. That's a legislator's version of patient rights, Dr. Spencer had implied.

In my philosophy courses, I wrote a paper on *natural justice* — the purest form of justice that exists *before* society imposes
its cultural forms of moral and legal justice. Philosophers never

tire of debating whether there actually *is* natural justice. I'm a Platonist on that topic—natural justice exists *a priori.*

The fact that this state hospital even *had* an office of patient rights contrasted with the Harrisville State Hospital, where patients had few if any rights other than basic safety and food. While I cringed remembering how little natural justice was honored at Harrisville, I was excited to learn how the humanistic orientation to patients here informed their rights.

Nurse Brownell had briefed the office supervisor, Mr. Wilson, before I arrived. An angular man with Groucho Marx eyebrows and a W. C. Fields nose, Mr. Wilson sported a brown billiard pipe with a well-worn stem. He used it as a sort of speech marker. Out of his mouth it came when he began to speak, back in again when he stopped.

He sat me at a tiny desk cluttered with folders, worn books, and index card boxes. Morning sun streamed through the venetian blinds, warming the room.

"These are our archives," he said, pointing the mouthpiece end of his pipe at a stack of folders and bound reports on the corner of his desk. "It would be best for you to learn the history of patient rights before we go on rights rounds."

"Rights rounds?"

"On the grounds. You'll see. I'll leave you with these," he said, sliding the stack toward me.

He left the room. I picked up a condensed history of patient rights at mental hospitals throughout the country. No such thing as "patient rights" existed before 1940. But during the war and post-war years when soldiers returned with an array of conditions, mental illness came to be seen less the result of immorality or idiocy and more a medical condition. Patient advocates argued that people who were mentally ill deserved the basic rights accorded to others who were not ill. Unfortunately, their views were not widely accepted, and so patients continued to have few if any "rights" other than the bare essentials of food, water, shelter, and safety.

I put down the little history and gazed around the room. *Not much different than how livestock is cared for,* I thought. I opened my diary to a clean page and wrote:

May 17:

Maslow never wrote about patient needs, but if he had, what might he have said?

Would he have said that patient <u>needs</u> should determine their rights? No. That's too broad and oversimplified. But it's on the right track.

<u>Physiological</u> (hunger, thirst, physical comfort) and <u>safety</u> (shelter, security, order) needs <u>must</u> be met. By law. That was Harrisville.

But don't they have the right to have other needs met? If society wants people to be "well," then what does "well" mean? I doubt that Harrisville could even have had that conversation. Questions such as "What does 'well' mean?" must be embedded in the hospital culture to even become part of a conversation.

So many patients are "well" here who couldn't be well outside. Here they have jobs, sports, outings, friends, belonging, predictability, and structure—and they are included in the grand operation of the hospital. These are things that are higher on Maslow's hierarchy. These are the things that constitute "wellness" for <u>anyone.</u> Why not for this population, too?

The room was now becoming stuffy, so I opened a window and gazed out over the lawn that stretched from Building 50 over to Cottage 45. The rain had let up. Three patients in wheelchairs were being escorted down the walk toward a cluster of newly planted walnut trees. They veered off on the grass and stopped. One patient reached down and plucked some dandelions. She placed the flowers in her lap and then pointed back toward the sidewalk, where the little entourage continued their journey.

I breathed in the fresh air just as Mr. Wilson returned and took a seat in the corner, where he began leafing through some papers. He appeared to be looking for something, but he could also have been killing time until I finished reading. We exchanged polite smiles and nods but said nothing to one another.

I opened another slim volume titled *The Office of Patient Rights at the Traverse City State Hospital*. There I learned the expanded rights every patient was entitled to—food, clothing, hygiene, medical and dental care; therapy; socialization "if appropriate"; and a host of others ranging from having approved visitors to being able to lodge complaints against other patients and staff. Patient rights recognized that "every human creature deserves the respect and dignity that their physical, emotional, and mental lives deserve."

My eye lingered over that phrase, *every human creature*. That elevated patient rights to a philosophical plane.

"The word *rights*," Brother Benedict used to drill into us, "is categorically ethical."

May 17:
The ethics of patient rights would be where human rights and natural justice intersect.

I came across the phrase *access rights*. I hadn't heard that one before. I asked Mr. Wilson what that meant. He put his papers down and explained.

Patients with *open tickets* had freedom to go anywhere on the grounds as part of their work. Others who did not work but who had earned trust would be granted *ground parole*. Ground parole gave them the roam of the campus, but they were not allowed in such work buildings as the livery, bakery, cannery, and so forth. Individual patients with *supervised access* had to be accompanied by staff, or they went in large groups with staff.

"It's what we call a patient's freedom to move about the grounds, or have that freedom restricted. When you see patients roaming freely about the grounds, they have *open access*. But they can lose that access if they violate rules or get into some sort of trouble."

For months, I had noticed that some patients move about the grounds freely for work or pleasure, while others were escorted by attendants, and still others always seemed to travel in groups. I knew there were differences among them as to freedom of movement, but I didn't realize that that freedom was earned and could be removed. Making movement an earned right put the onus on the patient to be more responsible. And encouraging more responsibility was yet another way to advocate for wellness. I thought it was genius.

Mr. Wilson continued, "As with any right, you can earn it, *and you can lose it!*"

He punctuated these last five words with multiple thrusts of the pipe that seemed to hold special meaning for him. I would find that out soon enough. Then he pumped the base of his pipe into a cupped hand as if he were emptying ashes. I wondered when it was that he gave up smoking.

Next, he produced a clipboard with pages of typed information. These were the "Access Status Reports" prepared the previous evening by the night clerk.

Page one listed patients' **Name and Residence**; a numerical **Code** corresponding to the reasons their access was limited; the **Status** of campus access; and **Notes**. I read the first few:

> Graham Foley, Cottage 29; Code 7; ground parole; see note.
>
> Frances Markey, Cottage 17; Code 9; open ticket restricted; no notes.
>
> Constance Gilbert, East Wing; Code 16; supervised access; see note.

"What do these codes mean?" I asked.

"Ah," he said. He went to his desk, opened a Rolodex, removed a card, handed it to me. It listed a series of numbers — "Codes" — with explanations next to them:

1. Theft
2. Destruction of Property
3. Alcohol
4. Physical Assault
5. Verbal Assault
6. Indecent Exposure
7. Public Nuisance
8. Trespassing
9. Self-Harm

Twenty-two codes rounded out the list.

"Patients have been known to kill one another here," I said to Mr. Wilson. "I don't see murder here on the list." I was making a little joke.

"What would be the point?"

I went back to the clipboard. No more little jokes.

My eyes alighted at the last name on the bottom of the page: *James Quinn, Cottage 40; Code 8; Supervised; see note.*

"I know this patient," I said. "Code 8 means, what's that again?"

"Eight is trespassing."

"Trespassing? Where?"

He took the clipboard from my hands and thumbed through the Notes section.

"*WW*, it says. Women's Walk. Men aren't allowed in the Women's Walk. And vice versa for the Men's Walk."

"What was he doing in the Women's Walk?"

"Let me see. Security saw him walking away from the woody area adjacent to the Women's Walk. Asked what his business was there. Subject did not answer. Dried weeds and dirt on subject's clothing. Zipper on pants undone. Officers surmise subject went in woods to urinate and probably fell down in the brush."

I smiled. Peeing in the bushes sounded like something Jimmy would do: Probably rushing from job to job and just didn't take the time to find a proper bathroom.

"First offense for a Code 8 is two days, no access. We have a lot of trespassers, especially where the two sexes are concerned. We've had our share of sexual assaults over the years too, so we have to be vigilant."

"Of course," I said, "But this man, he wouldn't hurt a fly. He works with Mr. Harrison in maintenance. He'll be sorry to miss work."

In April, Jimmy had moved to Cottage 40, which housed men who worked on maintenance. Being in a different cottage than me meant he wouldn't have to explain when I "discovered" he wasn't at work. That would only have added to his embarrassment.

I was certain he had learned his lesson. Next time, he would hold it a few minutes longer.

A nurse showed up, one I'd not met before. Slim woman, late 50's, grey hair pulled back in a loose bun, Nurse O'Brien had traces of a youthful beauty in her fair skin and high cheekbones. Her voice had a soothing quality that could melt any patient's opposition when she had to pull their access rights.

Nurse O'Brien, Mr. Wilson, and I were to go out on patient rounds. We were to find individual patients who were to have rights reinstated or their restrictions extended.

First on the list was *Graham Foley*, a war casualty who believed he was God. An otherwise harmless man who chronically harassed other patients for "sins" ranging from heresy to harlotry, Graham was to lose access rights for badgering a paraplegic patient to "stand and walk with the Lord." *Code 7: Public Nuisance.* He apologized for being under the influence of the devil himself and promised to "leave the wheelies alone." Rights reinstated.

Second on the list was Constance Gilbert, a female patient with a Code 1: Theft—and a one-week suspension of access rights. She told us to go to hell. Suspension extended.

The most intriguing—and complicated—patient we visited was Frances Markey. We were to talk with Frances about reinstating her open access.

"What did she do?" I asked.

"I prefer that she tell you herself," said Nurse O'Brien as we ascended the stairs to the large porch at Cottage 36.

Frances sat on a cushioned divan in the parlor. She rose demurely, curtsied, sat down again, and straightened the pleats in her skirt.

Frances was young and attractive in a Myrna Loy-cute way. Early thirties as far as I could tell. Slight, rather athletic body, dark hair with curls and parted down the middle. Green eyes that would seem to look right through you when she stared, as she most often did, long and hard, until you looked away.

She suffered from severe depression. She was one of those patients who chose *not* to work on the grounds or in the other places where females were employed.

Large urns of red and yellow tulips graced the end tables and upright piano in the corner of the room. Frances sat timidly, legs tucked under her chair. She smoothed pleats in her skirt, and then draped a single red tulip on a long green stem diagonally across her lap. She gazed at the tulip as Nurse O'Brien nestled closer to her on the sofa. Frances smiled at her. They were familiar. Mr. Wilson and I sat across, on separate chairs.

"Frances," Nurse O'Brien began. "This Mr. Henry. He is learning to be a doctor and he wants to be part of what we talk about today. Will that be all right with you?"

She looked at me, and then quickly looked down and fidgeted with the buttons on her blouse.

"Is he nice?"

"He's very nice, Frances. He'll just listen. We have to talk about, you know, what happened again. We have to talk about that if you want to have access rights again."

"Okay." The green eyes turned to me again.

"First, we're going to tell Mr. Henry your story. Is that all right?"

"Okay."

Frances had made many trips to the women's infirmary for the previous three years, the last one being the most recent reason for her restriction.

"I get sad. I cry a lot. I don't know why," Frances added. She reached down and rubbed at a scruff on her shoe. "I just get that way."

"When she has an open ticket, her sadness goes away. Isn't that right, Honey?"

"Yeah, I get happy again."

"She visits with other female patients; she plays board games in the cottages or she listens to patients play piano. But she loses her open ticket at roughly five-month intervals."

Mr. Wilson chimed in. "Frances is a swallower."

"A...swallower?" I asked, breaking my silence.

He explained. Frances had an unusual penchant for swallowing things that one would not imagine fitting in one's mouth, not to mention swallowing. But apparently she can. And does. Pencils ranging from four to six inches. Spoons, both tea- and sugar-sized. Door keys and nail files, bobby pins, screws, rocks the size of grapes.

"I ate my toothbrush," Frances added.

Nurse O'Brien took over. "The first few surgeries to remove the offending objects kept her in the women's infirmary for weeks at a time. The doctors questioned her about her strange behavior but she wouldn't talk about it—with them anyway."

"They were not nice," Frances interjected. "I don't like to talk with them."

She put her hand on Frances' knee. "We understand, Sweetie."

"They never made any headway. Before long, she had to have another surgery to remove the toothbrush. The surgeon swore that he would not remove one more toothbrush, spoon, pencil, quarter, or anything. Is that what he told you, Frances?"

She fingered the tulip stem and whispered, "Doctor said, no more—or else!"

"The surgeon told her that the next time, she would languish in Cottage 36 until she just stopped right up and died of stomach cancer. He spared no detail in describing a slow, agonizingly painful death."

"Not the best bedside manner," added Mr. Wilson, "but he'd had enough."

"Doctor said my stomach will boil up and my guts will burn and smoke will come out my mouth and I wouldn't breath. He told me to hold my breath for twenty minutes."

"Seconds."

"So I did. But I started choking. Doctor said that's how I will die if I swallow anything again. Just food."

Nurse O'Brien continued.

"Frances thus spent a lot of time recovering in the infirmary. Oddly, her spirits usually perked up during these recovery periods. Staff noticed this pattern; they alerted Nurse Brownell, and she had a hunch. She called in one of the new nurses—that was Nurse Swandler—and introduced the two of them."

"I *love* Nurse Swandler."

"Nurse Swandler is the youngest of the nursing staff, her hair done up in waves and curls, like Gene Tierney. Among all of our nurses on staff, she not only has a good clinical understanding of patients' challenges, but she connects with them on a most basic human level. She's a treasure of smart empathy."

"She's a dreamy baby doll," said Frances.

"And a good role model," said Nurse O'Brien. "She just completed School of Nursing here and hadn't been assigned yet. I requested that she spend a few hours with Frances one day, and, on a hunch, I asked her to bring some women's magazines with her. They were like two teenagers ogling over the outfits and models in the fashion magazines. Nurse Swandler and Frances get on very well."

"Fashion, romance, and dreams," added Mr. Wilson.

"She is so-o-o pretty. She's a dolly."

"Slowly, Frances opened up. Eventually she told the real reason for her eating habits — she was lonely. She wanted a boyfriend."

"Yeah, like Roland."

"Roland was her boyfriend before she came to the hospital. Right, Honey?"

"Yeah, Roland. I miss Roland. So much."

"I know, Sweetie."

To me again: "Nurse Swandler promised Frances that she would visit her every week if Frances would promise that she would stop swallowing bad things."

"That friendship changed everything," added Mr. Wilson.

"No more chances, doctor said. No more bad eating."

"No more chances," repeated Nurse O'Brien.

Frances looked up at her. "I never liked swallowing those things. I just did it. I was lonely. When I swallow things, I'm real important."

"You are important just the way you are," said Nurse O'Brien. "But, I have to ask, are you not lonely anymore?"

She twisted a button on her yellow sweater, stretched both

feet out before her as if she were comparing them. Her answer came slowly but decisively.

"Yeah, still lonely. I want to be pretty like Nurse Swandler. Someday she'll get married and have a family and a big home with a cat. I want to get married too and have all that—and cats, lots of cats. Like in the magazines and in the movies. I get sad because maybe I'll never get married. But Nurse Swandler says maybe I will someday, when I get better. She is my best friend. I love her so much. She brings me fruit and we eat it together. Fruit is very good for me. I like fruit now. I don't like spoons and pencils. They're not good for me. So I am going to try real hard, every day, to get better."

Mr. Wilson asked Frances if having an open ticket again might help her get better.

"Oh, yes. Can I go see Nurse Swandler then, on my own?"

"Well, I think that would be fine, as long as she's not busy with her other duties. I'm sure she would like that. She might even take you on outings."

Nurse O'Brien and Mr. Wilson exchanged glances. They nodded slightly, in unison.

Frances could resume open access in the morning, Mr. Wilson said.

Frances jumped up and twirled around, her curls whirling about her head. "Whoopee!" she shouted. She handed her tulip to Mr. Wilson, gave Nurse O'Brien a big hug, and curtsied to me.

At the door on our way out, she gave Nurse O'Brien another huge hug. "Whoopee! Whoopee!" sounded behind us as we descended the stairs from the cottage porch.

We walked east, toward the women's side of the grounds.

"I'm just astonished," I said. "Frances' case is so simple—and yet so complicated. She just needs Roland, or *a* Roland."

"I'm glad you see that, Henry," said Nurse O'Brien.

She stopped, turned to face me. "But will it surprise you to learn that Roland doesn't exist?"

"Doesn't...exist?"

"Only in her head."

We saw a handful of other patients that day—a psychotic woman who had cupped her own feces and rubbed it on the windows in her room (Code 2). A deaf mute who scaled the fence around the water tower in a failed attempt to climb and jump to his death (Codes 8 & 9). And a naked man with one tooth in the middle of his upper jaw who was found in the orchard, covered with leaves and brush, asleep (Code 6).

Back at the office around five, Mr. Wilson retired his pipe to his little pipe stand on his desk and bid Nurse O'Brien good-bye for the day. He briefed me on what to expect the following day—more rounds. Then he stood before a large window, stared at the pools of water that had formed on the lawn.

"Time is often our enemy here," he mused. "In institutions that are severely understaffed and underfunded, seldom do staff have the time to go beyond simply curbing the behavior. Restraints and punishments, unfortunately, are too frequently our only recourse. Not all patients can teach us about what motivates their behaviors, but for those like Frances, we sometimes get a break."

At the window, he pointed to something. I stood up and moved for a closer look. A small herd of deer was crossing the open space. The fawns followed the does in a straight line until they reached a wooded area and then disappeared into the thicket.

"Visitors," he said.

I didn't want to change the subject.

"She has to believe she has a future," I said. "She has the right to enjoy *some* form of intimacy. And the hope to have more, one day. Isn't that what keeps her going?"

Mine wasn't a rhetorical question. I'm not sure he heard it.

"Pardon me," he said. "I'm getting tired. It's been a long day. And it's nearly suppertime. We start at nine in the morning. Let's call it a day."

I thought a lot about *time* when I wrote in my diary that evening:

May 17:

How critical it is for a woman like Frances to have others acknowledge her need for intimacy. How critical it is for caregivers to take time to understand her needs. Time to construct her history. Time to sort out her complicated psychology. Time to learn all she has to teach us.

Time is the enemy, for time eats up human and financial resources. It's partly a matter of funding mental health care. Ultimately and most importantly, it's a matter of a philosophy that would illuminate this dark corridor of patient care.

How can an institution this large, with this many patients, afford the <u>time</u> to truly understand each patient? Understanding may be vital, absolutely essential, but is it humanly possible given the numbers of patients, the range of disorders, and the paucity of knowledge about mental *illness? And yet, understanding is the crucial point where human rights, patient needs, and human resources intersect.*

But it's not just a matter of time; it's also a matter of recognizing and acting upon fundamental human needs. In the context of this ethos at this hospital, patients have more opportunity to express their needs the way typical people do. Such increased opportunity begets more complications, however. With freedom comes more opportunity and with more opportunity comes the likelihood that patients will push the limits of those rights.

So, does society deny those rights through the practices of Harrisville-type institutions? Or does it acknowledge those rights — and provide the right supports for them to be acted upon, within limits, as much as there are limits accorded typical people?

That is the moral question: in ignoring — or denying — this basic human need, do we violate this basic human right?

Frances is one of the fortunate few. Jimmy may be another. But what about the hundreds, thousands of others?

**What about Cousin Ethel?

In all the time we were growing up, not once did I think about Ethel dating or Ethel having a boyfriend. When it was May and prom time for her school, it never occurred to me to ask if my own cousin would be going. Even worse, how must she have felt when no one asked her to go? Not once did I ever ask if Ethel ever went on a date. I could not ask about what I could not see. Like most of society, I was blinded by my own ignorance.

Frances and Ethel . . . it is all coming home to me.

Richard VanDeWeghe

Shouldn't a nineteen-year old autistic girl be understood
to have the same drives, the same longing, the same needs
as any nineteen-year old? Isn't there something wrong
when a cousin, a brother, a family, a community ignores the
needs — the rights — for intimacy that everyone has? Yes,
there is. And I'm as guilty as anyone.

CHAPTER NINETEEN

Bernadine's Hatchlings

THE NEXT MORNING, I DISCOVERED A NOTE FROM NURSE Brownell taped to the door of my room.

Henry,

With the spring weather setting in, it is time for you to gain more familiarity with the farming operations and the vital role farming, livestock, and the orchards play in the lives of patients and in the well-being of the institution.

In the morning, please find Mr. Meyer in Greenhouse 2. You have already met him. As supervisor of the greenhouses, he is familiar with the entire farming program. He is also quite knowledgeable about the hospital's relations with the community, a topic in which you have expressed interest. Mr. Meyer will direct you for the next two weeks.

Sincerely,
Nurse Brownell

I knew little about farming. I had never even been on a working farm. I grew up a city kid in Philadelphia, far removed from any farming communities other than seeing them through the window of a car or train. It was another world for me. Yet what I now understood slightly was that this "other world" of work—like art, beauty, and human relationships—*was* patient care.

So I was eager to learn more about the farm program. What I knew was that the hospital had hundreds of acres of rich farmland and orchards full of apple, peach, pear, plum, and cherry trees. Raspberries and strawberries covered acres, and grapes grew in abundance on well-maintained vines on rolling hills. The hospital had one of the best Holstein dairy herds in the state; those cows grazed throughout the green acres on the southwest side. The piggery provided meat for the hospital tables as well as a functional place to dispose of some of the garbage.

I needed to know more about how the farm program worked as therapy. Mr. Meyer would provide that, for sure, but he might also illuminate for me some of the mystery surrounding vandalism and harassment at the asylum.

Mr. Meyer stood next to me in the doorway of Greenhouse 2, waving goodbye to a group of male workers as they made their way up the path and then disappeared behind a cluster of large pine trees. Mid-fifties and balding, Mr. Meyer had the ruddy cheeks of an outdoorsman and the dirt-encrusted fingers of a farm hand. He spoke in a soft voice, his eyes constantly surveying his surroundings.

"Next Monday," he said, pointing toward the southeast, "we begin moving these seedlings out to the fields. We'll have ninety or so workers, mostly men, and a few hardy women. Greenhouse work will continue, but it'll be the early spring crops that get started Monday—lettuce, mustard and chard; spinach; carrots, radishes, asparagus—those will be our first harvest. What the hospital doesn't need, we'll take to market. We all look forward to spring planting. God's green earth returneth."

"Dr. Spencer said part of my experience with farming here would include market sales."

He scuffed the dirt with the toe of his boot until a small rock emerged from the ground. Then he patted it back down with the same toe. It seemed his way of taking time to think before responding.

"Well," he said slowly, "we'll be interested to see how things go at market this year. You likely heard about how they ended last year."

"I heard there had been some kind of trouble. I'd like to know more."

He turned and opened the screen door.

"Let's go inside."

I followed. A group of women sat at a long worktable. Before each of them was a large pot of soil, a bucket of seeds, and a stack of egg cartons. Some spoke to partners in low tones, barely audible; others worked silently.

He motioned to a long bench beside a worktable a short distance from the workers. "Why don't we sit down over here?"

We sat and stretched our long legs out before us. We put our elbows on the table behind us and leaned back. We studied the females as they worked.

"I can't get those ladies to stop for the day. They get real excited when planting time approaches."

He crossed one leg over the other and sat back, arms folded.

"Strange things going on these days," he said. "Never had any trouble at market in all the years I've been here, but then last year, some fellows, farmers themselves by their looks, started saying things when they passed by our stall."

"What kinds of things?"

"Ignorant, coarse remarks. They'd call the patients names like Loonies, Nuts, Crazies, Goofballs — that sort of thing. And they'd say our produce came from the Funny Farm, or the Nuthouse. One day a fellow said in a loud voice, 'I hear they use cow piss to water their fields over there.' Vulgar things. Every week different men would pass our stalls, never the same fellows, say the same things. One fellow announced to anyone who'd listen that people were being poisoned by our vegetables. Bastards. Pardon my French."

"The patients must have been terrified."

"Yes and no. Some were frightened, yeah, by the tone of the men's voices and some understood they were being called names and they got mad about that. Some thought it was all in fun and so they laughed and clapped and whooped — hell, they didn't understand. Every patient who goes to the market gets groomed on how to behave properly and how to talk with folks. They wouldn't say anything back that was mean. I was real proud of how our people handled themselves. Wish I could say the same for the scum that harassed them."

"What I don't understand," I said, "is why the, scum, as you call them, were so hostile?"

"No one really knows," he said.

No one really knows. I was beginning to see the pattern. No one *really* knows who slashed the tires. No one *really* knows who threw rocks through windows. No one *really* knows how Rosie the cow got killed. People here may not *really* know, but, like Mr. Meyer, they have suspicions. I hoped he would be more forthcoming than Dr. Spencer had been.

"Don't get me wrong, son. Most farm people in this area are real decent folk. They mind their own business and don't get upset just because there's competition. They let our patients visit their farms, see the animals. We have good relations with them. But others? Well, they think a state hospital has no right to act like a business. Period. Some think we're driving down prices, but think about it: why in the world would we want to do something like that?"

"But don't you?" I said. "I mean, the fact that the hospital is at the market selling comparable goods, it's competition, by definition. It seems reasonable, then, that if you sell at a lower price, you're driving down prices."

It seemed logical to me.

"Well, you have a point there. When you put it that way, the hospital does compete, no doubt about it. But we don't compete to make more money than our competitors. True, we do need to make money. Period. We don't need to make *a lot* of money, just enough to cover what the state doesn't provide us with, which is almost nothing. If the hospital had enough money from the state in the first place, things would be different."

When I thought about it from the farmers' perspective, it didn't really matter if one vendor had to support his family of four and another had to support his family of three thousand. It was a difference of scale, not a difference of intent.

I said, "But don't they have a legitimate point? About competition?" I was careful not to say *unfair* competition.

"The hospital would *really* have to be in business for itself," he said. "Really *intend* to drive out competition in the open market.

But it's not that way. You don't have labor overhead to pay for, so you don't have to make more money than what you actually need. There's no profit involved, the way it would be in a business."

I was beginning to see both sides better.

"Look at them," he said, pointing to the women. "Do they look like they're trying to achieve the American Dream?"

"Good point."

"Running this entire hospital doesn't cost the state a bushel of cabbage. What does it hurt if we feed ourselves and then sell a little surplus so we can buy a few things for patients and pay a few supervisors decent wages?"

"But," I said, "that's what farmers *themselves* do — they feed their own families and then sell the surplus — to buy a few things and pay their workers' wages."

"Yeah, I suppose. But selling is their *business. Taking care of people* is ours. There's a difference there."

"Dr. Spencer says that work is therapy. Do you agree?"

"Myself, I don't like to put it that way. They say that with therapy, if you get enough of it, you can be cured. Once you're cured, end of therapy, and you're gone. I'm saying it's more than just therapy. They don't want their work to end. They won't let it. When the work ends, they end. For so many of them. Like I told you a while back, son, *work* for them is not the same as it might be for others who think of work as a *job*."

He stood and pointed to a female patient seated at the worktable. "See that woman over there, the one in the blue babushka?"

I craned my neck to see the women at the long table. They were filling the egg cartons with soil, slowly, carefully. I could make out the woman in blue from the side of her face.

"I recognize her," I said. "Bernadine."

He sat back down. "Yes. That's Bernadine. I call her our Earth Mother. She's checking the sprouted seeds cartons. Watch her."

I stood up to see. Bernadine was carefully pressing dirt around tiny green stems sticking out in soil-laden egg cartons. Humming to herself. Each planted egg carton in front of her sported a tiny stick with a colorful paper flower attached to the top.

"Bernadine's hatchlings," he said. "She cares for each one like it was her own. Like she has to nurse until it leaves the nest. Next week she'll be out in the field planting what she's potting today. She'll weed that very part of the field. She'll make sure that part gets enough water. When it's time to harvest, she'll be the one to do that, too. She grew up on a farm in the upper peninsula. Parents brought her here when the fits got so bad they couldn't keep her home any more."

"She looks so happy."

"She is *now*—with planting season coming. Her spirits are way up from May to October, during the season. Then they take a dive through the winter months. Deep depression. That's her illness. Come spring, and she's as bright a spark as you'll ever find. Right up to the next winter season. Then it sets in again, poor girl."

"Seasonal depression?"

"I'm no doctor; I just know it changes with the seasons. She shrivels up in winter like a pulled weed. Serious stuff. But you see how she is here, not hot *or* cold, just right. Truth be told, she's just an extreme version of so many other patients who work on the grounds. The way they weed the rows clean as a whistle, look after the trees in the orchards. They do everything like they're grooming a prize horse or sending a kid off for the first day of school.

"You'll see the way they load the bushel baskets for market. They strip the lettuce heads of any brown edges, bunch the spinach in just the right way to make it a damned work of art. Same with root vegetables, all bunched and arranged just so in little groups tied with string. The ladies even put little ribbons on the bunches."

"*Sounds* like *art*," I said.

"For them, it's the art of caring. They water down the baskets in the evening to keep them cool all night before market day. At the market, they arrange and rearrange the produce on the tables and in the baskets so everything always looks picture perfect. When the fall produce comes, they polish apples and pears, shine pumpkins, and paint flowers on the jars of jellies and jams made in the cannery."

One of the ladies from the planting table stood. She looked up and down the length of the table. Then she came over to our area. Her hands were caked with soil and she had brown sweat streaks on her face. She wore a red bandana over wild brown hair that stuck out around the edges of the bandana, and a grey apron over a flannel shirt and oversized trousers. She spoke so fast I could barely understand her. She spoke with her hands, too, as they moved in jerks and starts in cadence with her hurried words. It looked to me like the onset of a panic attack.

"Mr. Meyer," she said breathlessly, "We got to have more planting boxes right away. I got no more and Bertha, she's on her last one. What are we gonna do?"

Mr. Meyer slid off the bench. "You ladies just work too fast," he said, a wide grin spreading across his face. "How is your supply of seeds?"

"We got plenty of seeds and we got plenty of dirt, but we got no cartons. No one was minding the cartons and now we're out and...oh my, I just don't know..."

He went over and kneeled down on one knee in front of her, his eyes looking straight into hers. Her eyes were wide, like a frightened deer; the upper part of her torso rocked back and forth.

"Now just calm right down, Ernestine. It'll be all right. When you can be still, I can help out. Can you try to be still?"

She continued rocking as she began rubbing both hands together. He stayed in front of her until the rocking and rubbing eased.

"That's better now. Tell you what, Ernestine. Do you know where that storage shed is behind the chicken houses? The red one with the creaky door?"

She looked to the rear door. Eyes the size of drink coasters, her face froze.

"I know where that is, but...but..."

"That's where there's more egg cartons. Get another fifty or so."

"But...but...there's a mean bear. And he sleeps in that shed and he ate one of the men who went there. He's gonna eat me when I open the door."

She shook her hands at her sides as if she were air drying them.

"Big bear, big bear," she whimpered.

Mr. Meyer stood in her path and crouched again. She stopped pacing. Their eyes met as he leaned toward her.

"Well, what if you took your friend Bertha with you? She's not afraid of bears. She can open the shed door and get the cartons for you."

"But what if the bear runs out and gets me? What if he bites off my arms?"

"Hmm. I know: you just stand behind the shed and the bear will never see you. Bertha can get the cartons and close the door and you'll be safe."

"What if he eats Bertha? Maybe we need a gun to shoot the bear."

"Oh, no. We need that bear. He's a good bear. He protects the egg cartons there. If you shoot him, who will protect the egg cartons so you can plant the seeds? You stay behind the shed. You'll be safe."

"Oh … oh … okay. I'll try. I'll get Bertha."

She went back to the table and whispered in the ear of another woman, who promptly got up. The two of them left, one behind the other.

Mr. Meyer settled back down next to me. He smiled.

"Now then, where were we?"

"You were talking about harvest, but can you go back to what you were saying about local farmers who are upset?"

"Just *some*, mind you, not all. For some of them, things have moved from being upset to lobbying our state legislators to do something about their cause down in Lansing. If they do have the ear of a couple of representatives or a senator, why, those politicians can see some votes in it, and that's always dangerous."

"How come," I asked, "more people who work here aren't more vocal? Doesn't it seem right that they would be more, I don't know, more *public* in their support of the hospital? I mean, the hospital writes their paychecks. Why aren't they more assertive?"

He looked past me and shook his head. "I can't say. People keep to themselves. They work long hours, and then they go home. Besides, nothing *really* bad has ever happened. A few broken windows or porch lights here and there, slashed tires. Though, I will say, someone crossed a line when they started in on the animals."

"Dr. Spencer thinks *kids* are behind the vandalism."

He shot a sudden sideway glance at me.

"Dr. Spencer *thinks* too much," he remarked.

"What do you mean, thinks too much?"

"Now, don't get me wrong," he said. "He's a good man. He's served this hospital well all these years, mostly."

"Mostly?"

"What I'm saying is, he takes good care of the hospital. He personally examines each patient when they arrive. He spends a lot of his time with the patients — too much, in my opinion. He could just give someone the once over and pass them along to the other docs. No, he actually examines them. He does rounds every week, in every ward. The patients love him, so do the staff."

"All that sounds like an ideal supervisor. What's wrong with it?"

"Nothing is *wrong* with it. That's what superintendents here have been doing for fifty years. But, like anything, that priority takes time, and a lot of it. Time that might be spent in other ways, given current circumstances, if you know what I mean."

I wrinkled my brow, as if to imply I didn't know what he meant.

He was blunt: "I think this hospital needs a different kind of man at the helm."

"Like who? Someone who does more public relations? More *schmoozing*?"

"I don't know that word," he said. "What I think is we need some toughness, some brawn."

President Truman? I thought, *Audie Murphy?*

"Let me put it this way. My wife, Gail, she's a reader. She read this book that won a big prize a few years back. *King's Men* or something, I don't recall the exact title. In the book, there's a politician named Willie something or other. Stern? Shark? Stark! That's it, Willie Stark. Anyway, he got himself all embroiled in corrupt state politics and eventually became corrupt himself. But he had what our superintendent lacks, and that is the guts to get involved in the *politics* of running a state institution. Willie Stark was ruthless, but he was also smart about how to talk to who and how to play the game."

"So, how would Dr. Spencer become a Willie Stark?"

"I'm not saying he should become a Willie Stark. All I'm saying is, that instead of spending so much time plucking brown leaves off the plants, so to speak, he ought to raise his head and see that the weeds are gathering and they're choking those plants. He ought to use his precious time in ways that matter most for the institution *now*. He ought to get some political clout himself, go down to the capitol, and make a ruckus. A tree don't move unless there's wind. A little bit of Willie Stark would go a long way. Times have changed. Leadership has to match the times."

I told him about Dr. Spencer's unsuccessful sit-downs with the local legislators.

"Well, I credit him there. It's a good start. But it's not enough. He needs to go out on that limb a lot farther."

We stood up. Mr. Meyer brushed off the back of his trousers, pulled out a pocket watch, and glanced at the time.

"Time to get a few more chores done before I go home, too."

Ernestine and Bertha returned with arms full of cartons. They plopped them down on an empty space on a planting table just as Mr. Meyer stood and moved closer to the patients. His loud voice boomed.

"Ladies," he announced. "Quitting time for today. You did good work, thank you. But you have to leave some for tomorrow. No more planting today. Time to go home."

With that, they dutifully rose and shook the dirt from their hands or wiped them on their aprons. One by one, they found their way out.

The patients gone, Mr. Meyer came back to where I sat. We shook hands. I thanked him for taking the time to explain to me the way things were with the farm operations. His eyes fixed on the last patient as the door closed behind her.

"We can hope, young man. We'll see in a few weeks when we get our folks and our produce back on the market. If some lawmakers are cooking something up in Lansing, we'll learn about it before long. In the meantime, we need to get on with planting and harvesting."

His gaze shifted to the furrowed fields to the east. "Time to go home," he said, and he walked out the door.

When I sat down to write that evening, I felt a deepening loss of confidence in Dr. Spencer:

May 21:

Dr. Spencer has good intentions and he has cared deeply for decades, and I admire that. But yesterday was yesterday and today is today. He falls short of today's mark. The hospital troubles are getting worse, not better, and he should take the bull by the horns. This is a storm that will not simply pass.

Mr. Meyer is right. Times change, and those in charge must change with them. Why, he can't even fire a colossal mistake like Daryl.

Remember what Brother Benedict said.

Ecclesia non solum boni, quod sacerdos potest hilum. The Church is only as good as its least able priest.

"Only as good," he said, "as the least competent priest in the smallest, most remote parish. And the St. Joseph's boxing team is only as good as its least able boxer."

CHAPTER TWENTY

Mayhem

A SUICIDE IN EARLY JUNE BROUGHT VIGILANT ATTENTION TO those patients with open access privileges. According to the official report to staff, a female patient (one Mrs. Kozelko) with open access failed to show up in her cottage late one evening. Staff went looking. But with the increasing darkness, and following a fruitless examination of every building on the grounds, the search was abandoned until daylight.

Shortly after dawn, two attendants found her body behind a shed in back of the old carriage house. She had cut her own throat with a serrated kitchen knife. Hers was the second suicide in two years, the previous one being a mongoloid female who threw herself under the coal train as it was leaving the powerhouse.

Death was a regular part of life at the state hospital. People died of old age and serious illness just like those who lived in town, but with more frequency. The patient population had more deaths per capita than the town population, for the simple reason that they came with more life-threatening and age-inducing problems, like alcohol poisoning, syphilis, and progressive brain disease. Suicide, it appears, seemed to some patients as the way to end the pain of living—and, in that respect, the patients were not much different than anyone.

There were occasional murders, too. Years earlier, a male attacked another male with a rake and killed him in reprisal for stealing his bottle cap collection. In another, a female patient beat a senile male patient to death with a large rock after he grabbed her butt while she was bent over pulling weeds in the fields. Generally, however, murders were rare, but even their infrequency served as a reminder that the potential for violence at the state hospital always loomed.

Unless family claimed the body, the remains would be buried in town, at Oakwood Cemetery over on Eighth Street, in a section reserved for hospital residents. The grave markers carried numbers that were recorded in hospital records. No names. Eventually, as hospital records were buried deeper and deeper in storage boxes, the identities of the deceased were buried too. Over time, their legacy would be reduced to no more than a number on a metal peg stuck in the ground.

Staff heard about violent events such as beatings, murder, and suicide through word of mouth or during rounds. Some witnessed things first hand, like the day Jimmy and Captain Jessup went at it in Cottage 34.

I felt I had seen enough violence myself: Jimmy threatening to crush my skull with a log; Daryl the recreation attendant standing ready to punch my innocent eyes out; and, of course, Rosie, the prize cow, slaughtered with malicious intent by who-knows-who.

But these were only preludes to that June morning at the farmer's market in Grand Traverse County.

The late spring produce from the fields had yielded hundreds of pounds of harvest weekly—greens, asparagus, fava beans, peas, and rhubarb. Again this year, milk and butterfat from the dairy herd was bountiful, as were the chicken eggs. The earlier harvest of beets and spring onions had all but ended, and the patients in the cannery had worked zealously putting up thousands of mason jars full of pickled beets to be stored for year-round consumption; the surplus would be sold at market or to the eating establishments in town who were regular customers.

The hospital offered good produce and dairy products at good prices. While most working patients spent their summer hours in the fields, orchards, greenhouses, barns, and cannery, a few delivered fresh and canned produce to a number of restaurants and to the open market.

On a typical market day, two large trucks full of produce were packed up the night before, watered down after dark, and kept in a cool garage. By 8:00 A.M., patients and supervising staff would be on their way to making deliveries, one truck headed to the restaurants and the other to the tri-county open market along the Boardman River. A Chevrolet station wagon would transport the women and men who would set up the market stalls and load them with produce. With supervision, they would also sell produce.

Since mid-May, when the market opened for the year, the hospital had sent three security men to keep an eye out for any potential troublemakers of the sort that had come by last year. But it had been quiet for three weeks, with no disruptions or threats, so they eased off their vigilance and decided that sending just one guard instead of three would be good enough.

On this unusually chilly Friday morning, nighttime temperatures in the upper 40's were slowly rising as Nurse Pearson drove Alice S., Tina, Brewster, Mr. Paplowski, and Jimmy in the station wagon. I drove the truck. We wore coats, gloves, and hats as if it were still winter. I followed the Chevy to the market, where we arrived 30 minutes early in order to set up for when sales opened at nine.

We arrived just as other farmers were setting up their stalls and unloading their produce. The parking lot was congested, so the truck and the Chevy had to be parked a short distance from our sales stall. There wasn't any room in the lot to maneuver the truck to get its rear to face our stall, which would have made it more convenient to move produce from truck to sales. From the stall, we wouldn't be able to see the rear of the truck. We could only see part of one side that had TRAVERSE CITY STATE HOSPITAL in bold letters printed on it.

Everyone had their designated job. Nurse Pearson would supervise the patients, making sure that they spoke politely and gave the right change; Alice S. and Tina were responsible for arranging produce for display; Brewster would take care of the cash box; and Mr. Paplowski was to help Jimmy haul produce from the truck to the stand for setup and then spray water on the produce with a squirt bottle. Jimmy was the only one who didn't work in the fields, but he had been selected to go that morning because it was often necessary for someone from Maintenance to repair or shore up the portable wooden tables and food trays that displayed the hospital's bountiful harvest. Since I was the fifth wheel, my job was to support everyone else wherever needed.

Jimmy would also put up the colorful banner that hung over the hospital stall—"The Traverse City State Hospital" it read in gold letters on a white background, with patient-drawn apples, carrots, and rhubarb stalks adorning the edges of the banner.

Frank, our security agent in blue uniform and cap, drove

himself in a hospital car he had to park on the other side of the parking lot, it was so crowded. He did not like that the rear of the truck was not fully visible from the stalls, but there was little anyone could do about the congested conditions there. He said he'd make the most of the situation.

Mr. Paplowski and Jimmy got the tables and trays off the back of the truck and into place in our reserved area off to the very end of the long line of vendors. Jimmy had to shore up the side of one of the display boxes with a few strategically placed nails. Once the stall was assembled, Jimmy and Mr. Paplowski began hauling wet bushel baskets full of produce from the truck.

Tina and Alice S. draped another hand-painted cloth banner, this one from two poles attached to the ends of our tables. It read, "Good Food from the Good Earth" and had daisies hand stitched between each word. Both ladies then dangled lines of tied garlic bulbs from tiny pegs sticking out from each pole.

The two banners made it clear where the state hospital stall was located. Neighboring vendors smiled and greeted us as they put up their own signage at their stalls and began hauling their produce from their trucks and cars. In the cool morning air, the market was alive with what seemed to be thirty to forty vendors busily setting up.

The two women and Brewster began laying out the produce in neat clumps until the trays were adorned with the lush greens of various hues. Mr. Paplowski's and Jimmy's next load consisted of carrots, rhubarb, green onions, chives, and asparagus, all of which found their resting place judiciously between the stacks of greens in the wooden troughs.

Tina and Alice S. took their work arranging produce seriously—here and there pulling out brownish threads from chives and the occasional lettuce wilt, and instructing Mr. Paplowski to "give these green onions a good squirt" from the spray bottle he kept tied to a belt loop. Nurse Pearson sat with Brewster at the small wooden money exchange table as the two of them counted out dollars and change that would be used for the day's sales.

Unless his construction skills were needed at the stall, Jimmy was assigned to stay with the truck and keep the produce wet by spraying it with water we brought in two-gallon spray cans. Frank would provide security at the stall itself while keeping an eye on the truck as much as he could see over there. I would do the same.

By 9:00 the market opened. Bulk buyers and families prowled the long line of stalls and eyed the array of goods. At our end, the rush began early and continued strong—steady business all the while. It was clear to me that the hospital's reputation for high quality produce and fair prices had garnered quite a following in the tri-county area.

Because they had worked in the fields and loaded the truck themselves, these patients could share with customers the very details of planting, nurturing, and harvesting, often personalizing produce with comments like "Yes, mam, I picked this rhubarb myself just yesterday and kept it close to my heart all night so it wouldn't get too lonely away from home," and "These are called the baby carrots 'cause they been in the nursery all week. But don't you worry, they're old enough now to be out on their own."

For the next two hours, sales continued at a brisk pace, with all patients busily attending to their respective jobs. About every twenty minutes or so, Jimmy showed up with bushel baskets full of produce which the others hastily placed in the bins. Mr. Paplowski kept the produce moist with his squirt bottle, Brewster oversaw the money exchange, and the two women kept busy arranging and rearranging.

Soon came the usual morning lull, the time between when the early birds had all the produce they needed and when the more casual shoppers showed up. As had been the case for the previous three weeks, there seemed little for security to do because things had been so quiet. That being the case, Frank announced that he needed to excuse himself for a few minutes to "use the facility at the other end of the market."

I said I would keep an eye on things in his absence. I left to retrieve the sandwiches for everyone for lunch. Leaning idly against the back of our truck, hands in pockets and passing time, Jimmy was bored but otherwise fine. I walked to our station wagon to get the sandwiches, handed off two to Jimmy on the way back, and returned to our stall.

I must have been twenty yards away when I saw two men approach the stall. They looked to be of farmer stock in their jean overalls and red-checked hunting jackets zipped up to their necks, collars turned up. Both wore stocking caps pulled down nearly to their eyes. As I got closer, their shoes caught my attention. They wore dress shoes—black and shiny, way out of step with the rest of their attire. I thought that was odd.

Both carried long poles. From my distance, those poles looked like walking sticks.

The shorter of the two men was standing before Tina and Alice S. as I came within earshot. Then both men began shouting.

"Look at the nuts from the nuthouse!" yelled one.

"Selling your shit laced with cowshit!" screamed the other. Nurse Pearson stood up quickly.

"What's going on here? What are you *doing*?"

"Shut up bitch!" the short one yelled, and swung his stick like a baseball bat at the bin supports on the right side just as the taller man swung at the supports on the left side. Nurse Pearson grabbed Brewster by his shoulders and pulled him away. I made it to the stall just as the left side collapsed. I pulled Alice S. and Tina backward, away from the mayhem.

Mr. Paplowski ran back from the stall a few yards, fell to the ground, and curled into a fetal position with his hands over his ears and his eyes shut. Onlookers froze in their tracks, speechless, as the men stepped into the mass of produce lying all over the grounds. They mashed their heels into bunches of kale and spinach and kicked lettuce heads along the ground, swinging their sticks wildly from side to side. No one dared challenge them.

"Take yer gooneyhouse shit and stick it up your crazy asses and keep the hell out of town!" one shouted. I held the arms of Alice S. and Tina. We stared, wide-eyed, helpless.

"If you know what's good for you," growled the other voice, lower now, "you'll keep your poisonous goddam fruits and vegetables the hell away from here or next time we'll break your arms and legs, you hear?"

Mr. Paplowski lay on the ground shivering and whimpering. Brewster's eyes were closed, his mouth stretched wide open but wordless. He cowered behind Nurse Pearson, clutching her coat.

I had one arm around Alice S. who had both arms clinging to me. Tina hung on my neck, fingers locked tight. They were terrified. The men continued to demolish everything they could; splintered wood and vegetables littered the ground. If I could have released myself from the tight grips of Tina and Alice S., I might have been able to fend off the attackers, but it came on so fast and the two women would not release their grip.

Then, just as suddenly as the two men had arrived, they ran toward the parking lot and disappeared among the cars and trucks. The six of us huddled together behind the shambles they left.

No one moved. Crying, Tina and Alice S. clung to my coat, quivering with fear.

I looked toward the parking lot. I feared the men would return. They were nowhere in sight.

I heard a man's voice yell, "Call the police!" as other vendors rushed toward us to help. Another voice shouted, "They went that way!" Two women ran up to the crouching Nurse Pearson but she waved them off.

"Wait. Please," she said. "Let us, just, get, calm," referring to our patients. The last thing we needed was a stranger touching them.

After a few long moments, Tina S. and Alice stopped quivering but still held on to me. Brewster huddled behind Nurse Pearson. "Bad bad men," he said.

Mr. Paplowski still lay on the ground, motionless. His hands still covering his ears, he was reciting aloud, "Hail Mary Full of Grace," over and over.

Frank burst through the onlookers.

"What the hell happened here?" Then, "Oh, Christ! I never should have left. Is anyone hurt?"

I looked up to Frank. "Two men," I said. "Swinging poles. Looked like farmers. Shouting and cursing. They ran somewhere, I'm not sure where."

He surveyed the produce and pieces of wood strewn everywhere, and then he stepped through the strewn vegetables to reach us. He stood next to Nurse Pearson. Brewster peeked out from behind the nurse.

"Bad men," he said to Frank. "Bad men with big sticks and bad words and..." he looked around, "everything everywhere." No one else spoke until Nurse Pearson looked to me with wide eyes and said, "Jimmy?"

I looked behind me to the parking lot. The men had been running in that direction when I lost sight of them. All I could see was the front of our truck.

I pulled Alice and Tina S. over to Nurse Pearson and she put arms around them as onlookers came closer with renewed offers to help.

Frank and I raced to the truck, slowed as we passed the truck cab and approached the rear. A grey-haired man holding bags of vegetables in both hands turned when he heard us come up. He wore thick glasses and he pointed with one bag to a spot beyond our line of sight.

"Mister," he said, "That man's hurt. He needs help."

Behind the truck, Jimmy lay crumpled on his side, motionless. Fruits and vegetables spread like a garbage dump around him. A bushel basket lay on its side, its load of collard greens spilling forth onto the dirt.

Blood poured from his nose. One eye was covered with dirt. From a gash above his eyebrow, blood poured down his cheek and soaked the collar of his coat. One arm was outstretched, the other unnaturally bent below the elbow.

"Jimmy?" I called to him, kneeling down by his side. "Jimmy?"

No response, no movement. I leaned my ear into his face, listening.

"Is he ..." asked the old man.

"He's breathing," I said. "Call for help, please. Call police, call an ambulance. He's hurt."

"My son, over there. He went to call. At a payphone," he said, pointing somewhere. "I hope this man's going to be all right."

More people emerged from the crowd of onlookers. One woman put a shawl over Jimmy's legs. Another offered a thermos cup full of water and a white handkerchief. "You can wipe his face with this," she said, "and give him a drink." She poured water into the cup and put it on the ground next to me. She poured water on the cloth and handed that to me.

Jimmy was unconscious. I wiped blood from his face with the white cloth.

Frank went down on one knee. He leaned in to get a better look at Jimmy's face.

"Son of a bitch," he said, "son of a bitch. I never should have left."

I held Jimmy close to me.

"They were watching us," I speculated, "from somewhere. They had our stall staked out and they had the truck staked out. They saw you in uniform and they saw you leave. This was all planned. They knew exactly when to strike."

"I'll be goddamned," Frank said, looking at Jimmy.

I don't know how long we waited until I heard the sirens approach. I knelt beside Jimmy, my hand on his shoulder. Onlookers spoke to one another in hushed tones. They kept a safe distance.

Two sheriff's cars arrived first, and then an ambulance whirled into the parking lot behind them. The medical people pulled a stretcher from the rear of the ambulance and hurried over to us. They placed it next to Jimmy.

One cop ran up. "What happened here?"

The old man with thick glasses pulled on the officer's arm.

"Two men beat up this man," he explained, "with big sticks. They ran that way." He pointed toward the maze of cars and trucks in the lot. "They were wearing red coats."

The two officers went off in that direction. Frank followed.

My attention was on Jimmy.

"Careful," I said to a white coat. "His arm. I think it's broken. There may be more broken bones, I don't know."

The medic kneeled to examine Jimmy. He first checked his breathing, and then lightly examined the rest of his body.

"Right arm fracture," he said to the other medic. "Facial contusions. Possible nasal fracture. No other visibles. Possible concussion. Let's stabilize the arm. We can take his vitals on the way. No time to lose."

I stood up and they went to work. Within five minutes, they had Jimmy's arm in a sort of brace ready for transport. They lifted his limp body and gently laid him on the stretcher. They carried him to the rear of the ambulance and slid him, gingerly, into its rear.

Just then the two police officers and Frank returned, empty-handed. I told them I was going with the patient in the ambulance and they could find me at the hospital if they needed a statement. They would.

Frank pointed toward our stall and said they needed to see what had happened there. "We're from the state hospital," Frank said. "There are more of us over there," he said, pointing, "where this all started."

He led them toward the stalls and the huddled patients there.

I climbed into the back of the ambulance. Jimmy lay still. I put his good hand in mine and rubbed his hair above the gash in his forehead.

"Hang on, Jimmy. Hang on, my friend. You're going to be all right. I promise you."

CHAPTER TWENTY-ONE

Lines In The Plaster

"WHAT HAPPENED TO THIS MAN?" SAID DR. STEELE, THE AT-tending doctor at Community Hospital's emergency room.

Jimmy's right eye was swollen shut like the bottom of a puffer fish. The gash on his forehead had strips of adhesive tape to stop the bleeding. The rest of his swollen face was lined with dried blood; his left arm lay across his chest, stabilized in a splint-like apparatus. He had been brought in on the stretcher, laid on a gurney, and moved to a curtained room.

I explained that we were from the state hospital, selling at the market. He glanced at Jimmy and then back at me.

"And you are?"

"Henry Mershartt. I work at the state hospital. Jimmy is one of our patients."

He pushed skin around Jimmy's head laceration.

"What happened to him?" he repeated.

"He was beaten up … at the market … our stall was attacked by some men …"

He leaned over Jimmy, gently probed around his right eye.

"I see," he said. His fingers traced the valleys on either side of Jimmy's nose. He traced around Jimmy's forehead and temples. He turned his head upward toward me.

"This man has had significant head injuries. We won't know just how significant for a day or two. At this point I would say that he's had a concussion, at least. Perhaps internal bleeding. We'll have to wait and see."

I had to ask the worst question. "Will he...live?"

He stared at Jimmy while he answered me. "His vital signs are stable. That's good. He's badly injured, as you can see. We don't know the extent yet. Broken arm, bruises, contusions—all *that* he'll recover from. It's the head injuries that most concern me. And his vision. Unfortunately, all we can do now is wait and pray for the best."

Tears welled up. I wiped my eyes with my sleeve. Guilt for having left Jimmy alone at the truck hit me. It was foolish to leave him alone. We all should have been more preventative. They let the extra security go too soon. It was too much to ask of just one security guard, especially with the truck parked the way it was and Jimmy out of sight. I wanted to blame someone, including myself.

Dr. Steele must have noticed my distress. "Let's be hopeful," he said.

He reached for a clipboard hanging on the end of the bed.

"Let's start with his name," he said, "for the admitting papers."

Nurses came and went. One checked Jimmy's blood pressure while another applied wet compresses to his face and wiped away dried blood. He lay motionless, breathing evenly. Dr. Steele sat on a stool while I paced.

He put down his clipboard.

"I'm going to sedate him now, so that he won't wake up prematurely. I would ask that you stay nearby. We'll move him to Special Care. If he stabilizes significantly, he can be moved to a regular room. We'll see."

"I'll stay with him," I said.

"Good. We'll keep him in Special Care until he's fully conscious. He may be disoriented — and very afraid. He'll need to know where he is and why he's here. Most important, he'll need a familiar face to greet him. You or someone else he trusts."

I looked at Jimmy's battered face, "He won't be left alone, I can promise that."

"One more thing, Mr. ... ah ..."

"Merchartt, Henry."

"Merchartt." He picked up his clipboard again and wrote on it. "Is there anything I should know ... about his mental condition?"

"He has mental retardation and a history of trauma that affects his moods — under certain circumstances." He wrote on the clipboard as I spoke. "And — he's an all-around general repairman. He's part of the maintenance crew at the hospital. He's a friend to nearly everyone."

I held back tears again as I muttered, "He has a great sense of humor, and ... I know him very well ... he's like a ... family member."

"That's okay," interrupted Dr. Steele. "Say no more. We can start prepping him now. You can travel with him once he's ready. I'm going to turn him over to one of our internists. He'll take it from here."

While staff prepped Jimmy for the move to Special Care, I went to the nurses' station to take the call from Dr. Spencer. I briefed him on Jimmy's condition and sketched some details about what had happened at the market. I told him I expected the police to come soon to interview me.

Dr. Spencer sounded exasperated. He was in the middle of a crisis with an out-of-control male patient who was running naked throughout the grounds, eluding security, but he would be at the hospital as soon as he could. In the meantime, he would send others to be with me.

In Special Care, the internist cast Jimmy's broken arm and treated other visible injuries. Over the next twenty-four to seventy-two hours, the internist, a Dr. Jonson, would examine him for internal bleeding, more broken bones, and possible brain and vision injuries. A new medical procedure called *intravenous feeding* would be used until he awakened—they would insert a needle hooked up to a tube into a vein in his good arm, from which he would receive liquids to keep him sedated and hydrated.

Dr. Spencer came within an hour. He had spoken with Dr. Jonson; he felt confident that Jimmy was in good hands and would recover before long. Was I all right? Yes—but worried. Was I comfortable making any non-urgent medical decisions? Yes. I insisted that I stay with Jimmy myself, take meals in the cafeteria, and sleep on a cot in Jimmy's room. He agreed. Staff would bring me anything I wanted.

For the next 48 hours, others from the state hospital would come and go regularly. Attendant Frank brought me a change of clothes. Nurse Brownell visited twice; she brought snacks and magazines.

That evening, the police interviewed me in the hall outside Jimmy's room. I reviewed once again everything from the attack. I remembered the men's shoes.

"Their shoes were incongruous with the rest of what they wore," I told the officer. "They were dressed for farm work, but the shoes were black oxfords, not work boots, not the kind you'd wear in a barn or on a farm. More the kind you'd wear to church or an office."

The officer tapped his pencil on his pad a few times, nodding his head.

"Yeah," he said, "that *is* interesting." He glanced at his partner, who nodded in return.

I said, "I think they were hired thugs who didn't remember to bring the right shoes with them."

"That may be," said the partner. "In the meantime, we'd like to speak with the man who was injured—Mr. Quinn—and we would appreciate if you could call us when he's stable enough to be interviewed."

The partner gave me a card. "Call us if you remember anything else." They thanked me and left, said they'd let me know if "anything turned up."

Dr. Spencer visited again. He brought a big greeting card signed by nurses and staff. I was to share it with Jimmy when he regained consciousness.

He told me the police had interviewed him. When he told them about other incidents of violence toward the hospital, they were *very* interested. Could the market attack have been related to the previous incidents, they asked? Dr. Spencer said he thought so.

I was astonished to hear that they had asked *that* question. I said the police already knew about all that from what was reported and why were they acting like it was *new* news?

"These officers are county, Henry. Sheriff's deputies, not city police. City police investigated the other events. But the market incident occurred outside the city limits. The Boardman River area falls under the jurisdiction of the county sheriff's office. They didn't *know* we have had problems before. Now they do."

I said, "Well, I hope that now that the crimes have escalated to assault and battery, the police will be more aggressive." He agreed.

He sat back in a cushioned chair next to Jimmy's bed, stretched his legs before himself. He wanted to talk.

"Everyone who knows Mr. Quinn is hoping and praying for him. We tried to keep a low profile about what happened, but you know, word travels fast. We've had to talk quite a few patients down who are really scared about going into town. Some who know Mr. Quinn think he died, no matter what we say. One fellow put up a makeshift monument—a sort of shrine—next to the reflecting pool. He put up a sign that says, 'St. James the Martyr.'"

I smiled. "Would that be the man who thinks he's God?"

"That's him. It's a good thing, what he did there. Patients come to that spot to place flowers. They pray there. They leave candy, handkerchiefs shaped into animal forms, all manner of mementos. It's especially a good thing for those who can't find words."

Imagining that scene brought tears to my eyes. "I didn't realize so many patients knew Jimmy. He's been here such a short time, not even a year."

He leaned farther toward me. "It's not that so many know him personally. It's just an awareness—that someone in their community is suffering. Many don't know exactly what happened, but they *do* know love."

Dr. Spencer put his hand on my sleeve, shifted his chair more directly in front of me.

"I just wish I could do *some*thing," I said, "to help him."

He removed his hand, sat back in his chair and sighed. He removed his glasses and wiped them with a handkerchief. He looked tired.

"I know," he said.

"I *saw* them," I stammered. "They were thugs. I...I should have done more, to protect...I should have stood up to them..."

"You did the right thing. You protected the others."

He continued. "We have to be hopeful that the sheriff's department will do what they can to get to the bottom of this tragedy."

Once again, Dr. Spencer remained naively hopeful and trusting. In other circumstances—or were our relationship on a more equal basis—I would have challenged his blind faith in law enforcement. But that is not the way things were between us, and I understood that, hard as it was to keep my opinions to myself.

"Until the police can capture whoever did this, we won't know why they did it," he said.

"We should stay away from the market, then," I said. "We should never have had just *one* security person there. So many mistakes, mine included."

"I'm not sure we should have stayed away," he said. "Many staff are saying that, but others, well, they think we shouldn't buckle under this sort of thing. Increase security and protect our patients, like we did before, they say. Don't allow ourselves to be bullied seems to be the general opinion."

"What do *you* think, sir?"

"I think our first priority is to protect our patients. Stop market sales for the time being. Exercise vigilance whenever our produce trucks make deliveries. Increase campus security coverage."

He looked at his wristwatch and rose suddenly. He was late for something.

"I'm kept informed every few hours," he said. "Immediately, if there is an emergency."

I thanked him for coming by. But something in his docile manner didn't set right with me. His strategy was to circle the wagons and protect patients and staff—but from what? What exactly *were* we up against? Two hired thugs? Angry farmers? Legislators who were courting voters? Greed? Ignorance? Fear of difference?

In my mind, it was all related. It could be a coordinated conspiracy. Or it could be a conspiracy of unknown partners, each working separately to dismantle what they perceive to be a threat to their prosperity. That was the local issue. Or, perhaps they perceived a threat to their vision of who really counts in their community? That was the larger, universal issue of justice and equality.

I thought he should have been over at the sheriff's office raising hell. I thought he should have been offering a public reward for information leading to an arrest. He should have gone to that spineless excuse for a local newspaper editor and wrung his neck for allowing spiteful letters to appear in the paper. He should have hired private investigators to dig up the facts.

Dr. Spencer, I was now convinced, exhibited what psychologists Bruner and Goodman call *wishful thinking*. He had an *optimism bias* that made him believe that everything will be fine in the end. I was also convinced that that bias hadn't served him very well.

Jimmy's sedation ended after the second night. I had barely slept for two nights. Jimmy mumbled some unintelligible sounds as he slept, but otherwise he seemed to breath evenly. When he woke up late Sunday morning, he could see slightly out of one eye, which peered at the ceiling and around the room before it landed on my face next to him. I grasped his right hand, squeezed it ever so slightly. His lips barely moved as he spoke those first words.

"Mister...Henry?"

"It's okay, Jimmy. I'm here. You've been hurt, very hurt, and you're in the hospital. You're going to be all right soon. You're going to be all right."

"Mmm," he said, his one eye blinking slowly open and closed. "Mmm...can't see..."

He tried to move his broken arm, now in a plaster cast.

"Ow! My arm."

"Try not to talk, Jimmy. Just lie still. I need to get a nurse in here, tell the doctor you're awake. It's all going to be okay now. All okay."

His eye closed again and in a few seconds, he was asleep. For the next 24 hours, his time awake would increase as he recovered.

I fed him soup and juices, and I helped him get to the bathroom; the intravenous tube, attached to a sort of tripod with wheels, went with him. He didn't understand what had happened to him—or why—but all would be explained to him in good time.

Slowly the swelling went down enough for him to be able to use both eyes. His vision returned, though he continued to squint out of the injured eye for days. The bruises on his face and shoulder went from reddish to purple/blue by Tuesday, greenish by Wednesday as his body healed itself. His headaches began to diminish as the effects of the concussion receded. His casted arm had to be elevated on a hanging apparatus to help the swelling. He had to carry his casted arm with his good arm when he began using the bathroom alone on Wednesday. That was the day he began eating solid foods. I fed him by hand, until he could raise his good arm sufficiently to feed himself. He loved the unlimited supply of Jell-O loaded with fruit cocktail.

Throughout the week, people visited. Mr. Harrison dropped off Jimmy's work gloves, telling him that he'd need them when he got back and how the crew couldn't get along without him. Then he looked at Jimmy's casted left arm and retrieved one glove, remarking, "We'll just keep this one safe for a while," with a wink.

Nurse Brownell brought two of the women patients that Jimmy knew well — Eunice, who did a little twirl sort of dance in the room that ended with her arms outstretched when she bellowed out "Ta Da!"; and Bernadine, who brought a large bouquet of bright orange and yellow marigolds arranged in a blue vase — tiny paper orange-yellow-black bumblebees were suspended from the budding sepals.

At the sight of Bernadine, Jimmy giggled and squirmed like a first-grader at his birthday party. His toes wiggled feverishly and he slapped his good hand down on the bed like he was keeping time to music. His one good eye followed her as she moved around the room searching for the perfect place to put the flowers.

Others also visited. Francisco brought Almond Joys and a bag of Cheetos; Ruth Greenfield brought shelled peanuts and a bag of grapes; and Mrs. Dorman brought dozens of homemade get-well cards signed with patients' names or a variety of X's.

Before she left, Nurse Brownell handed me a letter from the Michigan Department of Civil Service. "This came for you," she said. She had this strange look like she suspected I was up to something. Which I was, of course, but I just thanked her, without explanation.

Finally, a response to my letter about Daryl! Finally, something might be done. I was excited. I went into the bathroom to guarantee privacy. I opened the envelope. There was one short paragraph.

> *Dear Mr. Merchartt:*
> *Your letter dated April 27 has been received. The observations have been taken under advisement and referred. Your communication is much appreciated.*

It was signed by a Mr. Thomas Warnock, Administrative Aide, Division of Public Relations.

Three sentences. That was it! A masterpiece of bureaucratic distance intended to discourage me from writing again. It was successful: I would waste no more energy on the Department of Civil Service.

There would have to be another way.

On the following day, Jimmy was transferred to the men's infirmary at the state hospital. The gash on his forehead had required twenty stitches, and the multiple abrasions on his body were covered with gauze bandages. The swelling around his eyes had nearly disappeared, leaving only dark bruises around each one. He looked like he'd been in the ring with Joe Louis.

The infirmary in Cottage 20 had beds for twenty residents on the first two floors, a mortuary in a back room, and rooms for staff on the third floor. Physicians, nurses, and attendants — all on eight-hour rotations — cared for the sick and the occasional dying. One aged fellow died of advanced dementia the first day we arrived. He was four beds over from where they put Jimmy.

Nothing could fully rid the ward of the stench of vomit, urine, and feces on patients' beds, clothing, and skin from daily accidents. Some patients would pee in their beds and *then* ask to be taken to the bathroom. Others would make it there on time but then return with the rear of their pajama bottoms brown with feces. Every bed was equipped with a vomit pail, but no one could vouch for a patient's aim or timeliness when his stomach started to churn.

Standards of hygiene were the highest one could expect, and the ward was scrubbed regularly with antiseptic, top to bottom, all week long. Nonetheless, the smell lingered, no matter how much they cleaned and scrubbed.

I stayed with him for a few hours on that first day. Ruth Greenfield was on duty, so I knew he would get all the special attention she could give him. She changed Jimmy's dressings and she called food services to bring over some chocolate pudding, just for him.

When I said I would feed him, she put her hand on my shoulder and said, "Time to go, Henry. We'll take over now. You need rest." She was right, of course.

I returned to my cottage, with no other duties for as long as I needed. I slept for at least a full night and then more, got up to eat a meal, and then went back to my room. After the constant, intrusive noise of the hospital ward, I relished the silence in the cottage as the residents went about their own daily routines. For my sake, they had agreed to keep all talk to whispers.

Word quickly got around that I needed to be alone, and my need for solitude was honored.

I lay on my bed, gazing up at the cracks in the ceiling that formed little rivers and streams in the plaster. For the first time in the many months I had slept there, I studied the cracks as if they were the lines in a person's hand being deciphered by a palm reader. What do the lines say about me? I wondered. Where have I been? Where am I going? Who *am* I? With this last thought, I sat up, swung my legs over the edge of the bed, and picked up my diary.

June 13:

Jimmy has changed me. I am no longer the same person I was nearly a year ago when that train from Kalamazoo pulled up to the platform and delivered him on that warm September day. I care for him more than I do anyone at the hospital. He could have been the brother I never had, the one I would have taken to see the Phillies play, the one I would have defended when tough guys made fun of him. I am the man from the City of Brotherly Love who has found brotherly love.

The lines in the plaster kept me thinking. The attack on Jimmy had changed me, too. I was no longer a spectator to events that threatened the hospital. I was now a participant. It had struck too close this time. What that meant for me, practically, I didn't know. In different circumstances, I would have become the fierce advocate Dr. Spencer was loath to become. I would have mobilized political allies and people in powerful positions who would put a stop to all this. Brother Benedict would have expected nothing less.

CHAPTER TWENTY-TWO

Sheriff Nederhousen

I KEPT TO MYSELF ALL WEEKEND, EXCEPT FOR AN HOUR ON
Saturday afternoon. I went over to check on Jimmy. He was
"coming along nicely" reported the doctor. His recovery speeded
up as his eyesight returned to normal and he gained some agility
when they issued him a cloth sling for his plaster cast. It wasn't
long before he was up and shuffling around the ward, visiting
others at bedside, and annoying staff with his requests to oil
the squeaky hinges on the doors, or repair a leaky faucet in the
bathroom.

During my brief visit, a deputy sheriff stopped by to interview him but Jimmy said he didn't know what happened. He
said he was standing at the back of the truck, where he was
unloading bushel baskets of collard greens. He heard some noise
and when he turned to look something hit him in the face. Then
he woke up in the hospital. The deputy took notes and left, and
I went back to my ruminations and rest in the cottage.

By Monday morning, I was all thought out. It was time for
action—again. My conspiracy theory was no longer speculation; it was now personal—and real. Along with conviction
and determination, I now had had direct experience of violence
against defenseless citizens. At the very least, I was a witness to

criminal acts. That had to matter to someone in the judicial system. I would appeal to the county sheriff, whose officers seemed to be taking the market crime much more seriously than the city police had taken the previous crimes that beset the hospital. I just needed to know where the sheriff's office was located.

I called Mrs. Dorman, my talkative friend from the Records Office. She was like a living phone book for addresses from her days in the post office.

She knew, of course, where the county sheriff's office was located because her "poor sweet neighbor Diane Marie who was still married to that good-for-nothing, rotten two-timer Eddie — god knows why she puts up with him" — answered phones and "did odds and ends" in the front office there. As usual, a simple question had brought forth a parade of clauses.

Sheriff Ned Nederhousen's name appeared on a collection of wall commemorations I noticed when I entered — County Officer of the Year for 1951; 1949 Little League Coach of the Year; and Bravery in the Line of Duty, 1950, Police Officers Association of Michigan. The photos revealed a square-jawed man in pressed blue uniform shaking the hand of another man handing him a certificate.

At the front desk, Diane Marie sat, worn blue cardigan sweater over white blouse, dishwater blond hair cut pixie-style. She looked tired — worn out in a way that suggested she had had a hard life with Eddie the Sleazeball. When I came up to the counter and looked over, she had one hand poised over a phone, about to dial. I noticed that her fingernails were chewed right to the nail bed. She put down the phone receiver and asked, "Can I help you?"

"I am here to see the sheriff," I said, "if that was possible. I was involved with the attack on hospital patients at the market on the Boardman last week and I have some information to share." I didn't mention that I knew Mrs. Dorman, not knowing if "poor, sweet Diane Marie" even liked her neighbor.

She rang up the sheriff on the intercom to say that a young fellow was out here to talk with him about the Boardman market investigation.

"Send him in!" a gruff voice boomed. It was a knowing smile that came on her, one that suggested our award-winning sheriff really *was* busy or was simply having a bad day. She pointed to the closed door across from me.

"In there."

I knocked first and then opened the door. He looked up from a single paper on his desk as I came in. The office was small by hospital standards, but very neat. On his desk, he had only the one paper in his hands. A pen-and-pencil stand stood beside the telephone that lined up next to the intercom. No stacks of files littered the floors and the one bookcase had notebooks stacked tidily one next to the other. The whole place suggested order, predictability.

He looked exactly like his County Officer of the Year photo, except he wasn't wearing a police hat. Jet-black hair neatly parted down one side, blue tie pulled up tight to his throat. He stood, came around to my side of his desk, and put out a large hand to shake.

I introduced myself as Henry Merchartt, from the Traverse City State Hospital. He was Sheriff Nederhousen, he said. No frill like a first name would be included.

He offered me a seat and went back to sit in his swivel chair. He pushed a button on the intercom and growled, "Hold all calls, Diane." I thought it was significant that he would consider my being there important enough to curtail interruptions. I was encouraged. Anxious, but encouraged.

I explained who I was — the year-long field experience student from the University of Pennsylvania; and the victim of the melee at the market that day. I recounted for him the series of events that I had witnessed or heard about at the hospital since I had arrived the previous August. I did my best to give my account of what had happened at the market and I emphasized how Jimmy had nearly been blinded, if not killed, in the attack. They were patients from the hospital, I said, innocent citizens targeted by who-knows-who.

He took it all in. He said that since the market attack had occurred in his jurisdiction, his office had acquired files from city police that had reports on all prior incidents. He hadn't read any reports himself, but his investigating officers had. He didn't realize that here had been a string of incidents. Occasionally, he asked for clarification, like just how many dogs had been drowned (none drowned, one beheaded, I said — and the slaughtered cow, and the frozen chicks, I added).

He looked puzzled. "I don't understand why you came to see me in particular," he said. "My men *are* investigating, you know."

I said I needed to be sure that the recent history of violence would be considered, that this should not be seen as an isolated event. I said I believed there was some sort of collusion (I avoided using the provocative word *conspiracy*, having learned a lesson at the *Sentinel*) among members of the community and certain legislators and maybe even members of the local press. I said I had heard talk in a restaurant (I avoided saying it was a bar) that made me think the attack at the market, the other incidents at the hospital, and the letters in the paper were all related. Somehow the dots needed to be connected.

He sat quietly, taking in all that I said. The gruff side of him seemed to mellow as he listened. I felt more encouraged, so I went on to the main point. I said I thought city police were dragging their heels in their investigations, that they had not found any evidence in all these months, and isn't that just plain strange?

He rose to the defense of the city police.

"Well, Mr. Merchartt, I hear your frustration with the lack of progress from City, but like all jurisdictions, they have priorities and just so much manpower to put on investigations. I'm not saying they've dragged their feet, as you seem to think. I'm just saying that, up to now, frankly, the hospital has not had any *felonies*. Vandalism just doesn't get much attention, to be honest, when there are other, more serious crimes to put officers on."

"Animal slaughter? What about that?"

"You have a point there. It's inhumane and awful, but it is not a *felony* in this neck of the woods. It's not of the magnitude of a crime against a *person*, which *is* a felony. Up until now, city has considered the hospital's troubles to be misdemeanors, and low priority, I would guess. But what happened at the market is *now* in the jurisdiction of county. And that was felonious assault. That changes the game, so to speak."

At last, I thought. *At last there was legitimate cause to do something!* I asked if he thought the vandalism and the market attack were related. He didn't know, he said, because he hadn't read the files. But he assured me that he would personally take part in the investigation.

Personally? I thought. I was surprised that he wouldn't just instruct his deputies to step up the investigation.

"Sheriff," I said, "do you always get personally involved in investigations?"

He stood, walked around his desk to a wall full of photographs in frames. I counted four photographs of the serious faces of men in uniforms, each wearing a badged cap.

"See these?" he said. "These are men from this department who've given their lives in the line of duty."

"I'm sorry. I'm sure they were good men."

"Yes, they were, every one of them. But do you see this one here?" He pointed to a thick-chested, black-haired man wearing medals on his uniform, his police cap tilted slightly to the right.

"This is my father, *Big Ned* they used to call him. I was always *Little Ned* growing up. He was on this force for fourteen years when he was shot trying to stop a party store robbery. Two bullets. One bullet tore out part of his lung, and the other crippled his brain—left him unable to fend for himself. He didn't die, fortunately—or unfortunately. I was sixteen years old. My mother was thirty-nine and had three other children."

"I'm so sorry," I said.

"I appreciate that," he said. "Those bullets ended his career. He lost his speech and his vision blurred. He got confused real fast and he never lost that ringing in his ears. He had seizures and sometimes he had screaming outbursts. We couldn't take care of him, no one could. My mother had to go to work and we kids, well, we were all in school.

"I'm telling you this because my father had to be put in the state hospital here. They treated him as if he were part of *their* family. Even with the outbursts, they never put a straightjacket on him, never gave him any electric shock therapy. He was always a tough cop, and he was a tough patient, but they treated him with respect until the day he died, which was October 18, 1945. I became the second Sheriff Nederhousen two years later."

I could see that the sheriff still carried the pain of losing his father. But his allegiance to the state hospital reinforced my own view of what amazing things the hospital does for its patients. I said I had only been at the hospital for about a year, but what he described is the very reason I came here — to learn first-hand how people like his father are cared for in such humane ways.

"So now you understand why I take a personal interest in this case."

"I do, thank you."

He sat back down.

"What happened at the state hospital was wrong," he said, "and illegal. But what happened at the market was far more serious. And now that this department is involved, we will see if the dots of the past connect with the most recent dot."

I felt more encouraged than I had in months. But I still had to keep a low profile. I explained my predicament to the sheriff: I could not afford to be seen as meddling in the internal affairs of the hospital — in spite of my anger and my sense of personal violation, not to mention the near loss of a friend. I only had another month to completion, and even though I felt valued for my contributions so far, I still had to keep separate my role as a student and any other roles I might *appear* to be taking on.

"I made that mistake once before," I said, "and, without going into detail, I can't afford to make it once again."

He smiled. "We all have histories," he said, "some more open than others. I don't need any details."

Then it occurred to me to tell him about my failed attempt to convince the *Sentinel* editor that the paper needed to show more discrimination in publishing letters to the editor. I mentioned that I was pretty sure the editor had been drinking on the job and, if so, then it might be the case that he was driving drunk after work. I said it would be unfortunate if someone as prominent as the *Sentinel* editor were to be stopped for a DUI, but I wondered if such an occurrence might somehow influence that editor to exercise more balance in the ways he represents the interests of the state hospital.

Sheriff Nederhousen stared at me, one hand stroking his cheek. I thought I detected the slightest bit of a smile. He nodded his head and squashed that hint of a smile as he cleared his throat and thanked me for my "citizen's tip." He would *personally* look into the matter: *he just happened* to know where Mr. Remington, editor, lived, in Garfield Township, which *just happened* to be in his jurisdiction and *just* a few country blocks from his *own* home. In fact, he often sees Mr. Remington driving in the neighborhood, and he would now notice the man's driving habits more closely.

Denique, aliis successus. Finally, some success.

The intercom buzzed. Diane Marie's voice announced that there had been a multiple-injury collision out in Kingsley, officers on the way. He needed to go. He ended our time together with a promise to get some results. If I could leave a phone number with the girl out front where I could be reached, he would contact me with any news. Call him if I thought of anything pertinent.

CHAPTER TWENTY-THREE

Hindsight is 20/20

MRS. KRUEGER HELD THE PHONE RECEIVER TO HER EAR WHEN I entered. She waved hello and nodded toward Dr. Spencer's door. Hand over the receiver, she whispered, "Go right in."

I knocked anyway, heard, "Come in," from inside. He was seated behind his desk, as usual.

Normally, he wore a coat and tie, always a starched white shirt, and he was always clean shaven. This morning was different. A patch of uneven chin whiskers suggested a morning that began too abruptly for a close shave. Starched white shirt and necktie as usual, but the knot was slightly off center. He held what looked like a letter, as if he were about to read it.

He blinked slowly. He looked exhausted.

We greeted, I sat. He offered tea, I accepted. We had not talked since he had visited me at Community Hospital.

"How're you getting on, Henry? Did you rest?"

"I did. I'm feeling much better, and I'm ready to get back to my work."

He said, "Oh, that's good," in such a way that I sensed his mind was on something else. I wondered if he had forgotten why he invited me to see him.

"Mrs. Krueger left a message. You wanted to see me, sir?"

Glasses perched halfway down his nose, he looked down at the letter in his hands and then at me again.

He began abruptly, "The county police are investigating, but they still have no leads. I'm not hopeful that we'll ever know who did this. But there's no doubt that it was an attack on the hospital itself, on its most vulnerable."

I knew more than he did, but what I knew was privileged knowledge. I could not share my meeting with Sheriff Nederhousen. I was duplicitous, but I felt that duplicity was justified.

"Maybe they'll find something," I mumbled.

He cleared his throat, as if he were about to give a speech. "Have you spoken with any staff about what happened here last week?"

"Here, at the state hospital?"

"Yes, here, while you were occupied with Mr. Quinn and his recovery."

I said no, and he took the next few minutes to brief me.

First, Governor Petersen did not renew Dr. Spencer's appointment as medical superintendent, effective August 31, at the end of his current three-year term. He was to be reassigned, location to be determined. The new superintendent will be one Dr. Michael DeWitt.

"This news came from a call from the governor's chief of staff." His voice was matter-of-fact, like he'd told the same story many times.

I sat there, stunned. I couldn't come up with something to say other than a weak "How can he ... ?"

He raised a hand to signal wait. "There's more."

He looked at the letter in his hands.

"This letter is from the Michigan Department of Health.

It arrived the day after that phone call. The governor has appointed a commission, whose job it will be to inquire into the effectiveness of every mental hospital in the state, starting with the Traverse City State Hospital. The commission will begin its work in the fall, with a full report on this institution due by ... let me see ... here it is ... December."

"Why do they need a commission?" I asked. "Is something wrong?"

"In some people's minds, apparently yes. We've talked about this, you and I. Local politics seem to have reached the capitol."

"So much for your meeting with those legislators."

He raised his shoulders and shook his head slightly, as if to agree.

"It's impossible for victims to make their case to their victimizers," he returned.

There it was again: that defeatist language. For a while now, he had been morose but sort of hopeful, sort of convinced himself that things would change for the better. Someday. Somehow. Go about business as usual. This too shall pass.

He stretched in his chair, leaned forward and craned his neck to stare past me, out the window at the expansive lawn now browning with the summer heat. He spoke in a reverie about his appreciation for the "many men and women who've devoted their lives to patient care here — and in so many other institutions — nurses, administrative staff, orderlies, maintenance, grounds, cooks.

"So many good, good people! They don't get paid enough for the vital work they do; they don't get enough vacation commensurate with the hard work they do; and they aren't accorded enough respect outside these walls. Except for the respect of those kindred spirits who suffer mental illness themselves or who care for damaged souls in their own family.

"They're too busy working to involve themselves with the politics of the institution. Nor should they. That's not their job."

He looked directly at me then, and he sighed. I felt awkward, sitting there silent. But it seemed that he was not inviting a conversation as much as looking for someone to just sit and listen. Someone he didn't employ. Someone neutral.

That's why he invited me here, I thought.

He peered into his tea, swirled the tea bag.

"And, in that respect," he said finally, "I have failed."

"Sir?"

"I should have done more. I should have done…differently."

I waited.

"Money and power can go a long way toward corrupting a system at any level, from the very bottom to the very top. Forgive me. I know I'm being abstract. But so much of what is going on *is* abstract. Up here in the north, things happen at a distance from the center of power downstate. And vice versa. Things happen down in the capitol that we don't get wind of. People say and do things who have never set foot on these grounds, have never had any experience with patients *or* caregivers.

"*We* are abstractions, to *them*. The lives of our patients are so removed from the lives of, quote, normal people, unquote, that those people have *no* idea what patients' lives are like. And as for us, the caregivers, our lives are so remote from theirs, they have *no* idea what it takes, to provide care day after day. Or what it costs. *No* idea."

He put down his cup, pulled his spectacles off his nose and

cleaned them with the bottom of his necktie. He put them up to the light and peered at the lenses as he spoke.

"I believe that because they have *not* had the experiences with patient care that you and I and so many others have had, they *cannot* understand. Or, because they have more important priorities, they just *don't* care. In my darker hours, I believe *they* believe that our patients here are less than human, less deserving than people they consider normal."

"I know that attitude," I said.

He then launched into an explanation of state inquiry commissions, how they are appointed when someone—a governor, for example—wants to find out more about something, like why a fish species is dying out, or why bridges are crumbling.

Commissions gather facts and report those facts to the governor, he explained. But inquiry commissions can also be political agents who can find what they are inclined to find. They exude *objectivity* as they report the findings and make recommendations, but they aren't always quite so objective. Commission members are appointed officials who can select—and, unfortunately, omit—facts as they please. For those commissions that are politically motivated, their work is less about objective finding and reporting, and more about *not* finding. And they *report* as they are inclined, often in the face of facts to the contrary.

"They wield immense power," I said.

"Indeed they do. And we're susceptible to the decisions of those people who will come to their own conclusions and make their own recommendations, exclusive of us."

"Justice always butts up against power, Brother Benedict used to say," I said. But Dr. Spencer's mind was still somewhere else. He swirled the tea bag again, and then put his cup down on the desk.

"I hope you will do a better job than I have," he said, out of the blue.

I shifted uncomfortably in my chair. "Sir?"

"I hope you will be a stronger and more vocal advocate for *your* institution — some university, health organization, or state hospital, wherever you end up. I hope that you develop allies up the food chain who will rally for you when the time comes. I have not done so well in that department. Hindsight is 20/20, they say. How true that is."

He looked so worn, so distraught. My mentor. Apologizing to *me* for his shortcomings! Awkwardly, I asked for some tea. He poured me a cup.

"All we can do is all we can do," I said. "That's what Brother Benedict drilled into us."

I didn't tell him the rest of what Brother Benedict used to say: "We cannot be more than we are; nor can we be less than who we may become." Then he would quote his favorite Roman writer, Terence: *Forest fortuna adiuvat.* Fortune favors the brave.

He smiled. "He was a smart man, your Brother Benedict. Your successes loom large before you, my young friend."

I expected him to apply the opposite to himself — *My successes are behind me.* He didn't. But the implication hung in the air between us.

The phone rang. He looked at it as if it were the whining of an irritable child. He let it ring. When it stopped, Mrs. Krueger opened the office door ever so slightly; her head peered inside. "Sorry to interrupt, " she said. "That was me. I have Lansing on the line. Somebody named Smithson. Office of Budget and Planning."

She waited.

"All right, Bettyanne. We're just finishing."

I stood, leaned across the table and shook his hand. "I appreciate your taking the time to talk with me today, Dr. Spencer."

"You're welcome, of course. I appreciate *your* time. In you, I see a lot of myself…a long time ago."

"I only hope…" I started to say, but he cut me off.

"I *must* take this call. Enjoy the rest of your day, Henry."

Once outside Building 50, I headed toward the greenhouses. Recalling the conversation I had had in May with the supervisor, Mr. Meyer, I wanted his perspective on what Dr. Spencer had shared with me. I had become involved, willy nilly, in the political landscape, and I needed some perspective on that landscape.

As I rounded the corner by Cottage 39, a high-pitched woman's voice called out.

"Hi ya! Hi ya! Hi ya!"

I stopped in front of the building; white flower baskets full of petunias and green fern hung from the front porch railings. Two women sat in rocking chairs; they stared at me — rocking, silent, suspicious.

"Hi ya! Hi ya! Hi ya!" came again. Above me, at a second-story window with vertical bars outside the frame, a brown-haired woman in a purple and yellow shift stared down at me. She looked to be in her forties. She shoved open the window and put her hands out between the bars, beckoning.

"You look like a nice man," she said. "Come in here and we can have sex. I have a sexy body and a sexy look. I won't have any babies, don't you worry."

She cocked her head and smiled at me, beckoning me with outstretched fingers. "C'mon, Honey. C'mon!"

She closed the window, pulled down the front of her dress to reveal her large breasts and then flattened them against the glass.

I looked at the two women on the porch. They continued rocking, wordless, staring—the one expressionless, the other holding a hand to her mouth as if she were stifling a laugh.

I turned, walked a few yards and stopped when I heard the window open again.

"Look at me, you! Look at me!"

I looked up once more. She pushed one breast out between the bars, propped it up with one hand while, with the other, she beckoned again with her fingers.

At first I thought it would be best to just ignore her. But I was still thinking about what Dr. Spencer had said about outsiders thinking people like her were less than human. And though what she did was undignified, something in the back of my head said I should at least acknowledge her. So I smiled up at her, waved in a friendly way, and continued on my way toward the greenhouses. It was the right thing to do.

I passed through Greenhouses 1 and 2 before I found Mr. Meyer in Greenhouse 3. Seated on a high stool at a table in the corner, he was labeling wooden sticks with a black pen. He smiled as I approached.

"Well, look who's back. Pull up a stool here and take a load off." He nodded off to the right where another stool was parked under an adjacent table. I pulled it over and settled in next to him.

"I need to talk with you, Mr. Meyer, if you have a few minutes." I asked what *he* thought about the attack at the market.

He spoke quickly. "It's part of a pattern, don't you see?"

He arranged and then rearranged a pile of small wooden stakes on the tabletop before him.

"Like I told you once before, my friend. Someone—who knows who?—wants this hospital out of the local market. You can see how it has all escalated—from name calling and pranks to hurting animals, and now hurting people. They've become more brazen, more confident."

He confirmed my suspicions: collusion, conspiracy.

"Who's behind it all?" I asked.

"No one I know can say who did this…"

"Can't, or won't?"

"Either way," he said. "I just listen when I stop for a beer some afternoons on my way home. At Brady's Tavern, in town. Sometimes I hear the way some fellows talk about this place. Like that churlish Daryl. He's a regular there. Big mouth. Hates his job here. Hates the patients, too."

"Daryl from Recreation. I know him."

"That would be the same man. Big oaf makes up stories all the time. Thinks he's an entertainer. All brawn, dumber than a bucket of rocks. None of those fellows knows what goes on here. It's not their world. I keep my distance from them, just talk with a buddy sometimes. They don't know my connection to the hospital 'cause I keep that to myself. But I listen. Those men there, they don't hurt others. They talk big and they talk nasty. But they're not doers. They're just talkers."

"So, why don't you tell the police? Something they say might be a lead."

"Look," he said. "I start telling the police about their big talk and guess who's going to come after me? They're tough factory workers and farm hands. I'm not about to stir up that hornet's nest. People have always knocked the hospital and the patients, always called them names and made fun. Nothing new in that. But me calling the cops on them? Do *I* look like I just fell off the turnip truck?"

I just loved Mr. Meyer's metaphors. But we were having a serious talk and so I put a fist over my mouth to hide the emerging grin. A brief silence enveloped the space between us, until I blurted out what *I* had done with the police.

"I talked with the sheriff."

He looked sideways at me. "You did what?"

"I went to see the sheriff. I told him how I thought the market attack was related to the other incidents. I told him about what men talk about at that bar. The sheriff, he's a good man. His family had good experiences with the state hospital some time ago. So he cares enough to get personally involved in the investigation. I think it's his way of giving back."

"Well, I'll be damned," he said, smiling. "I'm right proud of you for doing that, son. You're no wilted stalk of corn."

Two men entered from behind us and clattered about with empty pails and gardening tools. They smiled at us, the smaller man waved a greeting, while the other grabbed hand shovels from a rack of hanging tools. They left by the same door.

I cleared my throat. "Do you think," I asked, "that what happened at the market is connected to Dr. Spencer's termination and the inquiry commission?"

"Does *he* think so?"

"He does."

Mr. Meyer turned full toward me. He put down the sticks he had been fiddling with, and picked up a green planting pot, turning it round and round in his hands. He turned it upside down on the table. Dirt and some dried root parts fell out. He rubbed a finger in the dirt on the table, partitioning it into two sides.

"The market attack and the termination are connected like white on rice," he said. "What's more, I think our chief medical superintendent can't do a thing about it. Or won't. Now, don't get me wrong. Dr. Spencer is a good man, does good work, like I told you. He's been good for us here. But he has his boundaries. Like this line in the dirt. He just doesn't cross it."

"Can't you or someone convince him to step up more, get tough, like you told me before? The Willie Stark thing."

"You remember that, eh? Well, I tried that and it didn't go very far. Went over to his office, sat down, and gave him my view of things, what I hear at Brady's. That would've been, oh, months ago."

"And?"

"I talked, he listened. He rubbed his temples a lot like he had a headache. Sorry to say this, but what I had to say, he didn't want to hear."

Or couldn't, I thought.

The two workmen stepped in again. The taller of the two looked distressed.

"Mr. Meyer," said the tall one, "you better come out here. Bert is at it again. Keeps fillin' up the baskets with pure cow shit, not mixin' it with the soil."

Mr. Meyer winked at me and jerked his head backward toward the voice.

"Okay, Tiny. I'm coming. Just hold your horses."

We both stood up. I brushed off the rear of my pants and put my stool back. Mr. Meyer lingered.

"Anyway," he said, "that's just my opinion, from where I sit. I trust you'll keep our conversation between the two of us. I don't mind if you share *your* speculations with others, based on what we talked about, just don't bring me into it. Deal?"

"Deal."

"Always a pleasure," he said, with another wink. He went out the rear door while I walked the length of the greenhouse and emerged from the front.

After supper, I visited Jimmy in the infirmary. I opened the door just wide enough to peer in. Ruth Greenfield was sitting at a desk doing paperwork. Jimmy was sitting on the edge of his bed, fully clothed. He was to be released that evening and he was dressed and ready. Release couldn't come soon enough.

I got one step into the ward. He saw me and started talking madly: Mr. Harrison had invited him to return to the Maintenance Department for work. They had a backlog of jobs that "only a good one-armed mechanic can handle," Jimmy boasted as I approached.

"See, Mr. Henry," he beamed, "like Gram used to sing, 'All God's critters got a place in the choir!' Even one-armed Jimmies!"

After a final once-over, Nurse Greenfield signed his release and handed it to me. I walked him over to his cottage. Along the way, I reminded him that the doctor had ordered rest for the next three days—"NO WORK" was written in capital letters on his papers, which I delivered, with Jimmy, to the attendant in his cottage.

He was cheered by his buddies in the cottage when he stepped over the threshold—Captain Jessup stood at attention and saluted; Siederman accelerated his chair-rocking speed; and a couple of others held up a hand-made sign:

WELCUM BACK JIMMY

Francisco came up from behind, threw his arms around Jimmy's good side and hugged him.

"Ah-mee-go!" Jimmy shouted. He was glad to be back. As for how much he would actually rest, I had my doubts.

CHAPTER TWENTY-FOUR

Guardian Angel

BY THE MIDDLE OF JULY, MY REMAINING TIME AT THE HOSPI-
tal was getting shorter and I wanted at least one more outing
with Jimmy before I headed back to Philadelphia. That outing
finally came on a day when the temperature was to rise above
ninety, with the humidity close to the same mark. Jimmy's arm
was no longer in a cast and it was getting stronger every day; he
had healed from all his wounds. I planned an outing that would
include two other male patients who lived in my cottage.

Walter was awarded a Purple Heart because he lost his hearing and his right eye when the Japanese bombed his ship during
the war. But the Purple Heart did nothing to prevent the horrible nightmares he had suffered ever since. Or the hallucinations
every time a plane flew over the hospital or a truck backfired. He
had been committed not long after the war ended.

Ernie was Walter's frequent companion at the hospital. Ernie's Tourette Syndrome caused him grimacing facial tics and
corprolalia—verbal utterances that were usually socially inap-
propriate. His other symptoms included impulse control and
learning problems. Unlike many TS sufferers, Ernie's tics did
not improve once he passed through adolescence. Learning dis-
abled and challenged at times to control himself in public, Er-

nie's family had him committed for better care than they could provide at home.

Both men were in their late twenties, both lived on the second floor of my cottage—and both loved to ride bicycles. Occasionally an attendant would get them bicycles to ride around the hospital grounds, but they never ventured off the campus. They knew that I sometimes took male patients on outings, so every day one or the other would ask me when they could go on a bicycle trip.

I borrowed bicycles from the hospital warehouse, gathered my group right after breakfast, and showed them the map of Old Mission Peninsula, where we would be heading that day. Peninsula Drive clung to the sandy shores of West Bay and extended about fifteen miles north of town. Tiny summer cottages and year-round homes dotted the road, and here and there a wooden dock with motorboat or sailboat stretched twenty or so yards out from the shore. We packed sandwiches, pickles, and apples for a lunch along the way, stuffed them in a basket mounted to the front of my bike, and struck out across town by mid-morning.

Jimmy asked if he could stop at a drug store to pick something up, so I waited with Ernest and Walter in front of Wilson's Pharmacy on Cass Street while he went inside. He came out in just a few minutes and hopped back on his bike and pedaled away before I could even talk with him. I figured he had purchased some treat to surprise us with at lunch.

"C'mon, Mr. Henry," he shouted at me, "let's get going!"

Off we went, Jimmy always in the lead as we crossed town and headed up the peninsula. About eleven miles out, we stopped and ate lunch on the shore. Jimmy had some crumbled Ritz crackers in his pocket to feed the terns that swooped down and grabbed them from the water's surface. Walter skimmed stones across the water while Ernest took off his socks and shoes and waded up to his knees. Every once in a while he let out a monosyllabic word that was either a curse word or a reference to a body part.

"Tits," Ernest said as he came in to shore. Walter hit six bounces with a flat rock. Jimmy turned his pocket of crumbs inside out and tossed the remaining morsels on the water. I packed up the remains of our lunch and said it was time to head back. Walter and Ernest wanted to pedal to the tip of the peninsula, another four miles, but it was getting hotter and humid, so I suggested instead that we turn around and go for lemonade at the Woolworth on Front Street. We voted, and it came out two to two, so we flipped a coin and it came up heads for Jimmy and me. We pulled ourselves back on our bikes and pedaled south, toward downtown.

Jimmy led the way again. At the Woolworth's, we leaned our bikes against a trash basket in front of the store and went inside. I was dripping with sweat and dying of thirst.

"Hell!" Ernest said as we stepped into the air conditioning of the Woolworth's store. There was little I could do to curb his audible tics, so I grabbed a *Life Magazine* from a rack and gave it to him as a distraction.

"My treat this time," Jimmy announced, "I got money from changing the oil in Mr. Harrison's car and from putting a new battery in Mr. Axel's shiny Ford."

He led us to the soda counter and sat on a swivel chair on which he spun around a few times before landing with both hands on the counter. The waitress, a teen-ager with a bad case of acne and hair pulled back into two ponytails, came over to take our order. She looked at our sweaty shirts and foreheads with pimply displeasure. When Jimmy yanked a napkin from the dispenser and wiped his brow, she wrinkled her nose.

"Four big lemonades, please," Jimmy said as he spun the seat next to me and, with an open hand, motioned to the three of us to sit down. Walter scanned up and down the counter with his good eye while Ernest studied the remaining piece of chocolate pie beneath a glass dome farther down the counter. A large mirror on the wall facing us reflected our sweaty faces.

"Pie," Ernest said. "Shit Pee Pie." He opened *Life* and spread it on the counter between Walter and himself. The waitress glanced up and squinted our way with a look that clearly disapproved of Ernest's language.

"Sorry, Miss," I said. "He can't control himself sometimes. It won't happen again."

She rolled her fifteen-year old eyes the way she probably did when her father asked why she wore so much lipstick.

She carefully placed four soda glasses on a Coca-Cola tray and walked back to us without spilling a drop. One by one, she placed each down in front of each patron, icy frost dripping down the sides of the glasses. She gave Ernest an especially chastising look when she got to him.

I prayed he wouldn't utter a word. Any word.

"Anything else?" she said, looking directly at me and alternating from one foot to the other. I wondered if she had to pee.

"Nope, ma'am," Jimmy said, stealing her attention to himself. "We only got money for lemonade."

"Then that'll be forty-four cents, plus a penny tax. Forty-five cents in all."

I stood and started to get the money from a front pocket when Jimmy put his hand on my arm.

"Oh no, Mr. Henry, my treat, remember?" He reached down in his pants pocket. The waitress stood there in front of us drumming her fingers on the counter and snapping her chewing gum.

Jimmy's hand came out of his pocket with a fistful of coins that he plopped down on the counter. Right in the middle of the money, right in the direct sight of the pony-tailed waitress, right before my own eyes, lay a Trojan condom encased in its grey and red wrapper.

"Oh-oh," Jimmy said, low voice, eyes glued to the counter.

Our waitress's eyes grew exponentially as she stared down, too. I thought I heard a tiny scream come out of her but it may have been more of a titter that seemed to originate somewhere deep in her skinny throat. She stared in horror as if he had put a human ear there, or a picture of her grandfather in bra and panties.

In that instant, we three seemed suspended in time and space. Had the waitress not been there, things would have been different. But there she stood, in all her adolescent distress. So, I reached over and counted out the forty-five cents, slid them past the condom, and picked up each coin as fast as I could. I handed the coins over to her, which she took in her own palm, and, with a glare at Jimmy and me, she spun on one heel and escaped to the cash register at the other end of the long counter.

"No receipt needed, ma'am," Jimmy said to her as she punched the resister keys with unusual force. Then she disappeared into a back room, where I figured she'd be praying the rosary in two seconds flat.

Jimmy scooped the rest of his money and the condom into

his pocket and sat down. Straw in mouth, he sipped, his eyes staring straight ahead, blinking wildly.

I sat back down, too, said nothing for a few seconds. Then, "Is…that…what you wanted at the…pharmacy, Jimmy?"

He looked straight ahead. A barely audible "Yup," came out of him.

"Shit pee pie," Ernest announced again.

"Well…not that it's any of my business, but…why do you, you know, need one of those?"

A broad grin formed across his face as he sucked the last of his lemonade noisily. He turned to me; the giddy expression had returned.

"I don't *really* need it, Mr. Henry. Someone else does."

"Oh," I said. "So, you're buying that for another man in your cottage?"

"Nope. She's a woman."

I sat up a little straighter. "A…woman? Jimmy, you're buying a condom for a woman?"

"She don't call it a condom," he said. "She says it's a rubber. She says it's her guardian angel. The one who protects her."

"Her guardian angel? I can understand that. And how is it that you happen to be the one buying a rubber for her?"

The waitress, now surly and over-dramatically offended, emerged from the back room, marched toward us, but then breezed past us and slapped a receipt down on the counter in front of us as she passed.

"Thank you very much, sir," she announced, her back turned to us as she sought safety down by the ice cream barrels in the sliding cooler.

Jimmy had this sheepish look—the boy with both hands in

the cookie jar. He rolled his eyes toward the ceiling fan spinning over our heads. He looked past me, around behind himself, then into the mirror behind the Coca-Cola dispenser. That's where our eyes met, in the mirror. Walter and Ernest had by this time spun around, elbows on the counter behind them, and were surveying the merchandise in the store. They weren't listening to us.

"Bernadine," he whispered, "and me, we ... you know ... need it."

I sat back, raised an arm and rested it on his shoulder, "You and Bernadine? How? Where?"

"In the Women's Walk. In the bushes and the weeds behind the trees in the Women's Walk. I go in there from the woods and she goes in from the street and we meet in the middle behind the big bushes there. You won't tell, will you, Mr. Henry? It's our secret."

I was astonished! Here was Jimmy and Bernadine, having a sex life right here, at the hospital, under the radar. It was no secret that sex between patients occasionally took place *somewhere*. Babies *were* born, after all, and not by any immaculate conception. But Jimmy? And Bernadine?

So *that* was why he lost grounds rights! He never went into the woods to pee. He went in there to meet Bernadine!

I had mixed feelings. On the one hand, up until now, I hadn't seriously considered the simple fact that that mental patients, like everyone, have sex drives. It's human nature.

On the other hand, here was Jimmy having this rich, secret sex life while I lived celibate far away from Clara. I knew that taking this internship so far away from her would be really hard. But I had been true to her, my attraction to Nancy Brownell my only weak moments. I envied Jimmy, not the way guys envy other guys who wind up in the back seat of their dad's car on prom night. That would just make sex, well, just plain sex. I envied Jimmy because, as I had long suspected, he really loved Bernadine. For him, I figured, sex was a true expression of love. That was what made it different.

"Of course, I won't tell anyone, Jimmy. You can trust me."

"'Cause we're buddies, right?"

"'Cause we're buddies, that's right."

"Whew-*wee*," he sighed.

We made our way back to the hospital, and I never mentioned the condom event to Jimmy again. But that event marked a significant milestone in my understanding of patient care, which is what I wrote about that evening:

July 16:

Maslow's third level, the human need for belongingness: family, home, community, neighborhood, social groups, clubs, teams. Belonging includes romantic, intimate relationships — courting, marriage. Definitely includes sexual relationships.

Many opportunities <u>here</u> for webs of belongingness — clubs and work teams, art groups, CHOIRS, quilting circles, and special interest groups (Bernadine's Birders, for example, and the Fashion Shoppe).

But what about sexual expression as part of that belongingness? There was that Frances Markey patient who swallowed things and had an idealized lover named Roland. But I thought of that as romance, not necessarily sex. I've never given much consideration to sex in a mental hospital. More ignorance on my part. <u>Of course</u>

271

patients have the right to intimacy. But there are so many potential problems with patients and sex — their lack of factual knowledge, the boundaries of intimacy, personal responsibilities, not to mention the LAW and the consequences of breaking the law! All the problems of a society outside the hospital, but WRIT LARGE.

It's a Pandora's Box.

On the other hand, it could be a wellspring of health and healing. Would having sexual outlets, intimacy, the hope of marriage and parenting, would that be therapeutic?

Should I open that Pandora's Box in my thesis?

CHAPTER TWENTY-FIVE

Those People

MY TALKS WITH DR. SPENCER AND MR. MEYER DROVE ME BACK to research in the Office of Admission and Records. I figured that office saved newspaper articles or letters related to the hospital. I had seen a few such letters the past year, but I wanted to know if what I saw was atypical or an evolutionary trend. The academic part of me was curious.

By late morning, I was back in the archives. I was greeted by Mrs. Dorman.

"Cutie patooti!" came her never-cease-to-amaze-me greeting. I must have presented with an unusually stern, or at least impatient look, because she seconded her greeting with raised penciled eyebrows, a step backward, and, "Goodness Gracious Gladys Gillman! What's up with Mr. Serious?"

I dispensed with the small talk and told her I needed to see anything she had on local newspaper coverage of the hospital. Mrs. Dorman pointed me to what I needed and then, thankfully, left me to my own devices throughout the day. I retrieved a long box from the CORRESPONDENCE stack labeled NEWS CLIPPINGS, 1885 - 1950, and took it upstairs to my desk. Arranged chronologically in it were manila files dated by year. Each file held newspaper clippings and letters that featured hospital developments or patient outings in the community.

There were many stories about construction and expansion. Human-interest stories about patients' goodwill. Later, occasional photos of patients visiting the community fairs, concerts, beaches, baseball games, and the like. One writer praised the hospital patient who had saved his dog from drowning in the Boardman River. Another applauded the hospital administration for providing patient volunteers to help tidy up the beaches on City Cleanup Day. One large photo captured a group of patients frolicking in the water at the hospital's own beach on the west bay.

I thumbed through letters to the editor that appeared through the previous decade. They were similarly appreciative.

I had a flash of guilt. Had I been wrong about Mr. Remington, the newspaper editor? Here was proof that he had, in fact, published many stories and letters praising the hospital and its patient community. But wait—I didn't know how long he actually *had* been the editor. I only knew that the other, recent letters I had read, the ones that criticized the hospital, appeared *while* he was editor.

I flipped to those more recent letters and discovered that sometime during the early 50's, those with a more caustic tone started appearing. I figured it was a safe bet to assume that Mr. Remington was on board since at least 1950. Then I figured it didn't really matter. There they were, regardless.

In a 1950 letter, the writer claimed that he saw patients urinating on lettuce in the fields and defecating in an area where the writer believed turnips were being harvested for market. Another letter writer stated that "two lunatics from the hospital" sold watermelons at market that he said made his neighbors ill and "it was time for the city to do something about the tainted produce those people are passing off on us."

When I thought about it, letters that appear in the only news source in town reach thousands of people. What a great way to make gullible citizens believe dubious claims. People believe what they read in the newspaper, especially when what they read is written by their neighbors.

In the last file, from 1952, two letters praising the hospital for providing "lovely baskets full of bright red begonias for the Fourth of July parade float" and "gorgeous bouquets of rose sprays and sunflowers for the county hospital lobby" were outflanked by three letters damning the hospital. One blamed the hospital for "systematically and intentionally selling vegetables, fruit, and milk at ridiculously low prices, nearly a giveaway."

"This unconscionable practice," the writer claimed, "threatens to destroy the local economy and drive vegetable and dairy farmers out of business."

Another writer said, "something has to be done when fruitcakes who can't even count are underpricing our own good neighbors."

The third writer minced no words: "It is time for someone to take some responsible action. We have elected leaders. Why aren't they leading?"

I sat back. Sweat formed on my forehead. I thought, *Something ugly built up during the previous year. People had begun calling names and making cruel innuendos. Worse,* I thought, *it doesn't take many letters like these to convince a lot of other people that there really* is *a problem.*

I put 1952 back in the box and left it in the storage room.

When I emerged upstairs again, Mrs. Dorman was swatting pesky flies on a window screen.

"Buggers!" Whack!

"Vermin!" Whack!

"Get out, you sons of biscuit eaters!"

Whack! Whack! Whack!

She craned her neck sideways when she saw me. She slapped the swatter over a paper basket a few times, knocking off fly remains.

"You all done down there?"

"I am. Do you have anything more current, from the *Sentinel?*"

"As a fact of matter, I do."

She produced a cardboard filing box labeled CURRENT NEWSPAPER from a bookshelf. I went to work at my small table.

Minutes later, Mrs. Dorman left for the day. Finally, I had the place to myself.

Aside from the usual articles about social goings-on at the hospital and community outings for residents, there was a series of letters to the editor spanning May to September. The first, written by a H. J. Higgins, alleged that the hospital vegetables sold at the market had traces of "foul-smelling irritants. Why doesn't the city enact food safeguards for the public?" the writer asked.

A Robert McAdamson wrote, "Here we are, once again, having to put up with the shenanigans from 'those people' on the west side of our town." The purported shenanigans included patients cavorting in shameful ways at the public beach and making loud and offensive remarks at a city band concert.

Two other letters echoed similar complaints; both called

upon "the proper authorities" to do something about "the perennial problems emanating from the asylum culture."

But there appeared other letters from citizens who defended the hospital and its residents. Frank and Agnes Steiner chastised those "thoughtless people" who write "outright lies" about the good-hearted patients at "our" state hospital. Mr. R. Kentwood affirmed the right of the hospital to "run itself in whatever darned way it pleases," especially since it's a major employer for the area. "If they want to offer things to sell at the market, that's their God-given right. This is, don't forget, a DEMOCRACY," he wrote, "and a FREE MARKET!"

It was a community divided. Reason, compassion, and level-headedness on one side. Outrage, anger, and ugly accusations on the other.

I put everything back in the boxes and left. I walked a long time alone, thinking. I had learned so much about the humanitarian mission of this hospital that I could easily return to Penn and write my thesis. But the divisions in the community had me stumped. Why, after decades of positive relationships with the Traverse City community, did things go sour so fast? What had changed?

I decided to ask Nurse Brownell. After all, it was her idea that I get some historical perspective on the hospital, and it was her invitation to come to her with any questions. Did she intend to wean me away from the sanctity of the academic world and immerse me in the real world of regional politics? Was she nudging me toward the kind of education that Dr. Spencer lacked?

I knew she had been gone since Monday—professional meetings in Lansing again. *She may be back by now*, I thought, *it's worth a try.*

CHAPTER TWENTY-SIX

A Moment of Truth

THE SIDE DOORS TO BUILDING 50 WERE UNLOCKED AFTER hours but a night guard was stationed at each one. Just inside door B-3, a security guard recognized me and waved me in. The evening news was on the television perched on a stand behind his desk. "Heard the news?" he asked. "The war in Korea is over. Ike was just on TV. Stalemate. Both sides stalled at the 38th parallel."

I stopped and stared at John Cameron Swayze's face on the screen. He was saying his familiar good night to listeners: "That's the story, folks ... "

"Finally," I said. "A stalemate. Well, I suppose that's better than war."

The guard's voice was even, his tone critical: "Yeah, well, thirty-three thousand lives later, now they can stand and take pot shots at one another for the next hundred years. Here? We'll just have to take in all the other casualties with hidden wounds." He pointed a finger toward his head and spun it in little circles.

I headed down the long corridor to the Nursing Administrative Services Office and stood silently before the slightly ajar door. I could hear file drawers being opened. I pushed the door a bit and peeked in. The room was filled with tall file cabinets, bookshelves, and two desks. Nurse Brownell had her back to me as she stood before a file cabinet. She was alone. She turned when the door squeaked.

"Henry? How nice to see you."

"Nurse Brownell," I said. "I didn't know if you were back yet. I knew you had gone downstate."

"We just returned," she said. "The others have gone home. I was just about to do the same."

"If it's not too late," I said, "I just wanted to ask a few questions."

"Of course. Come into my office." She pointed and then led the way to her private office. I had been in her office before, but I never took in the view of the grounds from there. Large double-hung windows with white curtains spread to the sides revealed a stunning view of a stand of green ash trees. She closed the door to the outer office. We were alone in the darkening dusk of the day.

"Please," she said, motioning to a chair. "What is on your mind?"

"Thank you. I wanted to talk with you about…the research in the Records Office that I did last year, which I've been thinking about since—and the events that have transpired since then. You said to let the culture teach me, and that's what I've done over time. But now my time is running out, and…you see, Nurse Brownell…"

She interrupted me. "Henry, I think it's time to drop the formalities. Please call me Nancy. In a short time, you will leave us, and I hope that the two of us can stay in touch—as professionals—and as…friends. Please, call me *Nancy*—whenever staff and patients are not close by."

"Of course. Nancy, what I found, what I learned, about the

history of the hospital has sunk in in new ways. Things have happened, good and bad, and I've talked with so many others over these months. I'm now putting all this together, and I just want to, you know, get your perspective on the whole thing—the history, the culture, the conflict, the institution itself, and its future. I want to be sure I get things right in my own mind before it's time to leave. Not that I can't do that on my own, but I respect you so much, and I hope to incorporate your insights into my, for lack of a better word, my *worldview*."

I went on for five minutes or so—the highlights of my September research in the archives: Dr. Munson, his beliefs and extraordinary work; natural therapies; and the successful agricultural enterprise at the state hospital.

She smiled. "You have captured the essence of our history well. And so, now do you understand the present any better?"

"Yes, I do," I said, "and I am troubled by that understanding."

"How is that?"

Ignorantia Affectata. Feigned Ignorance. She was leading me to something. It was in her tone.

"Yesterday," I said, "I went back to the archives to read newspaper letters, from early on up to the end of last year. What people have written about the hospital—especially starting last year. I'd seen some letters like those all this year; staff have pointed them out to me from time to time. Now I've experienced that animosity first-hand. That day at the market. I myself have become an historical artifact. Certainly Jimmy Quinn has. That day, we all were objects of scorn."

"That was a horrible day."

"It was, and the men who attacked us, the ones who beat up Jimmy, I'll never forget what they screamed at us. I just couldn't understand what could bring them to do something like that. Now, though, when I reflect on the history, it's coming together."

"On the one hand," I continued, "something this success-ful—a huge hospital like this that supports itself? What's wrong with that? What's wrong with patients working? Feeling part of something important. Getting better through work and play and healthy living? How could anyone object to that?"

"And on the other?"

"On the other, I can understand when people resent an institution cutting into their livelihood. They have to make a living, too. I hate to say it, but there is something valid to their complaints. I guess they have the right to be angry. Now that I have the history, I can see the state of affairs both ways."

"Well," she said, "you have now grasped the complications and contradictions. People in this community are hard-working, decent people. They are kind, charitable people who see the hospital as an asset to the region. People in the community like us for what the patients contribute—flowers and volunteering. They like us because we provide them with jobs. They like us because families from out of town come to visit their loved ones and those families stay in local hotels and motels, buy meals, gas, and shop. In other words, the community has an economic incentive to support us."

"That's exactly …"

She held up a hand, a gesture for me to wait.

"But, at the same time, we threaten *some* elements in the community," she continued. "And they have an economic incentive to oppose us."

"So what do *you* think?" I said. "Who's right? And who's wrong?"

"You'll have to decide that for yourself," she said. "Truth always complicates what, on the surface, seems to be simple, two-sided matters."

I regretted asking who's right and who's wrong: it did seem to oversimplify things into an *us-versus-them* mentality. But I had heard just about enough about political forces out to destroy the hospital; mysterious hoodlums wandering around in the night killing defenseless animals; and self-righteous thugs beating up innocent patients. Most of all, I had heard enough about hospital "leaders" who cannot or will not lead. But I knew better, once again, to voice my personal criticism.

Damn those eyes on the prize!

I wanted to tell her about my conversation with Mr. Meyer; I wanted to echo his criticism of Dr. Spencer. But I couldn't go back on my promise to keep to myself what Mr. Meyer said. As a sort of compromise, what I *did* start to say was, "Should Dr. Spencer have ..." but she waved me off again.

"I know what you're thinking, Henry. But it's too late for Dr. Spencer — or anyone else — to do anything that would deter the tide of change coming our way. Now that he is to be replaced, and now that a special commission has been appointed ... no one knows what that will come to. We would be naive to think nothing will come of it. Local outrage takes many forms in the trickle-up politics of the state. No one really knows what is happening down in Lansing right now. It is all very secret. I ... I am worried."

"About?"

"About the possibility that, somehow, our finances will be dramatically reduced. We will lose our ability to function independently of what others think we should be doing. People in positions of power have strong opinions on how to run a hospital like this. They think they know. Or, worse, they don't know and they don't care, but they want to promote the illusion that they do. One way to exert that power is to make the institution dependent on the state. With dependency comes forced compliance."

She sat back in her chair. She looked tired. I looked out the window as the dusk shot long shadows over the lawn. We were silent for a few moments.

She forced an embarrassed smile. "Perhaps our heads have been in the sand. Clearly, we should have done much more to advocate for ourselves. At the very least, we should have had an assistant medical superintendent whose job it is to represent the institution to the public and to the legislature."

I couldn't agree more. That was the least they should have done.

"You should have had a whole PR department!" I said.

"We know that now," she continued, calmly. "But we didn't anticipate very well what was really coming. We thought we could weather the storm. That was wishful thinking, and, frankly, a flaw of leadership. It would be easy to blame Dr. Spencer, but the blame lies with all of us in positions of leadership."

She glanced down at her wristwatch. She had this exhausted look on her face. I had that lapsed urge to take her into my arms and hug her. Even in her weariness she was sexy.

She continued. "We are entering a new era in mental health care, an era where *our* expert knowledge and *our* best practices are no longer sufficient in ensuring our livelihood and our integrity. We thought that being economically independent would please the state, and for years it did, apparently. But when resentment and greed and politics entered the picture, all that changed."

"So," I said, "legislators are willing to provide more money to the hospital—in exchange for, what, votes?"

"In a word, yes. This is how economics and politics intermingle. For us, the hospital will remain, people will keep their jobs, and the community will continue to express its appreciation for the patients. But we will be *dependent* on the government, and that will bring with it all the downsides of dependency. I fear we will become just like so many other mental hospitals."

I thought of Harrisville and the bare-bones version of patient care I had witnessed there—the listless rites of boredom, the loneliness, the purposeless daily passing of the hours.

"The future of state institutions, *this* institution," she continued, "lies in the hands of the *next* generation of caregivers. If they are like you, then we have reason to be hopeful. It will be up to you to preserve *our* proven success, *our* ways of taking care of our patients that have been so successful for so many decades. *That* is why I asked you to do that research. The next generation of leaders must know history and politics, in addition to patient care. They must be smarter."

My own advanced education would become much more complicated than I had ever imagined.

I said, " In other words, they must know a lot more about a lot more? I understand that now too."

Tears formed in her eyes. She pulled a tissue from a box on her desk and dabbed at her eyelids.

"I am sorry," she said. "This has been my life's work. Forgive me."

She waved the hand again before I could say anything.

"There is already talk of certain drugs replacing therapy. That may be good or not. I don't know. What Dr. Spencer and I do know, is that these patients deserve so much more than what most state institutions can provide. You cannot simply tell someone — some legislator, some governor, some commissioner — what you have come to learn firsthand. They have to work here, live here, have a family member committed here, have someone close to them recover here. They have to do more than make an official visit and then go back to their tidy offices and write a report. They cannot just knock on the door of the state hospital and say, 'Hello in there' and then leave without ever knowing a soul. But I fear that is just what they *will* do."

"I ... I wish I could ... do, something."

She dabbed again. "What you can do, Henry, is what you set out to do. Finish your internship, finish your degrees, and work to change the system. Early on, Dr. Spencer and I thought we saw in you the same bright spark of hope that we see in so many of our patients and young staff members. Our hope is that you will become a leader, an advocate for patient rights. What Brother Benedict saw in you, we also see — that you have the intelligence and the moral courage to act on your deeply held convictions."

I half expected to turn around and see Brother Benedict standing behind me, hands folded over his belly, nodding his agreement.

"I hope to live up to your expectations," was all I could muster.

"As I said, we have hope. Now," she said, standing, "it is getting late and I am afraid I have come unraveled a bit. Long day and all. I am expected home now."

We stood. I asked, "I'm sorry ... I never asked ... your home? Don't you live here, in nurses' quarters?"

She shook her head. "No. I live in town. With…a friend. Head Nurse never lives with the other nurses. Besides, I am a private person."

She walked around from her side of the desk and extended her hand. We shook hands, though I wanted more.

I wanted to put my arms around her and caress her back and kiss her with abandon. She was just so sexy and I was…vulnerable. Away from Clara for so long. True, Nancy Brownell was nearly twenty years older than me, but she was so damned lovely. There was no doubt that I had feelings for her; I had since the very beginning. In that instant, and with no serious forethought but the rising attraction I felt in the moment, anything could have happened.

I held her hand in mine longer than was appropriate. She looked at me, surprised, and, after a second or two, withdrew her hand. She gazed down; she looked embarrassed.

I had overstepped a boundary—and we both knew it. I fumbled for words that would undo my thoughtless impropriety.

Stultum. Dumb ass.

"I'm sorry," I said, "…about…asking where you live. I didn't mean to pry."

I was glad it was getting dark: if I had been turning red, she couldn't have noticed.

"I did not think you were prying," she said, looking directly in my eyes. There was now a chill in her voice. She turned back toward her desk and began to gather her things.

"As I said, it is getting late. I must leave now."

Though nothing explicit had passed between us, I suspected she knew, in that brief encounter, that I had feelings for her. But, other than the change in tone, she gave no clue as to her feelings.

Her eyes fixed on me once again, her voice firm, she said, "Good night, Henry."

I found my own way out.

Back at my cottage room, I tried to write to Clara but I couldn't. After what had happened with Nurse Brownell, I couldn't bring myself to write to Clara. I felt guilty. I rationalized: I just had had a … a weak moment. I had always found Nurse Brownell attractive, and there, alone, in that instant, something *could* have happened. I wanted it to happen. But it didn't—and that was fortunate, for I would have crossed a forbidden professional—and personal—boundary. Besides, Nurse Brownell had someone else waiting for her. I wondered who that person might be.

Later that evening, in my diary, I reflected on leadership:

July 20:

Nancy Brownell said the institution of the future must provide strong, determined, and innovative leadership—the kind Dr. James Decker Munson must have had in order for him to develop this amazing institution from the very beginning. He's my new hero.

Leaders with moral certitude, quiet wisdom, graceful ways with words, and tough hides. Leaders who are not afraid to stand up for those who cannot stand up for themselves, people who understand patient care from inside the institutional walls.

Could I become someone like Dr. Munson? What would that take? And what would it take to develop a streak of bold strength like what that Willie Stark character had in that book Mr. Meyer's wife read? I'm not talking about his moral corruption, just his backbone and tenacity.

CHAPTER TWENTY-SEVEN

Friends Don't Lie

THE NEXT TEN DAYS FLEW BY AS I PREPARED TO RETURN TO Philadelphia.

True to his word, Sheriff Nederhousen had taken over the investigation. I often saw his county sheriff's car parked on the grounds when he interviewed staff who had been at the market that day or anyone who had any connection with the spate of vandalism the hospital had experienced during the last year.

The sheriff re-interviewed me, too. He said he had tracked down others who were there when Jimmy was attacked. Someone saw the two men fitting the description speed out of the lot in an older model blue Plymouth. They didn't notice the plates. He had his deputies looking out for that car but he also said it was probably long gone by now. He said my recollection of their out-of-place shoes convinced him that those two guys weren't local, "possibly put up to this by locals, but hired from somewhere else, probably from downstate or out of state."

"Well," I said, "it's a lead. Better than nothing, which is all we've had so far."

He made some comment about did I know how many old blue Plymouths there must be in the Midwest? "Needle in a haystack," he noted.

Then he told me about what my "citizen's tip" about Mr. Remington had resulted in. Following my tip, the sheriff had pulled over the *Sentinel* editor one evening when he noticed, "what looked like careless driving." He suspected the man had been drinking, but he let him off with a warning—and his promise to "make some changes."

"Changes in what?"

"Personal habits, for one. And, other things," the sheriff said.

He winked at me, explaining that we could expect to see, for example, a full-blown editorial appear that would highlight how alcoholics are helped to recovery at the state hospital. The editorial would also cite the multiple ways the community benefits from having the state hospital farm products available in the community and at the county market. The editor would make a special effort to discredit the *now-loathsome* "letters to the contrary that have appeared in the paper."

I wanted to thank the sheriff for blackmailing Mr. Remington, but I just thanked him for sharing that news with me. "I'm always pleased to know that fulfilling my duties as a citizen really does matter," I said.

We left it at that.

Back with Mr. Harrison on maintenance, Jimmy would ride proudly in the back of a pickup as they went from job site to job site on the campus, Jimmy hollering as he passed, "Hey, Mr. Henry. Look! It's me Jimmy! You got anything you need fixin'?" His voice would trail off as the truck turned up the street.

I could not imagine a happier man riding in that truck than Jimmy Quinn. How far he had come since his timid arrival on the train nearly a year ago. How confident he had become, how full of affection. He was proof of what can happen when patient care nurtures happiness and bestows dignity.

On a rainy Wednesday, two days before I was to leave, I went in search of Jimmy. I wanted some private time with him before I left. He was in the Tool Shop, sharpening knives and wire-brushing tools. He was humming a song.

I rattled the door handle. "Jimmy?"

He looked up from his work. "Hi, Mr. Henry! Look. I'm sharpening blades."

He put down his stone and ran a finger across one blade. "Sharper than a Boy Scout knife. That's what Mr. Harrison says."

He cleared tools and mower parts off the table and cast out an arm for me to have a seat. He hopped up on the table.

"I'm so proud of you, Jimmy," I said, sitting next to him, our feet dangling.

"I'm proud of *you*, Mr. Henry! You stayed with me all that time in the hospital. You took care of me. You took care of me so I can take care of myself. I love you, Mr. Henry. And I'm proud I love you! I promise I'll take care of you, too, when you have to go to the hospital. I'll be there all the time. I'll bring you Kool-Aid and cookies and flowers and ... girly magazines.

"Oops," he said, grinning. "Not those kinds. Unless you want them."

Suddenly, I felt awful. Jimmy did not know that I was leaving. Not only leaving, but not coming back.

He was so talkative, I couldn't get in a word.

"And ... And Mr. Henry. I'm gonna tell you something else. It's a secret, so don't tell anyone. Don't tell Captain Jessup for sure, okay? No one. Promise?"

"No one, I promise."

"Bernadine and me. I'm sweet on her. And, she's sweet on me. She told me so. Bernadine and me, we're gonna get married. And move into a little house over in town and have little kids and I'll work for Mr. Harrison. And Bernadine, she'll keep on being a farm girl, that's what she calls herself. And she'll raise pigeons and sparrows at our house. And we'll come visit you down the street somewhere and have ice cream floats. And asparagus. Bernadine loves asparagus. And birds. Bernadine loves birding."

He scooted off the table. He paced back and forth in front of me. "I got so much to do," he muttered, pacing.

"Jimmy." I tried again. "Jimmy, I need to tell you something."

"Sure." He hopped back up and sat next to me again. "What do you want to tell me?" Our feet dangled, swinging back and forth.

"I...I should have told you this long ago," I began, groping for what words would follow.

"What?" He turned his face full toward me. I looked straight ahead.

"I...I have to leave. I have to go away. It's time."

"Where you going?"

"Philadelphia. I'm going to Philadelphia. Where I went for Christmas. It's a long way from here. It's my home. It's where I live."

I turned toward him, his face just inches from mine.

His nose crunched up and his eyebrows creased.

"You making a trip there?"

"Yes, I'm going on a trip, to Philadelphia. On a bus."

"How long will you be gone?"

"I...a long time, Jimmy. I'm going home. I won't be coming back."

He jumped down. He turned and faced me. He shoved his hands in his overalls pockets and looked to the floor.

"Not coming back? Why not coming back? This is your home."

I hopped off, too.

"Well, it's not the same kind of home, Jimmy. This is where I've come to learn, where I've continued my studies. But my time is over here. I have to go back to my real home."

He rubbed a heel into the dusty floor, looked up at me. Tears.

"*Real* home? Never coming back?"

"I ... I don't know, Jimmy. Maybe someday. But not for a long time, probably."

"Not coming back?"

Before I could say another word, Jimmy was hugging me. I held him, too, our arms around one another like reunited relatives.

"You're my brother," he said through sniffling. "You take care of me. Brothers. We're family people. Family, like Gram. You take care of me and ... and I take care of you."

I pulled my arms from him and looked him square in the eyes.

"Jimmy," I said, "we *are* like brothers. We *do* care for each other. Like family. But sometimes family members have to go away. My uncle went away to the war for four years. But he came back. I'll come back too, *some* day. To see you—and Bernadine, and all your children."

He broke from me. Fast pacing from one end of the shop to the other. He stopped each time in front of me, mouthing inaudible words under his breath, but then he continued the pace. I couldn't make out what he was muttering.

I waited.

His back to the door, facing me, it came out in a loud rush.

"Not the same!" he shouted, sorrow turning to anger. "You … you never told me you was leaving. You lied to me. You're my friend, and, and, friends don't lie. I'm mad at you."

"But Jimmy," I said.

"I got to go." He grabbed the sharpening stone and threw it across the shop. It broke into pieces against a table drill press.

"I don't like you anymore. You lied!"

He slammed the door on his way out. I stood, alone in my humiliation. Painful regret for what I hadn't said, hadn't done, from the beginning. In not even thinking about telling him, I had treated Jimmy as someone less important than others. Administrators and staff all knew I was temporary. But not patients. Why should I have treated patients any differently? I had been as ignorant as those I criticized. He had every right to be angry. Jimmy had taught me yet another lesson.

I leaped off the table, raced across the dusty shop floor and out the door.

He was gone.

CHAPTER TWENTY-EIGHT

The Dance of the Twirling Comets

A GOING AWAY PARTY HAD BEEN PLANNED FOR MY LAST NIGHT at the hospital. Staff were invited from departments where I had worked during the internship, except Recreation. More importantly, I was asked to name those patients whom I wanted to attend also. My list was not all that long, but it did include people I had come to know well—Bernadine, Eunice, Graham, Mrs. Hillman, Mikey the Milker, Jimmy's Mexican buddy Francisco, even Captain Jessup, and others whose names I knew just from talking with them here and there.

I wrote a special personal invitation to Jimmy and delivered it to his cottage while he was at work. I taped it on his door for him to find when he returned that afternoon. Since our falling out, I had seen him on the back of the truck, but when I waved, he looked the other way. Or, worse, he just stared at me, silent and sad looking. Three times I tried to corner him on the grounds to talk. Each time he turned and ran away, tools in hand. I tried knocking on his door in his cottage after bedtime, but he just said, "Go Away!"

I really needed him to come around—my stay at the hospital was getting shorter.

My bags were packed by the time of the party that Friday

evening. My bus would leave from the downtown station early the next morning. Dr. Spencer himself had called to say he would drive me to the bus.

"It would be my pleasure," he said. "I would like to see you off."

People gathered at 7:00 P.M. in a meeting room in the chapel. I made my way through the chapel proper, stopping momentarily to admire for the last time the tall multi-colored glass windows that stretched from just above the floor to the thirty-foot ceiling, windows that cast long morning and afternoon rainbow hues on the oak floors. Above me, white light fixtures ensconced in ornate bronze detail extended from poles that reached to the arched center of the ceiling. It had to be the most serene, most beautiful room in the northern hemisphere.

"Mr. Henry!" I heard behind me. "We're all waiting for you, over here!"

Eunice's cheery face peeked out from a door in the corner. "Over here, it's your party!"

"Eunice!" I returned. "How is the greeting business going? Any new gymnastics?"

She exuded a demur smile and shook her head affirmatively. "Just you wait, Mr. Henry. Just you wait. I do welcomes *and* farewells."

It was a lovely party. A table full of juices, ciders, and baked goods of every sort. Flowers in vases everywhere. A large sign taped to the wall read, CONGRATULATIONS! MISTER HENRY!

GOOD LUCK MISTER HENRY!

WE MISS YOU MISTER HENRY!

And, in smaller print, KEEP OUT OF TROUBLE MISTER HENRY! HA HA!

They were all there, the staff and the patients, Dr. Spencer and Nurse Brownell, Mrs. Dorman, Mr. Meyer, Nurse Ruth Greenfield, and even Mr. Harrison, his work boots caked with field mud. Mrs. Bradley, a patient whose piano music could be heard any evening when the windows to Cottage 19 were open, played her version of show tunes and popular music. After each song, she would stand and announce the next.

"And now, please listen to a piece I learned from my sister Hazel." Or, "For my next selection, I will play a request from Captain Jessup called 'The Marines' Hymn.'" Two versions of "Amazing Grace" also found their way into her repertoire.

As "The Marines' Hymn" trailed off, Captain Jessup approached. He stood before me as if it were to be an inspection. Erect posture, solemn voice. "May I wish you god speed, soldier. You have completed your mission here with honor, and I commend you for outstanding service."

He saluted, spun to the left on two heels, and marched to the oatmeal cookies.

I hugged Mrs. Dorman, Mrs. Hillman, and Mikey the Milker. I shook hands with Mr. Harrison and Mr. Meyer. In between hugs and handshakes, I scanned the room for Jimmy, but he was not there. Bernadine sat in a chair, one hand closed into a fist and resting in her lap. The chair next to her was empty. I figured she was saving it for Jimmy.

A series of others came up to wish me well or thank me for something they couldn't remember but thank you anyway.

When Bernadine's turn came to wish me well, she grabbed my hand and said, "Open, please."

I turned and opened my hand as her fisted hand hovered over it. Gently, she placed a tiny blue and white speckled egg in my palm.

"This one I found when one of them feral cats got after some robin's nest," she said, "and this little baby-to-be never happened. I been saving it for a special occasion. You take good care of it, Mr. Henry. It's good luck."

I was about to ask her about Jimmy, when Francisco pulled me around by my arm.

"Adios, amigo," he said. "Viaje seguro," which I knew meant *safe journey*.

Nancy Brownell approached. I spoke first, in a low voice.

"Nancy," I said, "I would really like to stay in touch with you. Can we correspond? By letter? I want to keep informed. I have…an investment here. That's not the right word but…"

"Of course," she said. "The right word does not matter. I am happy to correspond with you. Feel free to telephone me, too. Here is my home phone number."

She handed me a square of paper with a phone number on it.

I felt clumsy when I thanked her and we shook hands in the most professional way, though I wanted to hug *her* as I had Mrs. Hillman, Mrs. Dorman, and Mikey. But she was not one for hugging, apparently.

Dr. Spencer leaned into my side and whispered, "I'll have my goodbyes in the morning, Henry. My wife wants to send you off with some of her homemade brownies. She sends you her best wishes, too."

Mrs. Bradley announced in as loud a voice as she was capable of, "And now, everybody, our own Eunice Regina MacFarlane will entertain you with her famous…um…"

She pulled a card from her piano book and read from it.

"…Dance of the Twirling Comets."

Eunice cleared the center of the room, arms extended. She corralled people toward the walls. She strolled to the line of windows, took a deep breath as she steadied herself. She let out a whoop and proceeded to do a forward roll, followed by a failed attempt to walk on her hands (from which she recovered with modest elegance). She finished the routine with a successful one-handed cartwheel. Thunderous applause broke out as she did a series of backward rolls to where she began the dance, sprung up, hands over her head and then shot them down to her sides, like in the Olympics. A bright smile and a bow toward me. The applause continued as she ran to me, gave me a huge hug, and turned to her peers.

"Okay everyone! Ready? 1 ... 2 ... 3 Go!"

Mrs. Bradley struck up the piano. It was a number I remembered Billy Holiday singing, "I'll Be Seeing You." The group sang a verse and then started clapping on the last line that they changed to "We'll be seeing you."

I was deeply moved by their pure-and-simple farewell.

One by one, each guest left. Some turned at the door and waved to me. Captain Jessup gave a final salute. I remained alone for a few minutes while an attendant began the cleanup.

Then I left.

Jimmy was standing outside the chapel door when I emerged into the warm evening dusk. He was wearing a worn Detroit Tigers baseball cap pulled down low on his face. He stood in the middle of the walk, opposite the entrance.

I stopped, stood still. Our eyes met.

"Jimmy? I'm so ... I feel so bad. I'm so sorry for what I did." I walked toward him. He waited. As I approached, he removed his cap and handed it to me.

"This is my favorite hat," he said. "It's for you. So you can remember me. Here." He shoved the cap toward me.

I put it on. It was too small and it sat stupidly on my head. He looked at me and put a hand over his mouth. He stifled a laugh.

"Mr. Henry," he said, "You look like Howdy Doody. Or Mr. Bluster!"

"Well," I said, "You talk like Buffalo Bob!"

We both let it out. He doubled over laughing. I laughed like I'd never laughed in my life—full, hearty, relieved. He reached for me as I reached for him and we put our arms around one another. I patted his back, said quietly, "I will be back, Jimmy. Somehow, some way, I will be back. I will always be your friend, your brother."

We parted. He pointed to the cap.

"Maybe your mom can let it out some. So it fits," he said.

"I'm sure she can," I said. "She'll make it fit. Thank you very much. I love my new hat."

"Good bye, Mr. Henry. I won't cry in front of you again. I'm a strong man now."

I was up and dressed early. I had coffee downstairs in the cottage and sat alone, clearing my head for the long trip ahead of me. Dr. Spencer arrived just as men began moving around upstairs. The cottage was waking up for yet another Saturday.

In the car, Dr. Spencer reached into the back seat and pulled forward a paper sack. "Mrs. Spencer's going-away gift," he said. "The muffins are blueberry; I hope you like them with butter. *I* do. The sandwiches are ham and cheese, with mustard. And, her award-winning brownies. It was hard, but I kept my hands off the brownies," he chuckled.

In the ten minutes it took to get to the bus station, he filled the time with idle comments on the comforts and discomforts of bus travel. We arrived early, so we sat in the car and talked.

"Henry," he said, "hard times have come to me in these last few weeks, and I regret that I have not been as ... available as I hoped to have been. But I want you to know that I think you're a fine young man with a solid core and a bright future. Your parents should be proud of you. So should your professors. I hope you've learned what you set out to learn here ... and more. I hope you go back with fond memories and a sense of mission that'll allow you to complete your long-sought degree. Wherever your life takes you, I know you'll succeed."

"Dr. Spencer ... " I tried to get a word in but he wouldn't let me.

"Let me finish, please. In you I have come to see what I once saw in myself, many years ago. The idealism, the ability to know what is important in life, and to act on that conviction. As for myself, I'm afraid it's time for the likes of me to make way for younger, fresher people to take the leadership a hospital such as ours needs."

Before I could respond to that, he opened the car door on his side, walked around and opened mine. A Greyhound bus started up, blue smoke spewing from its exhaust. We had time for a few more words.

"Thank you for everything," I said. "I'm so different from a year ago. I've learned ... so much. I've changed."

"Changed?"

"So much. The biggest thing is, that patient care is no longer some abstract thing to study or read about. Not any more. It's concrete, it's flesh-and-blood people with real needs and real lives, with all their challenges and surprises. You were so right to have me evaluate Jimmy Quinn. He taught me more about humanistic philosophy than any stack of books in the library could ever teach me."

He smiled and nodded. "Nurse Brownell and I hoped that would be the case," he said.

The call came over the loudspeaker that the bus to Kalamazoo was about to depart. I grabbed my bags from the back seat.

He took my hand one last time. "You've been more than *just* a student to me," he said. "You've been ... "

The loud bus departure warning startled us and drowned out whatever else he said. He clapped me on the back, and gave me a hardy "Better get aboard, my boy, or you'll be late for your welcome-home party."

I took a seat in the back of the bus. He stood by his car and waved as the bus departed in a haze of smoke. I looked out the back window at him waving, an image that became smaller by the second as the bus sped away.

CHAPTER TWENTY-NINE

Transitions

"HENRY," CLARA BEGAN, "I HAVE A QUESTION."

We were lying on our stomachs, stretched out on a blanket on the bank of the Schuylkill River. We had just finished my welcome home supper. It was the day after I arrived the week before Labor Day.

Clara had grown only more beautiful and smart and special since I was last with her at Christmas. Her auburn hair was longer now and she had a suntan from swimming in an outdoor pool all summer. The suntan brought out freckles I didn't know she had. We spent every day together until she would begin to teach again after Labor Day. Then her days would be long and consumed by work while I would have my own work to do. But for now, we were blissfully together.

"This Jimmy," she said, "You talked a lot about him. He was very special to you, more so than the others. The way you described him to me in your letters, and what his life was like there, I often thought of him the way I would a character in a novel. Someone I knew through stories about him. Can you tell me more about him?"

I hadn't realized how *much* I had talked about Jimmy in my

letters. Or maybe it was just that Clara was able to hear what was really important to me, however much I said.

"I just really took a liking to him. He rose above the hardships of his life. He was living proof that patient care, done right, works miracles. Not for everyone, but for some. Like Jimmy. And Bernadine, and so many others there."

"Was he unusual?" she asked. "I mean, compared to other patients? When I think of a state mental hospital, I naturally think of the worst sorts of things. Crazy people. A danger to society, and to themselves. I'm like most people. I've never been near a mental hospital. I only know what I've read about insanity in novels, or seen in movies."

"Well, first of all," I said, "they aren't *all* crazy. They all have problems, but insanity is only one of them and even *that* has many forms and degrees of intensity. As for Jimmy, in some ways, he *was* unusual, but in others, he wasn't."

I told her about what Dr. Spencer had said about people in the hospital becoming an abstraction to those on the outside, and about how lack of contact with people who suffer from mental illness leads to all sorts of conceptions and misconceptions about an asylum and its residents.

"Some of the stereotypes you see in books and movies ring true," I said. "Mental illness is hell and asylums are the *only* place for some people. I'm just not sure they *all* belong there. With the right support, many could live and work alongside the rest of us. The problem is getting the support. Most ordinary families can't provide the right supports on their own, and there's no community infrastructure for providing them. What's worse, the state thinks the only solution is to hospitalize, at minimum cost to taxpayers—out of sight, out of mind."

"Does Jimmy belong there? At the hospital?"

"At first, I thought he did. But then I began to have doubts.
Give him a job, a supportive community, relationships, affection—he's as normal as you and me. What *is* normal anyway?
Isn't it normal to have needs and loves and fears and talents and
longings just like anyone? If so, that simple fact has profound
implications for patient care. That was my theory when I came
there. I knew it in my head. For me, it's no longer theory. Now
I know it in my gut."

"And in your heart?" She said, twisting the lid back on a jar
of pickles.

"And in my heart."

She pushed the plates and silverware off the blanket and
rolled to her side. She cocked her elbow and rested her head in
an open palm. Laurel green eyes opened wide, her other hand
pulling me to her, she whispered.

"And what does your heart say right now?"

"That I'm being seduced?"

Labor Day came and went. We spent every hour we could together. Then we agreed (reluctantly) that the demands of her
work and my writing schedule meant we should see one another
only on weekends. On one of our dates, I told her about how
I had come to think differently about Cousin Ethel and how
little I actually knew about her. I shared my ideas about patients'
rights to intimacy, but when I mentioned that I never heard of
Ethel even having a date, not to mention friends, Clara said she
would do something about that. "Girl to girl," Clara said.

Clara introduced my cousin to the cosmetics department at

Penney's, where Ethel bought makeup. Clara took her around the store and had her try on dresses, skirts, sweaters, and anything else that would nudge Ethel toward a more glamorous look. With her saved-up grocery earnings, Ethel bought forty dollars worth of new clothing, though Clara had to color coordinate the tops and bottoms for her.

Over the coming months, Clara would mentor Ethel on how to talk with boys, how to accept or reject an invitation for a date, safety around dating; sexuality issues—all the things this young, attractive woman with autism never learned. I joined the program by taking Ethel to a dance at St. Julian's parish hall; and Clara and I often included her on our dinner dates so she could see how two people in love spoke to one another—and how, at times, they disagreed.

It was a crash course in courting, but we never could be certain what key ideas actually got through to Ethel. She watched and listened *as if* she understood, and eventually she got the makeup on perfectly. She bought more outfits at Montgomery Wards. Aunt Pat was grateful that Ethel was beginning to have more typical female experiences. Uncle Tony, on the other hand, worried that his "only daughter might become attractive to the wrong fellows," as he put it.

Still no fellow asked her out. Clara picked up on Ethel's interest in books and helped get her a full-time job at a public library near where Clara taught; Ethel became a whiz at checking in and reshelving books. It wasn't long before Ethel was promoted to librarian assistant, where she helped Mrs. Kunkel, the reference librarian.

Aunt Pat and Uncle Tony were astonished at the changes they saw in Ethel in such a short time. Clara was very proud of her and all she was able to accomplish with just the right help from us and a few others. But I wasn't surprised at all. I'd seen similar miracles over and over at the state hospital. I was writing about them in my thesis. Seeing this one first hand, in my own family, only made a stronger case for humanistic care—with the right support.

While Ethel was coming into her own and while Clara was fully occupied by teaching, I worked a part-time job in my father's insurance office. In October, I moved out of my parents' home in Chestnut Hill to a furnished apartment a few miles away.

Office work was dull routine but I was glad to have personal income again. I filed, wrote information onto forms for clients, and checked policies for accuracy. Working mornings in the office meant I could go down to the university during afternoons for library research. By evening, I was back at my apartment where I worked on my master's thesis late into the night.

When I had the first two chapters drafted, I took them to Professor Hilliger for her approval before I continued work on the others. I felt very good about what I had written so far.

"It's rough and at times confusing prose, Henry," she said, as we sat in her modest office that afternoon. "The introduction is too redundant of Maslow's theory. Your description of the hospital and patients in these two chapters lacks crisp verbs and has too much passive voice. And your explanatory footnotes wander."

What I wanted to say was, *That's why it's called a "draft," Professor. Did you forget that minor point?*

I said, "I know. I have a lot of revising to do."

"But," she continued, "It's also brilliant, groundbreaking work."

A hurricane-strength sigh of relief welled up within me. "Humanistic Psychology is a new field," she continued, "and an exciting one. It is young. It has the *theory of practice*, but what it lacks is the *practice of theory*. Someone like you," she said, "who has had concrete and direct experience with the practice of humanistic—as opposed to strictly behavioral—approaches, that's invaluable to the field at this time. The more it can gain *practical* legitimacy, the more it will gain scholarly acceptance."

She turned over a page on her desk calendar, a signal that we were about to wrap up. I stood.

"Good work, Henry," she said. "Keep it up."

Heia! Whoo-Hoo!

Nurse Brownell's first letter arrived at my parents' home in mid-October. Mother dropped it in my apartment mailbox on her way to bridge one afternoon.

Dear Henry,

So much has happened since that August day when you left, I hardly know where to begin. So that you will not become alarmed, let me say at the outset that we are all fine here. No one that I think you know is injured or in ill health. Life seems to continue on as usual.

Fall harvest has come in with great gusto. We had a record crop of watermelon and squash in September, and the apples and pears are hanging nearly to the ground on long drooping branches. Patients are busy every day with this year's yield, while the ladies and gentlemen in the canneries are putting up stores for the winter. We thank the Lord for a bountiful harvest once again. Just yesterday, the bakery put out five varieties of apple pie, seven kinds of pear tarts, and apple-butter cookies, spicy pear cookies, and my favorite, pear-oatmeal bars. Patients scurry about the campus delivering boxes of sweet treats to staff everywhere.

There is other news, too.

Dr. Spencer departed on August 31. Though he was offered a position at the Ionia Institution, he declined it. He and his wife have moved back to Oregon. He has a position there at another hospital.

We had a grand farewell party for him, much larger and more formal than yours, and attended by many dignitaries from the city. It was nice. He was gracious in his departure; he spoke with the dignity one expects of an honored and honorable man.

In his farewell address, he said that he was proud of every one of the residents and staff who live and work here. He said he had achieved a life-long dream of providing leadership and, he hoped, a better quality of life for patients. He said that the future was now in our hands, and although change may be on the horizon, he knew we would be strong enough to maintain our integrity in the face of change. He ended with, "Good bye, my dear friends."

Not one eye was dry. He will be greatly missed.

Dr. Spencer's successor, Dr. Michael DeWitt, arrived three days later, with his wife and two children. They moved into the quarters formerly held by Dr. and Mrs. Spencer. Dr. DeWitt held a meeting with head staff the following day, at which time he announced that he did not intend to make any immediate changes. We should go about our work as usual. He said he realized he has big shoes to fill, and then he said he wears his own shoes. I believe he meant that as a joke. But since he seldom smiles, I cannot be sure.

I introduced myself to him, as did other head administrators, before he left. Later that day, he sent out a letter of introduction to all other staff reiterating what he had told us that morning. He asked to be referred to as "Superintendent DeWitt."

The Study Commission on Michigan State Hospitals has been formed and members named, according to correspondence we have received from Lansing. The head of the commission is a Mr. Barnes.

Rumors fly about what this commission intends. A letter arrived last week announcing that the Commission is scheduled to visit here in November for a "fact finding mission." I am not sure of what that will consist. It sounds formal. I hope to know more soon. I will not share any unfounded speculation until I do know more.

Superintendent DeWitt has yet to speak about it with me—or about anything else, for that matter. He keeps to himself most of the time, which I suppose I could understand for someone just starting off in a new job. That is not the way I would begin to serve a large institution such as this, but that apparently is his way.

I hope this letter finds you well and enjoying your return to your loved ones and your previous life there. Patients often say how they miss you. Jimmy Quinn, in particular, asks about you each time I see him on rounds.

Yours sincerely,
Nancy Brownell

A few days went by before I responded. I told her about progress on my thesis and my dreary job at the insurance office. I didn't mention Clara, although that felt disingenuous since Nancy mentioned my return to my "loved ones."

It was very kind of her, I said, to fill me in on the details of hospital life. I asked why staff don't know what's on the commission's agenda. I thought they had the right to know. After all, it's *their* hospital.

It was sad to see Dr. Spencer leave, I wrote. I'm sure that was hard for everyone. Superintendent DeWitt seems like a very inward man. But I agreed with her: perhaps he *is* just different. Perhaps he just needs time to settle in and do things his way. I've known people who are like that—slower, more methodical. Maybe the new superintendent is that way, too.

I tried to be upbeat. But the new superintendent's detachment gave me doubts too.

CHAPTER THIRTY

The Harshest of Winters

FALL SLIPPED QUIETLY INTO THE HARBINGER OF WINTER. I divided my time between the university, my work at Dad's office—and Clara, with whom I could never spend enough time. We had long ago abandoned the silly notion of seeing one another only on weekends. We enjoyed suppers at her place or mine, long walks in leafless parks, plays and a concert at her school, and the Philadelphia Orchestra (Mother gave us tickets).

A letter from Jimmy arrived the week after Thanksgiving. It was written in a lovely thick cursive.

Dear Mr. Henry,

I got Mrs. Dorman to write this for me cause she's got good writing. I talk and she writes. She says to say hello to you in Philadelphia and she showed me where that is on the map. It is a long ways from here, sure.

I got alot of work to do these days with Mr. Harrison since he cut his ankle and broke his toe when the snowplow fell on it in the barn where we was fixing it. He says I'm his right hand man. He tells me what to do and I do it like he says. Pretty soon he can get the bandages off and not need the crutches any more. Last week he showed me how to fix a radiator on his truck when it had a hole in it and it was leaking. I like fixing trucks now. Or anything. Mr. Harrison says I got a knack for it like everything else.

It's getting real cold up here now. We got snow everywhere and the day ends early and the night lasts until 8 o'clock in the morning.

I'm sweet on Bernadine. I danced with her last week when we had a party for Thanksgiving at the big hall. She is pretty and I got new leather shoes for the dance and for church too. Not really new but new for me. Bernadine gets sad in winter. Real sad. On account of she can't be working in the fields that she loves to do. I try to cheer her up but it don't matter much. She don't even care about birds no more. She sits and stares a lot. And she cries.

My friend Francisco is teaching me more Spanish. I know how to say a lot of words now. He is the only person who talks Spanish here so I just say the words to him, no one else. No one understands him when he talks Spanish. He's my ah-mee-go. That means friend. He used to drink a lot but no more. He would if he could. Next time you come to see me I will say a lot of Spanish words.

I miss you Mr. Henry and you are still my friend. I remember how you come to visit me when my arm was broke and I was in the infirmary. Thank you very much. I hope you come and visit me pretty soon.

Your ameego,
JIMMY QUINN

*P.S. Mrs. Doman says to ask if you like Philadelphia cream
cheese. She says she is making a joke.*

I wrote back to Jimmy the next day with *my* news. I put in a
picture of Clara and me sitting on the fender of her Ford at my
parents' house back in September. Borrowing Jimmy's own turn
of phrase, I told him that I was "sweet on her and she was sweet
on me, too."

I also put in a map of Philadelphia. I circled the area where I
lived in Chestnut Hill and the Penn campus downtown. I didn't
say anything about my coming to visit him. I didn't have any
plans to go back.

In late December, a letter from Nurse Brownell arrived.

Dear Henry,

*I hope this letter finds you well and enjoying this holiday
season. Here in Traverse City, winter has set in, with snow
a yard deep and temperatures below zero on the coldest nights.
The city has opened the ice rink in a parking lot downtown
and we've begun taking residents there for sliding and ice
skating. The city waives their fees for skate rentals. They have
such fun on the ice. Staff skate with them, too, so it is all quite
a marvelous scene.*

*We see snow sculptures popping up in the strangest places
now that we have substantial depth. Early yesterday morning, a snow woman appeared at the intersection of Gray and
Silver Drives. She was dressed in a red striped dress and
straw hat with a dangling paper flower. By ten o'clock, a
group of male patients showed up to produce a giant snow-
man wearing a straw hat, scarf, and, of course, charcoal but-*

tons down his front. Before long, more ladies created a line of snow angels on a rise by the fire station. I watched all this from my office window.

The downside of winter is that occasionally a patient will elope from a cottage at night and freeze to death outside. So far, we have lost two patients to the elements.

In other respects, things are not the same. I feel I am at liberty to be direct with you, Henry, and I ask that our correspondence be kept private, for I may make statements that, while true, may offend others should they be made public.

Superintendent DeWitt, whom I introduced to you in a previous letter, continues to be isolatory. He meets with staff monthly; at these meetings, he solicits reports from the various departments. His secretary takes notes and he rarely talks. He frequently glances at his wristwatch. He seems uncomfortable, even with his chief staff, which includes me, of course. It remains a mystery to me as to why he was appointed superintendent here.

But to the point. Superintendent DeWitt briefed us on the "progress" of the Study Commission of Michigan State Hospitals. We are to call it "the Commission" from now on. That body visited the hospital in November. There were six members, led by a Mr. Barnes, who is the Committee Chair. They toured the grounds and many of the buildings and cottages. I was the tour guide when they visited the men's and women's infirmaries, the senility ward, and the nurses' training building. They said little and had few questions. That surprised me. Because their purpose was to gather facts, I would have expected more interest and curiosity, but that didn't seem to be the case.

The tour of the barns, stables, piggery, and greenhouses garnered much more interest, as told to me by Mr. Meyer, whom you may recall is in charge of the greenhouses and who is intimate with the farming operations.

He and I began meeting over coffee after the commission's visit here. Mr. Meyer thought the committee seemed especially interested in how patients accomplish so much work, given their mental health, how many actually participate in the farming operation, and of what their work consists. They asked about safety issues that occur, how many on average, that sort of thing.

They spent most of their time with Superintendent De-Witt behind closed doors or at dinner parties in his quarters. They spent three full days here. Our superintendent told staff to expect their report early in the new year. I was also surprised to learn this as I was under the impression that they were going to visit all institutions in the state and only then would a report be written — because, as I understood from the beginning, their charge was to study all of the state hospitals. I wrote this concern in a note to Superintendent DeWitt and he responded, in his own note, that they would issue a report on each hospital as their work progressed. He also said the individual reports would contain recommendations for changes.

When I consider the troubles we have had in the community during the last year, not to mention the letters in the paper (which you know well), I begin to think that this commission has us in their sights (pardon the metaphor). I know Dr. Spencer felt that way and expressed the same to me before he left.

At any rate, we'll know more when the commission report

*comes out next month. I will be happy to share its contents
with you at that time.*

*In the meantime, I wish you and yours a Merry Christ-
mas and Happy New Year. I hope your work on your thesis is
progressing as planned. Though I have never met your parents or your friend Clara, please extend to them my warmest
wishes for this holiday season.*

*Yours sincerely,
Nancy Brownell*

I wrote back immediately. I thanked her for her news and her interpretation of recent events. I wrote, *I understand how intertwined
local and state politics can become. Dr. Spencer (and you) did your best to
educate me on the subject, and that horrible day at the market was the
best—and the worst—education I could have had. For me, the hospital's
political problems became personal on that day. I am eager to learn what
the Commission says about the hospital. I will keep my fingers crossed.*

Shortly after the Christmas holidays, another long letter arrived. In it, Nurse Brownell dispensed with her typical update
on pleasant hospital goings on.

Dear Henry,

*There is no longer any doubt as to the intent of the Com-
mission. They have determined that significant changes must
be made at the Traverse City State Hospital, "changes that
should have been made years ago in light of the evidence,
changes that should be implemented immediately." I am
quoting from the report.*

They recommend that "patients no longer participate in the farming operations or in the harvesting of fruit in the orchards." They have taken the opinion of Superintendent DeWitt that "there is no viable evidence that patients benefit therapeutically from toil in the fields, barns, or orchards." Those are the exact words of OUR superintendent!

No one can understand HOW he could come to that conclusion, or, more important, WHY he would come to that conclusion. I can only speculate that he was put here, by the governor, with the specific intent to discredit the decades of work of his predecessors — from the zealous foundational work of Dr. Munson to the caring tenure of Dr. Spencer. In my opinion, Dr. Spencer was gotten rid of in order to smooth the path for this superintendent and this conniving commission. As you said in your letter, you understand the intertwining of state and local politics. In our case, that intertwining has had devastating results.

We among the staff are astonished and shocked. I hardly have the words even to write of this to you. Except to say that, in hindsight, as a hospital staff, we have been naive in our confidence that right would prevail.

But that is not all the news, I am sad to report.

The Commission also recommends that the Civil Service Statute, enacted in 1936, be applied to all mental institutions in the state. According to the report, "government has allowed a state of benign neglect to exist on the grounds of the state hospitals. That is to say, it is the law that any persons(s) whose work on the grounds is comparable to work outside must be civil service employees. As such, they must be paid on the civil service scale; receive the pay and vacation ben-

317

*efits accorded a civil service employee; and be provided full-
time employment (40 hours per week) with premium pay for
overtime. Only civil service employees may be employed on
the grounds of any state mental institution."*

*Henry, you can see what this means. The farming oper-
ation has been a success because the patients have done the
work. We cannot afford the costs of paying civil service employees to do the work. Even if the patients themselves were
to become civil service workers, the hospital could never afford to pay them the wages the law required. As a result,
our patients are no longer permitted to work in any capacity
related to farming. Not in the fields and greenhouses. Not in
the orchards, the piggery, or the dairy barn. Since the law
applies to work "on the grounds," patients will no longer be
allowed a role in grounds maintenance. That will include
building maintenance too, as part of "grounds."*

*I am sure that you can name patients whose entire lives
are bound up in the work of the hospital, whose mental and
physical health depend on that work. I cannot imagine how
this new policy will affect them. Nor can I imagine what
they are going to do once spring comes and they will not be
allowed to work.*

*To make matters even worse, the Commission notes that
the "era of farming with horses and wagons is long gone."
They recommend that outdated technology such as horse-
drawn wagons and snowplows be replaced by modern machinery, namely trucks and tractors.*

*"It is also the case," they write, "that, by statute, any per-
son residing in a state mental institution is prohibited from
operating any vehicle or machinery."*

Henry, that effectively removes any of our patients from anything connected to motorized work. Where they might have driven a tractor, for example, or backed up a truck to the barns, they cannot. What little dignity a few may have garnered, what little experience they might have gained—experience that may have served them once released—has been dashed away.

This is the state of affairs here. Patients who have nurtured seedlings in the greenhouses starting in March, will not. Patients who have prepared the fields for planting and the orchards for the coming fruit crop, will not. Patients who have beautified the grounds, swept the sidewalks and streets, and maintained the facilities and gardens, will not.

The Committee recommends that these procedures be put in place no later than March 1! Until then, patients will be allowed to shovel show and make maintenance rounds. After then, new hires from the community will be employed in civil service jobs. As you can see, the immediacy of the timetable is even more devastating for our patients.

I am still reeling from this series of setbacks. We are beside ourselves with confusion, dismay, and anger. Perhaps your distance will allow you a cooler head and a sharper insight than I have here in this state of crisis. I invite you to send me your thoughts.

Yours sincerely,
Nancy Brownell

I was waiting for Clara in the school parking lot when she emerged at 4:30 that afternoon.

We went to a restaurant near her school. In a booth there, she read Nancy Brownell's letter, slowly. She put down the last page and stared deep into my eyes.

"Henry, I'm so sorry. For you, for her, for all of them. They must all feel so...powerless."

"And betrayed," I added.

"And betrayed, yes."

"I want to do something. I have to do something."

"What can you do?"

"I...I...don't know. Something."

"You're not an employee, not a state politician, not an attorney. You couldn't do anything when you were there, what can you possibly do now? You're a thousand miles away. You have your life, here, now."

"I know, but...I'm not *no one*. I'm not like what the powers-that-be think of the patients there, as three thousand no-ones! But they are not no-ones, and neither am I."

She took my hand in hers. "I understand, and I think you'll know what to do when the time comes," she said. "But maybe now is not quite the time."

I didn't know if she was right or not—about *now* not being the time. But at the very least, I had to write back to Nurse Brownell. All I could do was express my own outrage and empathy. Which wasn't enough, to be sure, but it was all I *could* do.

I plan, I wrote, *to send a letter to Superintendent DeWitt, and make an appeal for humane decisions to be made on behalf of the hos-*

pital patients, and argue against decisions that run counter to their well-being.

Which is exactly what I did, for what it was worth.

Dear Superintendent DeWitt:

We have not met. Before you became Superintendent, I had just completed a university field experience at the hospital, from September 1952 to August 1953. I am soon to complete my Master of Science in Psychology at the University of Pennsylvania, where I plan to go on for the Ph.D. with a specialty in Patient Care.

My field experience at the Traverse City State Hospital proved to me that the quality of patient care for those who suffer from mental illness is directly proportional to the respect and dignity they experience on a daily basis. That is the subject of my thesis, and I fully expect to continue that project into the dissertation and then publish it as a book. When that happens, the Traverse City State Hospital could be recognized as a model for distinctive and progressive patient care. I hope to recognize you personally for preserving the philosophical and therapeutic integrity of the Traverse City State Hospital.

I am aware of the recent report issued by the Study Commission of Michigan State Hospitals and the recommendations they have made. If those recommendations are implemented, the extraordinary mental health care provided through the successful agricultural and work programs will be eliminated. Further, if mechanization of farm operations is mandated, then further erosion of patients' ability to find meaning and fulfillment through farm work will be utterly destroyed.

The combination of these two recommendations alone will overturn more than a half-century of progress made by your predecessors, and it will threaten the economic stability of the institution, which, as I understand, is a hospital that has demonstrated its financial success through the very programs the state plans to eliminate. It simply makes no sense — not through the lens of humane patient care, nor through the lens of fiscal responsibility — to destroy a model mental health program that is entirely self-sustaining.

I implore you to resist these recommended changes. I implore you to consider the real — and proven — benefits that accrue to the "work is therapy" philosophy that has informed this hospital ethic for decades. These are real people whose very lives depend on meaningful work and human dignity. I implore you to do the right thing.

Sincerely yours,
Henry Mershartt
The University of Pennsylvania

I had no real credentials that would garner his attention (no M.S. or Ph. D. after my name; no impressive title), so I borrowed some Psychology Department letterhead to make it seem more authoritative. I typed it up and mailed it the next morning.

Appealing to Dr. DeWitt's sense of moral justice and his own potential spot in the hospital's historical legacy ("I hope to recognize you personally," I had written), would, I hoped, make a difference. Nurse Brownell's misgivings to the contrary, I wanted to trust that his moral compass would point in the right direction. At my distance and without any real clout, it was my best effort.

His response came 10 days later.

Dear Mr. Mershartt:

Thank you for your letter of January 10, 1954. It is noted.

It is not my intent to comment on the particulars of your letter. You are entitled to your opinions. But know that I am in complete agreement with the recommendations made by the Study Commission of Michigan State Hospitals.

Sincerely,
Dr. M. DeWitt
Superintendent

Clara and I were sitting in a café sipping iced tea and picking at French fries. It was late afternoon, school over for the day. I had showed her the letter I wrote to Superintendent DeWitt. She read it and then slid the letter across the table toward me.

"Sounds just right," she said. "Logical. Compassionate."

"That's what I thought."

I passed the second letter over to her.

"Here's his response."

She read it quickly and then put it face down in front of her.

"My goodness," she said.

"What are you thinking?"

"I want to hear what you think first."

"Okay," I said. "I think he's an incorrigible puppet for the governor, the commission, the legislators who are behind this dismantling, and the local people who put all of them up to it. This is all about money, all about who can exert the most power to protect their greedy interests. No one really cares about who gets hurt as long as the vested interests get what they want. As Dr. Spencer said so well, 'these patients here, they are just abstractions to those on the outside.'"

She nodded. "I understand," she said. "You want to blame those vested interests and the new superintendent and the commission?"

"Not just them," I said, "but also the staff there for being so...passive. They just pretended nothing was wrong, that the threats would go away somehow."

Clara gave me *that look*.

"All right," I said, "I know what you're going to say: human motivation is too complicated to generalize, especially about an entire hospital staff of diverse people. I see that now. I think some put blind trust in tradition—'It has always been this way and it will *always* be this way, so why worry?' they probably said. Others probably said, 'What can *we* do? We're powerless, and besides, we can't afford to jeopardize our jobs.'

"And," I added, "there were—are—others who just don't care. A job is a job."

"That sounds like *my* world," she said, "to be honest. It sounds like the faculty at my school. Administrations come and go, they sweep in with changes and new policies, and, before long, they're gone. And all the while, it's the teachers who remain, doing our job in spite of administrators' grand ideas as well as the real changes they implement. From what you've told me, the hospital staff spent long hours every day caring for so many patients, and then, in addition, they had their private lives—children, spouses, extended families, *life*! There are just so many hours in the day, Henry. Besides, they had no experience with public relations and political influence."

"That was Dr. Spencer's job and he failed at it," I said.

"I just don't think it's fair to blame," she said. "From what you've said, it seems he just found himself out of his element, too late."

I repeated what I once told her—that I thought the staff should organize; they should take mass action the way labor unions do.

"Well," she said, "It's one thing to say a group should organize, it's another to say they know *how*, or they have the time, or they have the leadership. From what you've described, they didn't have any of that. From what you wrote, most staff knew something was amiss but went about their busy lives. They had their jobs to do, just as teachers are responsible for classrooms full of students, preparation, grading, meetings, *and* our personal lives. Their patients were their priorities, but the political process unfolded, and it left them behind."

"Dammit, Clara. It's just not fair!"

I swung my arm across the table, and my now-empty iced-tea glass shot across the aisle and shattered under an empty table. A few remaining French fries spilled to the floor. People at other tables and booths stretched and looked our way to see what the commotion was all about. A burly waitress hurried over with broom and dustpan and swept up the mess. She glanced my way as if to say are you okay?

"Sorry," I said, loud enough for the onlookers to hear. I was angry and I felt defeated.

"I couldn't even do anything about that sonofabitch Daryl."

Clara put her hand on mine, calming, reassuring.

"No, Sweetie, it's not fair at all, but it's how things go some-times. You asked me what I think? I think this thing is bigger than you, or at least who you are *right now*. Maybe someday you'll be in a different spot, maybe you'll be the one behind *posi-tive* change. I'm sorry you feel so helpless. But you couldn't fight the system when you were at Harrisville, you couldn't fight it when you were at Traverse City—and you can't fight it now. Now is the time for you to put the hospital behind you and focus on *your* future."

We paused, quiet for a few moments as her last words hung in the air.

"Of course, you're right," I said. "But I just can't get Jimmy off my mind."

"I know," she said, "I worry about your friend Jimmy, too. What will happen to him?"

I would soon find out.

The letter from Jimmy arrived January 25.

Dear Mr. Henry,

Mrs. Dorman is writing for me again. She is my friend. I am fine for now and still doing my job. With Mr. Harrison. His foot is ok now. And the daytime is starting to get warmer. But I won't be fine pretty soon.

Mr. Henry, we are not going to be able to work anymore here because they changed the rules. Some people came and said we can't do no more work and that's that. They are going to have tractors now and more trucks but I ain't going to be on maintenance with Mr. Harrison no more cause of the new rules.

I am very sad now.

Bernadine can't do no more work too. She has been very sad anyway with no fieldwork since winter came and now she can't even do any more when the snow goes. She cries all the time now and just sits and stares. She took down her bird feeders by her cottage and threw them in the trash. She won't talk much with me either. She says she is going to soar like a swallow so don't worry about me she says so maybe she will get better pretty soon.

Well I am going to go now and help the fellows with the snow that is so high from last night. Goodbye.

Your friend,
JIMMY QUINN

P. S. This is Mrs. Dorman now. Mr. Dziewa my boss is gone on sick leave for god knows how long this time. So I am in charge of the office. I'm telling you this in case you need any more of your research information or whatever. I got A's in grammar in high school. Can you tell? Jimmy is not so good and Bernadine is no good at all. I am sorry.

CHAPTER THIRTY-ONE

Soar Like a Swallow

JIMMY'S LETTER BROKE MY HEART, BUT THE LATE FEBRUARY
phone call from Sheriff Nederhousen broke my slim hope that a
conspiracy against the hospital would be revealed. He was terse,
as usual, in saying that the investigation into the vandalism and
animal slaughter at the hospital, as well as the attack at the market the previous summer, was closed. His office had questioned
ten people who had written damning letters to the newspaper
but "to no avail"; it had never gotten anywhere in the search for
the blue Plymouth from the market attack; and, although he,
too, believed there likely was some sort of conspiracy against
the hospital, he could not come up with any verifiable evidence.

"Without evidence," he said, "the district attorney's hands are
tied."

I recalled what Mr. Remington said that day at the newspaper office — "Do you have any actual *proof*?" The conspiracy
theory would remain just that — a theory.

He also said he believed that whoever may have been behind
the local violence had gained the ear of more powerful people
in the capitol because, as he understood it, the farming program
was going to end by order of the government. Since the threats
to and violence at the hospital had been dried up since fall, he

figured that someone, somewhere, knew bigger things were in the works. Therefore, there was no longer any reason to pose threats, etcetera.

"Because the bastards got what they wanted," he said. "And there's not a damned thing I can do."

I thanked him for all he *was* able to do.

I just wanted you to know," he said, "I'm sorry if I let you down."

I carried grief around with me like a heavy load of rocks but there was nothing I could do — once again. With Clara's help, I had convinced myself that I had to get on with my life and let events run their inevitable course at the hospital in northern Michigan.

And so, in spite of its sad beginning, early spring became a very good time in my life. Professor Hilliger approved the al-most-final draft of my thesis. By mid-May, I just had a couple more weeks' work on the footnotes and bibliography. I would be finished by June. The Psychology Department had accepted me into its Ph. D. program for the fall and awarded me a stipend to be a research assistant to Professor Hilliger.

Best of all, Clara and I became engaged, no date set. Her parents immediately invited us to come for a celebratory din-ner, so we drove over to Tom's River to their lovely home on Barnegat Bay one Saturday and stayed overnight — separate rooms, of course. They invited neighbors who knew Clara since she was a child and her dad kept giving toasts until her mother cut off his water before he got too drunk. At one point, he pulled me aside to say he had worried if she would *ever* get married, she was so headstrong and particular, always had been, he said, a slight slur developing.

Back in Chestnut Hill, Mother was ecstatic; so was Dad. They really loved Clara and, most important, they admired her for those very character traits—her authenticity and candor—that I loved, too. Dad cooked a big congratulations barbeque for the two of us the weekend following our trip to Tom's River.

He had spare ribs and hamburgers ready to go on the grill, while Mother prepared potato salad, roasted green beans, home-made rolls, and, eventually, apple pie with ice cream. Dad would serve very good champagne to top off the evening with a big toast, while Mother planned a little speech about welcoming their beautiful daughter-in-law-to-be into the family.

Uncle Tony and Aunt Pat joined the party, too. Cousin Ethel showed up late; she came from her library job—on the streetcar, on her own, two transfers. She looked terrific—lipstick applied just right; curls and waves in her hair that had a silky sheen to it; and a lovely black chiffon party dress she must have changed into at the library. She went straight to Clara and held both of her hands between the two of them; Ethel smiled unpretentiously, as if she were the honor student showing off to her teacher.

"Look at you!" Clara exclaimed. "Beautiful!"

Ethel stepped in front of me. She gave me an awkward bear hug that pushed her nubile breasts uncomfortably up against me. I felt her fingers dig into my shoulder blades. Her hug lingered until it exceeded the standard two-second hugging rule. Was this the same Ethel who recoiled like a haphephobic when I patted her on the back at Christmas dinner?

I eased myself out of Ethel's grasp with a polite, "Nice to see you, Ethel," and she made her way to greet Mother and Dad over by the kitchen counter.

I whispered to Clara, "It's time you gave your student a few lessons on boundaries and cousin hugging."

"I wonder what she's been reading in the library?" Clara said.

"She takes the streetcar and the bus everywhere now," announced Uncle Tony. "I gave her strict lessons on not talking with men at the stops or on the ride," he said, using the worst anxious father voice one could imagine.

"And guess how she responded to that advice?" he continued. "She looked past me and said, 'Lisbon is the capital of Portugal and has a population of over 150,000.'"

"What's a father to do?" he muttered as he walked over to take the beer Dad had extended toward him. Dad put a sympathetic arm around Uncle Tony and dragged him out to tend the barbeque grill in the yard.

"Oh, Henry, your Uncle Tony worries too much," Aunt Pat said. "Ethel is doing just fine. Did you know she has a young man calling her on the phone, someone she met at the library? He's very polite. He talks and she listens for the most part, but the call only lasts a few minutes and she seems giddy afterward."

Clara and I did a sort of Lucy-Desi double take. Aunt Pat noticed my astonishment.

"I know. Don't tell your uncle," she whispered. "He'll go through the roof. He just needs time to adjust to her ... newness."

Then she leaned toward Clara's ear and confided, "I can't thank you enough, dear, for helping my daughter learn to become a woman."

Clara and I exchanged glances. She winked; I raised my eyebrows.

My parents kept my room just the way I had left it years ago — baseball trophies on the bookshelf, Penn flag draped behind the door, and my favorite childhood books lined up like soldiers in a tall bookcase. Time seemed suspended in that room. As if earlier versions of me lingered. I noticed the way Mother doted over children she tutors at the library, especially girls, and the way Dad still liked to go out in the street to toss the football with neighborhood boys. You could tell. Why was I their only child? I always thought they wanted a larger family, but I figured there were medical reasons. They never talked about it, but the way they kept that room in a time warp, I thought that said something about unfulfilled dreams.

The turmoil continued at the hospital in Michigan. Since early spring, letters from Nancy Brownell kept me abreast of how much worse things were becoming. Following Clara's advice, I continued to try to put the hospital and its troubles behind me in order to focus on my future, not the hospital's past. But Nurse Brownell's reports about the hospital's present and future gnawed at me.

Nurse Brownell wrote to say that the committee recommendations had been implemented as predicted on the first of April. More people from the region were being hired as civil service employees to take over jobs done previously by patients. With more paid employees and no income from the farm, the hospital was forced to rely solely on the state for operating costs. And, like every other state hospital, that dependency meant that resources for patient care would be controlled by distant bureaucrats.

It was the ignominious end of a glorious era.

I recalled Jimmy whooping and hollering as he rode in the back of the maintenance truck. But no longer. And no longer squirting lubricant on rusty hinges, painting railings on the buildings, or changing the oil in Mr. Harrison's pickups.

The farm operations were closed down completely, she wrote. There was talk of selling the dairy herd and the pigs. New employees tended the animals for the time being. Modern milking machines billed as having "gentle massaging actions" took over for the gentle, knowing hands of patients.

Nancy wrote with moving elegance: "Where patients used to spend hours in the barns milking and grooming the dairy cows, they now stand at the fences watching strangers do the work, their faces strained with longing and confusion. Those who just last year tilled and enriched the soil with compost and those who had spring crops ready for market by May now sit in sullen silence on porches. Some roam empty fields with makeshift tools made of tree branches—hoeing imaginary rows, raking soil, and pulling weeds. The trucks that used to be filled to the roof with bushel baskets of produce and bound for market by early morning now sit idle behind the garages."

Reading the letters was unbearable. My heart ached every time. I tried to respond—barely—with weak condolences and attempts to be hopeful. *Things will improve*, I wrote, once *they see the way these decisions have affected the patients.*

But I *knew.*

It was the May 22 letter from Jimmy—that was the one that tipped the scales for me. I found it in my mailbox early in the evening. I walked down my street to a little neighborhood park and sat on the kids' swing. Rain threatened. The darkness would come early that night as a storm front pressed across the city. As I read, I pushed myself back and forth with one foot.

Dear Mr. Henry,
  I came to see Mrs. Dorman tonight because I need to tell

you that something awful happened and you are going to be real sad and sorry just like I am and Mrs. Dorman and other people too. Especially me.

Do you remember Bernadine saying she was going to soar like a swallow? She said it a lot lately when the work stopped and she got so sad all the time. I am crying now because when I tell you this it hurts so much for me. My heart will bust and flood all over. Mrs. Dorman is helping me with the words. She is having trouble with her words too.

Yesterday morning they found Bernadine with a rope tied round her neck and she was hanging from the railing on the big water tower behind the warehouse. They said she must of climbed up there in the night and tied it round her neck and then jumped off. The rope came from the warehouse shed back there. They took her down and she was dead. They said her neck was broke. They will have a service for her tomorrow.

Now my heart is broken in a hundred pieces. She is my best friend. You are my best friend too but you are gone and she stayed. I am sweet on her and I will be for all time.

You remember that patient who thinks he is God, Mr. Henry? Sometimes he acts nuts. Well, God says she is in heaven now and the angels Michael and Gabriel and Clarence will look after her. God will give a speech for her at the service and everyone will bring flowers and then they will take her over to Eighth Street in the town at the cemetery. We won't be able to go over there tomorrow cause we are too many, but sometimes we can visit and bring her more flowers. I will sneak over there anyway when I want to. I will bring her bird feathers that I found under the trees here be-

cause she loves birds. I started looking for feathers today and I found red ones and black ones.

Bernadine made me laugh all the time. She did jokes on me and everyone, but not so much when she got sad. I never heard her say bad words. She says Holy Cow a lot but that's not a cuss word because there ain't no Saint Cow. God says she will be Saint Bernadine in heaven.

Mrs. Dorman has to go home now and that's all there is to say. I am so sorry I never got a picture of Bernadine like you got a picture of Clara. I wish you was here to help me. People try to help me, but I just want to be with Bernadine. I just want to be with Bernadine.

Your friend,
JIMMY QUINN

I stopped swinging. Lightning a few miles away, then the rumble of thunder. A young woman pushing a baby buggy rushed by. Two dogs chased one another in the empty street. A raindrop struck the letter I held in my hands.

Two voices in my brain collided.

Bernadine's death was a tragedy, "but not uncommon," the clinical voice said. She was manic-depressive. Circumstances drive severely depressed people to do things like this. It was a familiar and not unexpected part of the condition.

But Bernadine was more than a clinical "case." Her simple joys had been denied her. All she really needed was to get her hands in the earth and her fingers on the crops. She needed to believe she was a significant part of something bigger than herself. But now that she no longer felt significant, what was the point of living? Suicide meant she could become *part of* the earth. In that light, I figured, Bernadine's solution made sense to her.

For Bernadine—and for so many others there—women in flowery dresses fostering tiny seedlings, sun-burned patients with calloused hands cultivating the fields, men in bib overalls milking cows and feeding pigs, men and women on ladders picking apples, Jimmy fixing leaky faucets. For them, it wasn't "work," the way it is on the outside. For them, "work" was their grace, their personal antidote for what life had given them. Any "normal" person could, at any moment, be forced to bear the same burden.

I wondered how things would be different were the governor of Michigan to have his wife or his child committed to the Traverse City State Hospital. What would *their* antidote become? Would it be painting? Music? Dancing? Sewing? Building maintenance? Bread baking?

Would *they* sit idly by while *their* relatives sat and stared the whole day long? Hardly. That wife or that child would no longer be an abstraction, not to *that* governor.

I remembered what Jimmy's grandmother told him: "All God's critters got a place in the choir." *All* God's critters, not just *some*.

Then it hit me—*I just want to be with Bernadine*, he said. Jimmy was contemplating Bernadine's solution. And now, with no work to fill his days, he would have plenty of time to mourn, plenty of time to plan how he could be with Bernadine.

I would not again write impassioned letters to indifferent administrators the likes of DeWitt. Write and talk, that's what academics do.

This time, I *had* to act and it had to make a difference. Things back there were moving too fast.

What *would* I do? I had no idea. Only that I would *not* do *nothing*.

Minima maxima sunt. Who is silent gives consent.

CHAPTER THIRTY-TWO

Rounds

I DECIDED TO KIDNAP JIMMY. SOMEHOW.

What could I tell Clara, or my folks? That I planned to sneak Jimmy out in the dead of night? That we would be hundreds of miles away before he was missed?

Then what?

I knew it wasn't much of a plan. It was vague and it was rash. It was illegal and it would get me arrested. If I got caught. And, it was stupid as hell. Should I risk everything on a stupid plan like that? Brother Benedict used to say, when it comes to social justice, only *you* can decide the *shoulds*. *Stultus in inferno, aut non.* Stupid as hell, or not.

No. I would appeal to the court for adoption. I would bring him home with me. No crime involved. But how long would that process take? Likely months. And would they even approve me, a 26-year old single male?

Just to be sure, I called the Probate Court in Traverse City and got a very friendly clerk to answer my hypothetical question: could a single 26-year old male adopt a 30-year old mentally retarded male if that male had no living relatives? She could not speak for the judge, but in her 18 years as clerk, she had never seen any judge approve an adoption by an *unmarried* person, male or female. This hypothetical person would be the first. The judge would likely place the 30-year old in an institution.

I didn't even bother to add that this hypothetical person didn't have a job with an income that would support two people. And I made sure not to say Jimmy was already institutionalized.

I didn't have the time to become a pioneer for adoption rights. I didn't know how long Jimmy could remain in that environment and be safe from harming himself.

Jimmy's clock was ticking.

I stopped by the law library. I knew a third-year law student who worked there. He had a specialty in criminal law. We sat in a seminar room in the library and talked. I told him I was thinking of writing a novel and needed some legal information. I described various hypothetical situations to him and he told me how the criminal justice system would view them.

"So," I said at one point, "if Mr. X does that with *intent*, then it's still a crime but not to the degree if he had just done it spontaneously?"

"Right," he said. "If he *planned* to do it, it's premeditated. The official term is 'malice aforethought.' Typically, the difference between first-degree murder and second degree is malice aforethought. But the principle applies to other felonies too, like robbery, or, as you mentioned, kidnapping."

I left the library discouraged but no less determined.

I arrived at Clara's school just as the dismissal bell rang. Students started pouring out of the building. I went around to the side door and up the wide stairwell to her classroom on the second floor. She was bent over her desk, marking papers when I entered.

"Henry? What a surprise!"

I came around to her side of the desk and we hugged. When we pulled apart, I said, "I need your sound advice."

I pulled up a chair and sat across from her. She saw the troubled look on my face.

"Something's wrong. What's happened?"

I told her the news from Traverse City and my plan to drive there and get Jimmy.

She sat back in her teacher's swivel chair, folded her arms. I had seen her look of disbelief before. I steeled myself.

"What are you saying, Henry? Just *what* are you saying? You think you can just go back there and steal a patient? And not get caught?"

"I don't know. Maybe I won't get caught."

"*Maybe* you won't?" she exclaimed. "*Maybe*? What, you'll write me from a cell somewhere—*Hi Clara, I can't wait to see you in a few years!* Are you thinking at all? Are you even thinking about *us*? We're getting married, remember?"

"Clara, Honey, listen. I didn't say I was going to steal him. I said I wasn't sure what I would do once I get there; I only know I have to get him out of there. Now. Before he hurts himself."

"Oh great. So you have no plan at all?"

"Not yet. But I will. It's just that, Jimmy means so much to me. I can't explain it but I love that man—like the brother I never had, I suppose."

She looked over at the wall of windows. Thinking. I never liked it when she stared in silence and didn't look at me. I waited, hoping her resistance might weaken.

"Even if you *were* to succeed," she said, "what does your friend Jimmy do once you two are back here? *Can* he even live on his own? How will he get a job? Who will support him?"

She was now *considering* the stupid plan. Consideration was progress.

Then she became sarcastic: "Or will he move in with us once we're married? Become our adult child. Is that your plan for *our* future?"

She was right on all points, of course. I was not being pragmatic. I knew that, but it didn't matter. What mattered was saving Jimmy.

Funny, I was proud that I *wasn't* being pragmatic—that I wasn't acting solely from my head. True, I didn't know exactly *what* I would do, but I did know I would be doing something *right*, and that was what mattered. I would save Jimmy from a life that he likely would not survive, given his history of loss. To paraphrase Professor Hilliger, it *was* humanistic theory in practice. In the moment, it didn't matter that it was illegal. To me, it was simply imperative. I feared that if I *did* think about it too much, I would talk myself out of taking *any* action.

I could not let that happen.

She stared down at her engagement ring on her left hand. With her right hand, she rolled it around between finger and thumb.

She just stared at me, silent. Thinking. The look.

"Clara," I said. "I love you so much. But this is one of those times that ..."

She pulled the ring off and put it on the desk. Tears streamed down her face. She stared at the ring between us.

" ...is going to test our love and our commitment to what we truly believe in," I said. "I don't know what *your* moment of decision will be or when it will come, but I promise you that I won't stand in *your* way when *your* time comes for acting on principle. No matter how much I may disagree with you. I love you more than that."

She stood and came around to my side of the desk. I stood up. She put her arms around me and I held her tight. We stood there for a long while in silence.

I whispered, "I'm asking you to trust my heart."

She sighed. I waited. She whispered, "I'm so scared. I'm-just-so-scared for you."

We held each other tight.

Minutes later, when we descended the school stairs to the parking lot, the ring was back on her finger.

Clara went with me to see Mother and Dad. She made it clear that she would be a reluctant supporter, at best. But I thought her being there would help. She wouldn't take sides. I didn't need their permission, but I couldn't just leave without them knowing what I was about to do. In the back of my mind, I also needed their blessing, just as I needed Clara's.

Then there was the little practical matter of my needing their car.

Clara parked on the street in front of my parents' home. Dad peeked out through the kitchen window curtain. Mother came out on the porch, dishtowel in hand. She waved. We followed her inside.

Dad was seated at the kitchen table. They had been enjoying tea and their regular late afternoon cribbage game—wooden board with pegs and cards spread out before them. He stood up and shook my hand briefly, then hugged Clara and gave her a huge kiss on the cheek. We all sat at the table as Mother poured tea for Clara and me.

I said I had something very important to discuss. I made

them promise to say nothing until I finished. Mother had this worried look; Dad turned over his spoon and started shining it with a napkin.

I talked in more detail than I ever had—about the relationships I had formed in Michigan; Dr. Spencer and Nancy Brownell; Jimmy, and who he had become for me; Mr. Meyer and the editor and the sheriff; Bernadine. I told them about the dead chicks, the murdered cow, the market attack, and my behind-the-scene efforts to affect local politics. I showed them the letter from Jimmy, and I shared my certain fear that he would "find a way to join Bernadine." I couldn't let that happen.

Then I said I was going there to get Jimmy and bring him back to Philadelphia before he killed himself.

"A strict interpretation of the law would see this as adult kidnapping," I said. "But a judge might see the whole scenario as a moral justification for saving a man's life. Some circumstances in life justify rash actions. This would be one of those circumstances."

Mother kept looking to Dad, muttering a frequent, "Oh dear." Dad kept at the spoon project.

I stopped.

Mother spoke first.

"Oh, Honey. This is so unlike you." She looked to Dad for more words.

I knew what he would say.

"Why don't you just let it be?" he said. "Why take a chance like this? Stay here, finish your degree, marry Clara. Don't screw everything up."

It took another thirty minutes. Clara sat close to me, her hand on mine. I told them about my call to Probate Court and why I couldn't expect that avenue to amount to anything. I emphasized that time was running out.

I reminded them about the principles of justice that the Jesuits taught me in the education they themselves had provided for me. I didn't need their approval; I needed their moral support. If I did get in a jam, I needed to know that they believed I had done the right thing.

Maybe it was Dad's own education in a Jesuit school. Or maybe, seeing my stubborn determination, he imagined what *he* would do in similar circumstances.

He lay the spoon down at last and parked it next to the cribbage board. He looked at Clara, at Mother, and then me.

"You should take the Packard," he said. "George just tuned it and put on new tires. It's ready for a road trip."

Mother had tears in her eyes. She wiped them with the edge of her apron. She was not one to disagree with Dad. Clara squeezed my hand.

"I'll pray for you, night and day," Mother said. "Just…be careful. Please, be careful."

Mother got up and went to the pantry. She pulled out a ceramic jar and returned with it to the table. It was full of quarters.

"Take this. It's my cribbage winnings from your father. A quarter a game adds up over time. You'll need it for long-distance calls."

Then Dad left the room. I heard him opening drawers in the den. When he came back, he handed me an envelope.

"Two hundred dollars," he said. "You'll need cash."

"Dad, I have savings."

"Whatever you've managed to scrape together, it won't be enough. Take this. We'll wire you more if you need it. We'll come *there* if you need us to. You know we will."

"I do."

"You can do work around the house to pay it back. Take care of the yard work and house repairs we need done around here. I'm getting too old to do all this myself. Someone has to take over."

We all stood. Mother hugged me and kissed my forehead. Then she went to Clara and hugged her. Dad shook my hand and then put his arms around me.

"Son," he said, "we will be here when you get back and we will do our part, don't you worry."

I didn't ask what he meant by *our part*. I don't think he knew. It was his way of saying family sticks together, regardless.

CHAPTER THIRTY-THREE

Convictions

I WAS ON THE ROAD LATE MORNING THE NEXT DAY. THE PACK-ard hummed along through sleepy Pennsylvania towns as I headed west toward Ohio.

Late in the day, when I crossed the Ohio line west of Pittsburgh, Dad's words came back to me: *I'm getting too old to do all this myself. Someone has to take over.*

We will do our part, he said.

That's when it came to me what their part could be.

What they need is a handyman. Someone who can maintain the property, someone who can fix things! Maybe even someone *who can fill that empty space in my old room.*

The real plan began to take shape.

I stopped for the night at the Sir Lancelot Motel in Norwalk, Ohio. I got out Mother's bag of quarters to make calls from the phone booth in the parking lot.

First call was to my parents. To protect them, they could not know how I would get Jimmy released — *if* I could — only that I had found a way to make that happen. When it was all over, when Jimmy was safely in Philadelphia (assuming all went as planned), only then I would explain everything — after the fact. I — we — would have to make up some story that accounted for how Jimmy came to be living with us. People would want to know.

On the phone, I helped them recall what Dad had said about how he needed help to keep up with all the yard work and house repairs.

"*'We will do our part'* were Dad's exact words," I said. "So now I'm asking you if you'll do that part. Now that I know what that part will be."

"We have the receiver here between our ears," Mother said, "so we can both hear you. Go on, Honey."

Then I asked the questions I had jotted down in my diary.

Would they be willing to accommodate Jimmy in my old room in exchange for him doing all the odd jobs around the house and yard that Dad needed to have done? Or that Mother needed doing so she could spend more time at the library or with bridge club, and so forth? *Yes, to all of this if it would help me solve my problem safely,* he said. Mother agreed.

Could Jimmy stay with them until he is independent enough to get his own apartment? *If I think Jimmy would be a good houseguest, then of course,* Mother said.

Could they imagine Jimmy starting his own neighborhood handyman business if I managed it for him and if Mother and Dad served as references to get him started?

"If he's as honest and hard-working as you say he is," Dad said, "then I suspect he can start a pretty good small business right here in Chestnut Hill. People always need something re-paired or maintained, and no one's getting any younger."

Mother's last words stuck with me: "You know, Honey, we never had any other children than you, and now we realize how empty the house is when there is just the two of us. Maybe your friend Jimmy, well, let's just say we will treat him as if he were our own."

Lucror–Lucror. Win-Win.

Then I called Clara. I gave her the big picture and said I would be contacting people at the hospital who would help with the details. On a slip of the tongue, the word "illegal" escaped, so I tried to balance that by saying a compassionate judge might see the ethical imperative in it all. That didn't work.

"Well, Mr. Idealist," she said, "good luck with that. What was it Aldous Huxley said? You pays your money, you takes your chances."

She was still opposed, not to the *intent* of the Save-Jimmy Mission but to me being the savior.

"No one will ever know I told you," I said. "As far as you know, I must have lied to you about how I got Jimmy released."

"I'll make that decision when and if the time comes," she said. Her voice was clear, her intention direct; she chose her words carefully.

Then, "If you manage to make this work," she said, "I will be with you one hundred per cent. If you don't make it work, I'm still one hundred per cent. I love you."

"I love you too, so much."

Next I called the Office of Admissions and Records at the State Hospital. It was after hours. I didn't really expect Mrs. Dorman to still be in, but she picked up on the third ring. My heart raced. I knew she would make things complicated, and I really didn't know if I could count on her. But it was my only option.

"Well, if it ain't my favorite ray of sunshine! You calling me up for a date finally, after all these years? Mr. Dorman ain't gonna like that."

"No, Mrs. Dorman … I'm calling because … " I explained that I had a serious matter to discuss with her and I needed to be sure it would remain private.

"Don't you worry. The girls are gone for the day. And me? Why, right now I'm sitting here in the boss's chair, at the boss's desk, talking on the boss's personal phone. You want to know why? 'Cause the boss is taking a paid medical leave and that leaves me in charge. What with all the cutbacks coming, they got no extra money to replace him since they're paying him for *not* being here. Besides, this is all clerical work, says Mr. Dim Witt the new super, and any simple-minded person can do that. That's exactly what he said, not to me, but to some ladies over in his plush office. So, this here simple-minded clerk is running the show."

Now this is a lucky stroke, I thought.

I laid it all out for her. I would impersonate a long-lost relative of Jimmy's who's come to take him home. "An uncle, " I said.

"Cousin," she said. "Second cousin, twice removed. From out of state. I'll figure that one out — I like the sound of this. Go on, gumshoe."

I explained that I needed her to prepare paperwork for Jimmy's release, then actually get him released and have all this arranged so I could get him out under cover of darkness.

"It must appear to be legitimate," I stressed. "People have to believe he's going to live with family. He has to be officially released. Can you arrange that?"

"Sugar pie, I am *the* place where *the* Admissions and Records buck stops. No one gets in or out of this place without yours truly arranging the paperwork, at least until you-know-who gets back and that ain't going to happen very soon, not when he's on paid leave to fish or snooze — whatever he does with his precious time."

"Good," I said. "But you must understand the risks. What I'm proposing is unlawful. Maybe not in your eyes, certainly not in mine, but in the eyes of police and the public, and especially in the eyes of your superintendent, we would be breaking the law."

She was silent on her end for longer than I felt comfortable.

Then, in a gush, "I love it! I ain't had so much excitement since Mr. Dorman got pissin' drunk and backed his truck straight through the garage and out the other end into Mrs. Randolph's tomato patch. Then he puked all over her squash and ..."

"Mrs. Dorman! You do understand the risks, don't you?"

"Risks smisks. I'm sixty-five years old and at the peak of my career here in Mr. Dziewa's throne. What can anyone possibly do to an old fart like me anyway? Send me to prison for helping some poor soul help another poor soul? Besides, I like a caper. Like that one in *The Big Clock*. You see that movie? Charles Laughton and Maureen O'Hara ..."

I interrupted. "And I need you to do something else, please."

"Let's whisper, just for effect," she said, her voice barely audible.

"I need you to talk with a couple of people there, people who only need to believe certain things about Jimmy's release. I haven't gotten that far in the planning. I know some people will have to be told *something*. I'll call you about that when I get into Traverse City."

"I know everyone and everyone knows me. Whatever you need, consider it done."

Then a long silence followed as we both caught our breath.

"Just one question," she said. "What about…" and her voice went to a whisper again. "What about, you know, him. I ain't gonna say his name out loud. But what about *him*. He's gotta know what's going on. I mean, *after all.*"

"I'll take care of that," I said. "That's *my* job. Your job is to prepare the paperwork and talk with others. I'll call you when I arrive and we'll go from there."

"Well, I only got one thing to say."

"What's that?"

"When the cat's away, the mice will play!"

Next, I dug Nancy Brownell's home number out of my wallet and put in *that* call. I didn't recognize the voice of the woman who answered the phone, but when I said my name, she held the receiver away and repeated it. Nancy was on the receiver in seconds.

After pleasantries, I got to the point. I told her, in general, what I intended to do and why.

"Are you certain, Henry?" was all she said, at first.

"I am."

"Then why are you telling me?"

"I'm telling you because you are my friend and, for some time, through letters, my confidante. As much as I have been your confidante. I won't share with you the details of how this is going to happen because the less you know, the better for you should something go wrong. As far as you know, I'm just upset over Bernadine's death and talking wildly. You can dismiss this call as the emotional rant of someone in great distress. Nothing more than that."

"I understand what you're suggesting, Henry. And though I appreciate your effort to keep me safe through feigned ignorance, know that I will act in a manner consistent with my own personal convictions. Should it come to that."

I wasn't exactly sure what she meant by the vagueness of those last two sentences, though her tone was determined and confident. In her characteristic way, once again, she was elusive and guarded. Still, I was relieved that I had shared the plan—what little I did share—with her. It was the right thing to do.

"God be with you," she said before we hung up.

CHAPTER THIRTY-FOUR

The Genie's Spirit

I PULLED INTO TRAVERSE CITY JUST AS THE SUN SPREAD PINK and purple hues above the hills to the west.

I got a room at the Whiting Hotel in town and then drove over to the hospital grounds. Lights were on in most of the cottages as patients settled in for the night or attendants assisted them into bed. A few people hurried on the sidewalks — attendants and staff, I figured. The place was quieting down for the night.

I drove toward Jimmy's cottage and parked a hundred yards or so away but with a good view of the wide front porch. It was empty. A few lights illuminated rooms inside. I turned off the engine and sat there a few minutes, staring up at the cottage while lights inside went off slowly, one after the other.

I was startled when a man appeared suddenly at the side of the car. His face peered in the driver's-side window as he knocked on the glass. He was not dressed in attendant whites, but rather in a grey long-sleeved shirt and green trousers. He was a patient.

"Mister, it's bedtime. You better get to your cottage and check in, or else." He pulled a round watch from his pants pocket and showed me the face.

"See here. It's ...lemme see myself."

He held the watch up to the light of a streetlamp. "It's past ten. Too late to be out. You better get in or you're going to lose your privilege. I can be out because I'm the night watchman."

With that, he disappeared behind me somewhere into the darkness. *A wanderer,* I thought. *Attendants will be out looking for him very soon. He'll lose his ground parole privilege.*

The last light upstairs in Jimmy's cottage went out. I drove back to the hotel for a second night's sleep.

In the morning, I called Nancy Brownell.

Would she meet with me somewhere off the hospital grounds? I needed to talk to her in person. Yes, in an hour, at Robert's Roundup—homemade muffins and bottomless coffee cups, on the east side of town.

I was sipping coffee at a table in the back of the place as she entered. A broad smile broke across her face when she spotted me. I waved. She looked the same as always—auburn hair perfectly in place, clothing freshly pressed, an erect stride that signaled restraint and confidence. I stood when she came over. We shook hands.

"You look tired," she said. "That is a long trip for one driver."

"Oh, I took a room along the way, and one in town here last night. Hard to sleep, though, you know."

"I know."

"So, here I am. Here we are."

She looked out the window toward parked cars, then turned to see who else was in the restaurant. I felt like I was in a B-movie—the familiar look around, the secrecy.

We sat.

As soon as her eyes came back to rest on me, I spoke quietly.

"I wrote to DeWitt, begging him to intervene, stop the machine. What he wrote back sounded like something a machine would dictate. Authoritative, and aloof. Basically, he told me to mind my own business."

"What did you expect?"

"Recognition, to begin with. Recognition that the hospital has a past that matters. That patients have needs and rights. That failure to step in is tantamount to endorsing the wrongness of what's happening. I guess I was naive."

"So, you had to learn, firsthand for yourself, that he's part of the problem?"

"I suppose so. I did what I could. I tried to make the ethical case."

She waved toward the waitress for more coffee.

"Thank you, Henry. But I do not believe that making any kind of case matters any more, if it ever *did* matter."

"I see that now, yes."

"Well, then. I'm afraid the news does not get any better. Let me fill you in on the latest calamity."

"Please."

"Two days ago, we had a supervisors-level meeting with the superintendent and Walter Stiggins. Walter is the hospital budget director. He has been here forever. At the meeting, he reviewed the bottom lines of fiscal reports for the past five years. Each year a surplus, each year very little or no money coming from the state for operational expenses. Some state money for building the new butcher shop, but almost nothing in operating expenses, because of the continued success of the agricultural program and the revenue it has generated. Breeding and the sale of cattle was part of the revenue-generating picture, too. Virtually no labor costs, no mechanization costs, and so forth — all of which you know full well."

I was incensed. "How could DeWitt just sit there, confronted with the undeniable facts of self-sufficiency, and not be affected?"

"As I said, he is part of the problem."

"A political puppet, I'd say."

"That seems to be the case," she said. "But, to continue, Walter then shared a projected budget for the coming fiscal year, which starts in October. We end this year with a significant deficit. With no income from the farm operations, we have no revenue. The state is prepared to rescue us with an appropriation commensurate with money given to other institutions in the state."

"I can see what's coming," I said. "*Commensurate,* just the right word. Sounds like 'fair,' or 'appropriate' to the public ear. Whether it's adequate or not, that doesn't matter."

"Unfortunately *adequate,* like *commensurate,* is a word with many meanings in the current climate. How they use it is not the way we do. Especially where the economics of patient care are concerned. But, by now you understand how those economics affect patients."

"I do."

"Basically, we are not broke — yet. But given the outlook, we are forced to cut back."

"How? Where?"

"Personnel, unfortunately. Salaries are the biggest line item in the budget. Until now, our patient-staff ratio has been exemplary compared to other state mental institutions. We could always afford to put resources into patient care, where it mattered the most. But now, attendant staff are being given notice."

I was astonished beyond words. The single area most vital to supporting the mental health needs of patients would be the first to suffer.

I asked, "How do they decide who gets fired and who doesn't?"

"Civil service rules give priority to seniority. So, older staff will likely stay. We can expect that patient load will increase significantly, and that increase will reduce our ability to give the time and care as we have for so long. Staff with less seniority have already begun looking for other jobs. There will also be reductions in the professional staff—the doctors and nurses. They are more skilled and in demand, so finding other work will not be as difficult."

"I can't believe they would just acquiesce. I can't believe others would abandon everything they believe is vital for patients and leave, just like that! I think there should be a major revolution. I think all the staff should revolt; say, 'No, you can't do this!'"

"I know you feel that way," she said. "But most say that what's happening is just the natural evolution of change, and they feel they'll just have to make the most of it."

Of course, I had to agree with her about change. Some change *is* inevitable, and natural. But this one was fabricated and avoidable. In my mind, no change is justified when it originates in greed and results in human suffering.

I told her as much.

"It is easy for you to be disappointed," she said. "But you are different. You are not someone who has built a career here, who has a family that depends on your paycheck, who has lived in a culture that instills trust and respect for authority. Economic livelihood, families, cultural ways of being—those things carry more value than creating a stir and possibly losing one's job.

"For those who intend to leave, they, too, have families and careers to think about. If they are to find another job, they need a positive recommendation, and the superintendent has promised to provide one. That's just the way it is."

The realist in her challenged the idealist in me. It was not an argument I would pursue. By now it was all academic.

"What about you?" I asked.

"Oh, I don't plan to go anywhere. Whatever happens, I have to do what I can to maintain continuity—from what we have been to whatever we are to become. That is now my principal work. Increased demands on nurses are certain, and I must help them support the patients through this transition to the new era. I am more needed now than I have ever been. But permit me to tell you more."

I poured milk in my coffee.

"Ironically," she continued, "key services like building and grounds maintenance, motor pool, are adding people from the civil service rolls. They will replace patient workers. As you know, patients are no longer permitted to perform work that is within the purview of a civil service employee."

"So, what about those patients who need to be doing physical work? The ones for whom work is their *only* therapy?"

"Well, that remains to be seen. You see, we are not sure how the patients will handle all of this in the long run. So far, their reactions are not encouraging. To address this set of new issues, the occupational therapy and behavior therapy departments are hiring more staff to help offset a significant rise in behavior problems among the patients and between patients and staff."

"Have there been more suicides?"

"Just one so far. I think you know about that one?"

"I do."

"Fighting and bickering among patients has increased. Wandering off, stealing, and various forms of making life miserable for others—including staff—have increased. We will need more security on the grounds, too. The superintendent believes our main work now is to contain negative behavior."

"*Contain*? Did he really say *contain*? Is he blind? Can he not see that once you let the genie of genuine patient care out of the bottle, you can't just stuff it back in?"

The waitress arrived with a fresh pot of coffee and poured. We sat back in silence. Our eyes followed her as she moved to other tables.

"I know," Nancy said. "You cannot put the genie back in, but you can take away the genie's spirit. They *are* patients at an institution. They do understand who is in charge. Some will complain. Some will act out. Many are indifferent."

I shook my head from side to side. "They should be pouring money into recreation, occupations, and arts. They should be funding the building of human relationships, not security forces. They wouldn't need to increase security if they would just pay attention to what truly matters."

She scooped a spoonful of sugar from the bowl and stirred it into her coffee. "Of course, you are right."

"What if it were their *own* children, their *own* spouses? How would they want *them* treated? Has anyone ever asked that question?"

"I doubt that question would ever come up. Other than our governor and our superintendent, we don't even know who *they* are."

"True. We only know who they are *not*. They are not the

Nurse Brownells of the world, or the Dr. Spencers, the Mr. Harrisons. They are not Mr. Meyer, Eunice, Bernadine, or Jimmy."

"You're right, of course." She sighed, continued, "Unfortunately, there is more. At the meeting, Walter said the state budget shows no increase for mental health spending in the next fiscal year, and with the current party in control of both the executive branch and the legislature for the foreseeable future, he foresaw little change."

"What was DeWitt doing through all this?"

"He took notes. He seldom looked up. He had no questions. He knew what was coming. He gave a little speech about how surprised he was by the results of the inquiry—a lie—but he believes the time is ripe for some belt-tightening and if anyone needed to leave, he would give a good recommendation."

"He knew all right."

"I'm afraid so. But that changes nothing. Now we have to do what we can to make life work for our patient population, no matter what. They did nothing to deserve any of this."

She looked down at her wristwatch. "I must go. I have rounds at eleven. I expect I will be hearing from you at some point?"

"Maybe. I'm not sure."

"Call my office or my home. I'm there after eight most every evening."

"I will. Thank you. For everything."

"You get the thanks, Henry. For being the kind and courageous man you are. Bless you, stay well, and godspeed."

I drove to the nearest phone booth to put in a call to Clara and then my parents. I let them know I was fine and things were moving forward. No other news.

I called Mrs. Dorman but she wasn't in the office. The girl

who answered said she would be back after noon and could I call back then.

I decided to peek around the grounds again, this time in daylight when the population would be out and about. I pulled my Tigers cap down over my forehead and put on my sunglasses for anonymity. The Packard had air conditioning, so I could keep the windows rolled up.

I made one slow tour of the grounds before parking in a lot opposite Cottage 30, which housed male field workers. Last year at this time of day, the cottage would be empty; they would be out weeding acres of melon; delicately picking robust tomatoes drooping from long vines propped by wood stakes; or, in the orchards, thinning fruits with signs of insect puncture.

But today, men sat on the wide steps leading to the porch. Many donned their working garb, as if they were just waiting for the familiar call to get out to the fields. Some wore wide-brimmed hats that *used to* protect their faces from the hot summer sun, while others wore black boots that *used to* protect their feet from wet mud in the sculpted field trenches.

They were ready — and waiting.

Others, still in pajamas, sat in white rocking chairs on the porch, watching the street. One batted flies from his line of vision; two men rocked in unison, holding hands in the space between their chairs.

Around the corner from the rear of the building came a short fellow carrying a long tree limb curved at the bottom like a hockey stick. He shouted to the others sitting on the steps.

"C'mon. It's time!"

He repeated himself two or three times, shaking the limb over his head as if calling troops to action.

"Get up. It's time. It's okay now. Let's go!"

No one moved. A few looked at him expressionless. The one on the top of the stairs shouted back.

"Go on. Get outta here. We ain't going nowhere. Dumb ass."

Another spit at him. "You heard right. Go on, you dumb ass. They're not coming for us." A few others leaned forward to see who was down there, then resumed their silent vigil.

The man with the tree limb turned back and walked to a patch of grass. There he began a motion that looked to me like frantic hoeing. He beat on the ground hard enough to raise a plume of brown dust. Soon, he heaved the limb far toward the next cottage, then walked over to retrieve it. He picked up the limb and began smashing it on the ground. Soon all that was left was a short stump in his hands. He tossed that aside. He sat down in the grass and raised a middle finger toward the others on the porch.

I pulled away slowly. I remembered another cottage that housed women who were part of the farming operation. They did the lighter work in the fields, like weeding and picking fruit, and they also packed baskets for market. This was where Bernadine had lived.

I drove to Cottage 29, another three-story yellow-brick building on the edge of a cluster of women's cottages on that side of the campus. Jimmy had mentioned this one to me in a letter: it was the only one in the cluster with a large red spire that rose majestically from the roof. Jimmy called the spire "a big red rocket."

I parked on the street opposite Cottage 29. Two women on the porch swayed back and forth on white rocking chairs. I imagined Bernadine leaving from the front door of the cottage on a typical day, leading a troupe of ladies toward the meadows for a good day's work or toward the woods for birding. She would be singing one of her familiar songs, like "Whistle While You Work." In the warm weather, she was always leading some group somewhere.

From across the street came three pairs of women strolling in their summer dresses. Arm in arm they walked, guiding one another. No hurry in their gait. They crossed the street thirty yards or so in front of my car and turned my way. As they approached, the first pair pointed toward me and said something to the others. Then the whole parade stopped and stared at me sitting there in the Packard.

They stood there in silence for a good minute or so until the second pair broke loose and walked toward me. I knew I could not afford to be recognized. I pulled my hat down even farther as the taller of the two approached from the passenger side.

She knocked on the window and beckoned me with a wave. The shorter one stood back a few feet, arms akimbo.

I leaned across the seat and rolled down the window.

"Hi," I said.

"Mister, you from the goverment?"

"No, ma'am. I am not."

"'Cause if you're from the goverment you got no friends here and we don't want you here no more."

"No, ma'am. I'm not from the government. I promise you."

"'Cause if you're goverment we don't like you 'cause you're the one that took our work from us and you're the one don't want us farming."

She looked over her shoulder. "That right, Junie?"

From the other, "That's right, darlin' Jeanette darlin'. Tell him what for, I say."

"Ma'am…and ma'am. I swear I am not from the government. I'm just a visitor looking around."

"'Cause we got nothin' to do now. 'Cause we can't go to work no more. 'Cause the farm, it's gone, see?"

"I know. I'm very sorry to learn that. I'm sure you miss it."

"Yeah, mister, that is right."

"That's right and that's wrong, I say," the other one muttered from behind her.

She leaned her head down and looked straight into my eyes.

"We ain't gonna hurt you or anything, mister. We don't hurt strangers. Well, Imogene over there," she pulled a thumb toward another pair on the sidewalk, "*she* might, but that's because she's got a condition."

"Thank you. But I'm just a visitor. Not government."

She stood upright as Junie came over and looked in the window. "You got any cookies for Junie?"

"No. Sorry."

"Thank you kindly then."

And off the two went, arm in arm, resuming their stroll with the others. As the group passed, the one who must have been Imogene waved a fist at me. I rolled the window back up and started the car to get the AC running again.

I slammed both hands on the steering wheel.

"Damn it!"

Another knock at the window. A tiny woman carrying a doll in a blanket. I rolled it down again.

"You okay, sir?"

"Yes, I was just upset. I'm fine now."

She held the doll over her shoulder and began patting its pack, as if burping it. "I get upset sometimes, too. I cut my arms sometimes. And my feet. Then I go to the hospital and they put the leathers on me and give me pills to sleep. I never hit anything. *You* hit things. Baby tells me how to get along better. Right, baby?"

She took the doll from her shoulder and held it up to me. "Her name is Priscilla Amelia Petunia, but I just call her Amy. Or Baby."

"She's...she's very pretty. You have a lovely child."

"Thank you. I must be going now. It's time for Amy's nap. You feeling better now? I can get someone if you want."

"No," I said. "No, I'm fine now. You get Amy to bed. I'll be all right."

And she was gone. I started the ignition and pulled out onto Grey Drive.

From a phone booth outside Dill's Cafe, I called Mrs. Dorman. As soon as I said my name, she said, "Hold on," and muffled the receiver. I could hear her bark.

"Tina? You and Paulette get going now. And don't forget to bring back those requisition forms from Central."

Another few moments passed before she came back. "Sorry, I had to get them out of here."

"Good," I said. "I'm here now, in town. Since yesterday. Is everything ready?"

"Ready as a horny rooster in the hen house. Let me see. Here's what I got so far. The whole admission file. The release papers, signed by Mr. Dziewa in what looks impeccably close to his wrong-side-of-the-tracks Palmer Method scribble. I learned that word—impeccably—last Sunday in church. I been using it all week with the girls but they have no clue what I'm talkin' about, so they just say, 'Thank you, Mrs. Dorman' and 'I try hard, Mrs. Dorman.'"

I intervened. "Wonderful. I can't thank you enough."

"Well, my clever cherub, you don't need to start in on the thank you's yet. We got a ways to go with this, so let's not start counting our bingo money. Besides, there's this little problem come up."

"Problem?"

"It seems your friend there, the one you spoke to me about? The one whose name we won't actually say in case J. Edgar Hoover is listening through the floorboards? The friend we'll call *X*?"

"Okay, X."

"It seems X got himself in a pickle yesterday, and, well he's sort of detained, in a manner of talking."

"Detained. How?"

"It seems he got into a row with another fellow over something I don't know what but had to do with the other fellow calling him a dick or some such thing. Wait, dickhead, that was it. So, X laid into him with a wrestling hold. Dang near strangled the other fellow. The two of them went at it for a while until staff broke it up. Then X got loose of them that were holding him off and he grabbed the other fellow by the throat and tried to choke him with his bare hands. They got him off that time, too, and took him over to Building 33 to restrain him while he cooled off."

I slumped against the window of the phone booth. "Is he still there?"

"Apparently."

"How long can they keep him in restraints?"

"Wrong word. Not restraints. Isolation. He calmed down after they got him away from the dickhead shouter, so no restraints needed. Just isolation."

"Oh boy, do you know how long they'll keep him in isolation?"

"Long as they want, usually. But the docs came by to look him over this morning and they said he was okay. Just lost his temper. They said they'd keep him there till tonight, after dinner. Then he'll go back to his cottage. We hope. If he doesn't fly off the handle again."

"So, he'll be back in his cottage tonight?"

"Far as I know, depending. He doesn't know about you being here or anything about what's going to happen. Not yet. I was planning to tell him today and then all this bugamaroo came up. Now I gotta figure out how to tell him."

"Maybe I can talk with him."

"Now don't get stupid, lunkhead. You don't want to have *anybody* know you're around. In the end, all's they're gonna know is that his guilt-ridden cousin finally came round to fetch him to live with his family in Tennessee. I got the correspondence right here to prove it, written in my sister-in-law's crappy handwriting and sent from Bull's Gap, Tennessee, where she lives with her alcoholic boyfriend and her two brats. But she's a good woman and she's smart enough to lie through her teeth when the time comes. *If* the time comes, which it won't."

"You'll talk with him then? Get him ready?"

"You just leave all that to me, bubble. I didn't get the role of co-star in this movie based on my good looks. I got a working brain, and I got connections. You just lie low. Go catch some fish. Learn braille. Call me up here after nine tonight and we'll see if Operation X is on or not. And bring some identification."

"Identification. What for?"

"So you can prove to me that you're really his cousin. It will just so happen that I can't find my reading glasses anyway, so I'll more or less just take your word for it. After all, I'm just clerical. And clerical ain't a very bright group to begin with. Ask Mr. Dim Witt. Oh, forgive me, I mean *Superintendent* Dim Witt."

CHAPTER THIRTY-FIVE

Punctum Punctum

EARLY AFTERNOON, BACK AT THE HOTEL. I BOOKED ANOTHER night. It was the longest afternoon and evening of my life. Useless attempts to get some sleep. I went down to the lobby and called Clara. I told her how much I missed her. She said she was still afraid but loved me even more for acting on my principles. "Some things are just right," she said, "and some are just plain wrong." She apologized for putting her ring on the desk.

I said nothing about the "little problem" with Jimmy. That would just worry her. I would call her on the way back.

I couldn't walk around the town for fear of being recognized. I took some magazines from the lobby and sat in my room thumbing through *Popular Mechanics*, *Life*, and *Colliers*. After a couple of hours, I went down to watch television in the hotel lobby. Senator Joe McCarthy was on the *Nightly News Caravan* raging about communists infiltrating the U.S. Army. I thought he suffered from obsessive-compulsive disorder and I thought his hearings were nothing more than witch hunts, so I changed the channel. *My Little Margie* was cute, as always; *I've Got a Secret* had me guessing; and *Amos and Andy* amused as they bumbled their way through yet another disaster. If someone were to recognize me, I would make up a story about just passing through on my way somewhere else.

Around seven I went for a walk. I didn't intend to go to Brady's Tavern, but there it was on my left when I turned the corner off Lake Street at Union. I had another hour to kill. *Why not?* I thought.

I sat in the same spot the two loudmouths had sat in months ago — on the curve of the bar, toward the rear. The same bartender, towel dangling from his rear pocket, nodded to me. I ordered a Carlings, pulled my cap down, kept my head low.

I realized my mistake the instant I saw Daryl walk in. *Damn,* I thought. Blue jeans riding high on his waist, thick black belt, and white t-shirt, biceps bulging, hair slicked back in the duck's tail. He looked around slowly, checking each person out. I pulled my cap down lower until the brim nearly touched my beer glass.

Raised voice, he ordered a beer and sat on a stool down from me. The bartender put a Pabst in front of Daryl, pulled off the cap with an opener. No words passed between them.

I didn't look up, but I knew he was staring at me. I heard him stand and I heard the clink of his beer bottle against the bar top as he picked it up. Then I heard him walk toward me. I should have just picked up and left, and I don't know why I didn't. Something kept me there.

"I know you," he announced to our half of the room, standing ten feet away, beer bottle in hand, blocking my only exit to the front door. "Pull up your hat. Pull it up!" It was a menacing voice, full of challenge.

"Sit down and shut up," came the bartender. "Don't you go starting anything here. Leave that fellow alone."

Daryl put up a hand toward the bartender as if to say hold

on. He leaned his head down toward the bar and peaked up at my face under my visor. I did not move.

"Why, I'll be god-damned. If it ain't the shit-for-shinola college punk. How you doing there, shit-for-shinola?"

A woman's voice from the other side of the room, "Get outta here, you mean son of a bitch. You're always looking for trouble."

He ignored her, too. His eyes were trained on me.

"Look out there, buddy," came a male voice near her. "That guy will tear your head off." Then, "Leave him alone, Daryl. Just mind your own business, for once."

"Shut the hell up, Harry, you know what's good for you," Daryl shouted over his shoulder. "Me and this boy got some business to settle."

Then, to me, "You gonna talk to me, college boy, or you just gonna play dead?"

I removed my cap, stood up. I pulled the bar stool back to clear some space behind me.

"Oh-oh," he said. He took a few steps forward and stopped just beyond arm's length. He squared off, one fist doing little circles in front of his belt, the other clutching the beer bottle. "You forget how to talk to your elders, little shithead?"

The bartender picked up a phone and started dialing. I knew I had little time.

Punctum. Punctum. Permeo! Jab. Jab. Cross!

The two jabs hit him in the left eye and the cross caught him in the lower jaw, right side. The beer bottle flew off somewhere as his head flung backward. He took two steps back, a shocked look on his face. He came at me again, right arm cocked low to his chest, left shoulder dipped slightly as he prepared to let me have it. I let another quick jab go, this time in his right eye. The follow-up right cross hit the left side of his nose. Blood exploded from both nostrils. His head swung to the right. He slumped. His body thumped when it hit the wooden floor.

"Son of a bitch!" came the male voice. "Did you see that, Myrtle? You see how fast that guy is? A regular Rocky Marciano! Ho-ly shit!"

"Got what's coming to him!" said his lady friend. Others pushed their chairs backward and gazed at the victim writhing on the floor.

A round of applause went up.

Daryl rolled from side to side, blood gushing. "My fucking nose," he screamed. "You broke my fucking nose!"

I stood over him.

The bartender replaced the phone on the phone stand. Our eyes met. "You better hightail it out of here," he said. "I called the cops. Sorry, but I did."

He looked over the bar at Daryl squirming on the floor.

"Thanks for cleaning up the place," the bartender said. "You better clear out the back door," he added, pointing toward the bathrooms. "Over there, past the toilets."

The door locked behind me as I emerged into the cool of the evening. I started to walk back to my hotel. My right hand was a little sore, but otherwise I was fine. I felt pretty good, actually. I had never hit anyone without wearing gloves; hadn't hit anyone since high school, actually.

I figured Brother Benedict would be proud of me. All that Latin had finally paid off.

When I passed a liquor store, another thought occurred to me: Daryl would probably miss a day or so of work, then show up with a nose splint, or some kind of bandage, and some visible

bruises. The point was, he would be *back*. Along with his animosity, which would likely be intensified by his own lingering
discomfort, and which he would then take out on patients or
anyone who crossed his path.

I couldn't let that happen. I knew the state would not protect its asylum citizens from the likes of Daryl, but in the back
of my mind I thought somebody might do something if a
quart of whiskey was found in his locker. How I would get it
in there — *if* I would get it in there — remained to be figured
out.

Daryl has to go, I thought, as I forked over three dollars for a
fifth of Kessler's. On my way back to the Whiting Hotel, I took
a swig and poured out half the bottle into the gutter. I stopped
at the desk and asked for some plain white paper, an envelope,
and a postage stamp, "to write a letter," I told the clerk. I sat at
the little desk in my room and composed:

Dear Superintendent DeWitt:

*I write to tell you that one of your employees, a man
named Daryl, who works in the Recreation Department at
your hospital, has a serious problem with alcohol. I have it
on good faith from others that this man frequents Brady's
Tavern nearly every evening, where he drinks himself into
a stupor and brags about how he keeps whiskey in his work
locker. He is reported to have said that the only way he gets
through a day on the job is by drinking.*

*Although I do not frequent this establishment very often,
tonight I did, when my wife and I stopped in for a highball
and late supper. He was verbally abusive to the bartender
and to other customers. I personally witnessed his brash be-*

Richard VanDeWeghe

haviors when he started a drink-inspired brawl with an innocent bystander.

This man is an embarrassment to the Asylum and to all Civil Service workers. I know: I rose through the ranks of the Michigan Civil Service myself. The state would not tolerate for one second this behavior from any of its civil service members — were they to find out what I am informing you of here. I feel it my duty to report this man to you and I trust you will take appropriate actions. If you don't believe me, a search of his locker will confirm what I have said here.

He is a menace to Traverse City.

Sincerely,
A Concerned Citizen

CHAPTER THIRTY-SIX

Cousin, Twice Removed

NINE SHARP.

Mrs. Dorman answered on the first ring.

"Hello," I said, "I'm trying to reach a Mrs. Dorman. I'm calling about picking up a patient. Tonight."

Her voice was testy. "And who would you be?"

"I'm … the patient's cousin. From Kentucky."

"Hah! Gotcha! It's Tennessee!"

"Oh for God's sake, Mrs. Dorman. Please."

"Honey bunny, you got yourself all fiddle-footed. All's you need to do is take two aspirins and get yourself regular, so to speak."

I was still calming down from Daryl. I didn't mention him to her, not yet.

"What about the little problem?" I said. "With my … cousin."

"Little problem, little solution. I'll tell you all about it once you get here. Park in the visitors' space out front, just like any other relative would. Best to wait a while, though, until it gets darker. I'd say, just before ten. And bring your identification, Mr …. What was the name again?"

I hung up.

I paid my bill at the front desk, said I would be leaving early in the morning and wanted to clear up the tab now. I went down the back stairs with my things and out into the back lot where I'd parked the Packard. I sat there for a good half hour with the lights out and then drove over to the hospital. Lights were still on in most of the cottages but the walks were empty. Two attendants in white uniforms sat on a bench next to the laundry, smoking.

I drove slowly past the Security Building. Three cars were parked alongside. I turned the car into a space for visitors in front of Building 50. Lights were on here and there in the building, as third shift began their night's work. The blinds were pulled in the Office of Admissions and Records, but I could see lights on behind them.

It was ten-thirty when I knocked lightly on the glass-paneled door.

"Just a sec," came from the other side.

I waited.

The door opened half way. Her voice was elevated, loud enough so anyone working late down the hall could hear her.

"Why, you must be Mr. Collins? Come to fetch your relative? Sorry, I get so many people comin' and goin' from here, I can't possibly remember their first names. But you come on in here now and we'll get us started."

She closed the door behind me, whispered, "How was that, Boston Blackie?"

"You are amazing," I said.

"Yes, I am. Though this ain't exactly in my job description. Now then, let's get busy. Come over here to the ex-boss's desk. I got some papers for you."

She handed me a manila envelope. "There's not much but

it's all there. I got to leave a duplicate of the discharge paper here and some other papers, too. That's SP, standard procedure. Relatives just get the discharge. Here, sign both of these, Mr. Collins. Now, where *are* my reading glasses? I left them around here somewhere."

She shuffled around the office, moving papers and notebooks. Her glasses were lying on top of a pile of manila files on a side table, in plain view.

"Well, I'll find those later," she said. "Show me some identification so you can sign these papers and we'll get you and your cargo on your way."

She handed me a pen. I signed both of them as Donald W. Collins.

Charge #1, I thought to myself, *Criminal Fraud. Charge #2, Criminal Impersonation.*

She put the papers back into the envelope and slapped it on the desk. "Let's launch this ship," she said.

"Thank you."

"Now then, your friend was sent back to his cottage around six today. Doc said he's fine, just flew off the handle more or less. I brought the doc some carrot cupcakes I made this morning. Buttermilk frosting. They were my diversion. He was stuffing his face when I asked him would he sign off on Quinn's release, too. Said his cousin was getting impatient about hitting the road before dark. I had all the papers in order. I flipped to the last page and pointed to where he had to sign. Which he did."

I sighed with relief. "Good."

"All right. So I went over to see the cottage staff there, to tell them about him being discharged tonight. They don't give a hoot and a holler anywhoo, just one less body to look after.

That's third shift—bunch of lazy louts, in my opinion. Why, you won't believe what they did when one of the patients there had diarrhea one time watching TV. Right in the middle of the *Arthur Godfrey's Talent Scouts* he started letting loose...on the sofa!"

"Mrs. Dorman, please."

She pinched an index and third finger together and stretched them across her mouth. "Zipped shut," she said. "Just for you, Mr. Nervous Knickers."

"You were saying...you talked with them...about the plan?"

"I did and it's all set as far as that goes. I asked if Earl—he's third shift—would bring Jimmy over here once I call. Earl has no common sense and never passed second grade, so he won't put two and two together. Couldn't, in fact."

"And did you talk with Jimmy, too?"

"Just hold your horses, there, bucko. I'm getting to that part.

"I just want to get going."

"Well, you can't rush this sort of thing. Now, do you mind?"

"I'm sorry."

"All right, then. I went upstairs to his room and sat down there on a chair and talked real low to him about, about you coming here. He didn't say much except he didn't know you were coming to see him. I told him you're going to take him for a ride in a big fancy car. I told him you would have some important things to tell him once you two were on your way. I said you two might be gone for a couple of days so he should take his belongings—which don't amount to much anyway—put them all in a bag to bring with him."

"What did he say to all that?"

"Well, ever since, you know, Bernadine, he don't trust too many people. He trusts me, though. And his Mexican friend, what's-his-name. Anyway, he said he only had his suit and his good shoes to bring, and his underwear and pajamas. I told him to bring his toothbrush, just in case."

"How did he look?"

"Like his gas tank been siphoned dry. Didn't seem to care one way or the other what was going to happen to him. I don' t think he believed you were coming to see him, because he just settled back into a slump again. Pretty much what I've seen of him since Bernadine...you know. Course, half the patients are like that nowadays. Jimmy Quinn, though, that's not him, not him as how I've come to know him."

"He's been through a lot, again," I said.

"So, Mr. Whoever you might be," her voice lowered, her tone turned solemn. "It's a good thing you've come here. With his temper and his gloom, who knows what edge he'll step over? I'd be a liar if I didn't say he's a worry."

"Then let's get going."

She looked at her wristwatch. "Let's see, it's nearly eleven. I'm to call over to the cottage to let Earl know to bring him here. Should take fifteen minutes or so. He gets here. You take off. That simple. Oh, and I got this going away present for him."

She pointed to a corner of the room where a small black suitcase sat. It had seen its better days but it looked usable.

"Plucked that from my neighbor Mrs. Pryzinski's garage sale. Fifteen cents. Ain't much, but I can't let that boy leave here with all his worldly goods in a common paper sack. What would people say?"

She placed the suitcase next to me and made the call.

While we waited, I pulled the half-empty whiskey bottle out of my coat pocket and put it on the desk. From my shirt pocket,

I pulled out an envelope, removed a hand-written note from it, and handed both to her.

"What's this?" she asked. "A present?"

"It's another favor. Please, read the note."

She grabbed her glasses from their perch on the side table. She brought the paper closer to the desk lamp and read.

She put the paper down, pulled off her glasses, and squinted at me, one eye closed.

"You're a sneaky one, you are," she said.

"It is my obligation," I said. "It is justice. Now, can you think of some way that this bottle can find its way into his locker tonight? And can you get this note, written with my left hand, into Superintendent DeWitt's morning mail? I hope Mrs. Krueger won't notice that the letter is missing a postmark. I have a hunch Daryl won't be at work tomorrow, and I have another hunch that the superintendent will order the search before Daryl *does* return to work. At that time, he'll have to account for how he got all the bruises on his face, and how he broke his nose."

"Son of a beeswax," she said, a broad grin breaking across her face. "I think this bottle and this note can find their new homes this very evening." She put the note back in its envelope.

A knock at the door ended our conversation. Quickly, she put the bottle and the envelope in a drawer. I sat in a chair at the desk, my back to the door. She went out into the hall, where I heard her say, "Thank you, Earl. I'll take it from here. You best get back to your duties."

I heard a door down the hall close. Then her voice again.

"Why, hello, Mr. Quinn. How you doing tonight?" She used that unusually projected voice again.

"Not talkin' much? That's all right. I got your relative in here waiting to see you."

Jimmy followed her in as I rose and turned. He stood at the door, paper sack in his arms, eyes and mouth wide open. The sack fell to the floor as he opened his arms. I came over and put my arms around him. We hugged, weaving side to side like two twigs swaying in the wind.

"Jimmy, I said I would come back and here I am. I always keep my word. I always will."

He spun us around in circles, a whirligig of two old friends.

"Mr. Henry!" he said. "Mr. Henry! Mr. Henry! You came back just like you said. Came back to see me. And we're going on a vacation. Just me and you."

I stepped back. "That's right, Jimmy. Just you and me. On a vacation. We're going to have a good time. We're going to drive a long way. I'll tell you all about it."

"I've been real sad, Mr. Henry. I miss Bernadine. I got in a fight and then had to be in the room. I'm sorry I got in a fight."

"I know, Jimmy. No more fights though, okay?"

"No more fights. I promise."

He was crying and talking at the same time. Saliva ran from his mouth in small white bubbles and mixed with mucus dripping from his nose. I handed him my handkerchief.

"Now, then. Mrs. Dorman has something for you. For the trip."

She set the suitcase on the floor between him and me.

"That's for you, Jimmy. From me. For your vacation trip."

"Thank you," he said as he bent over and emptied his belongings into the suitcase. He stood, suitcase in hand. He told her he would tell her all about the vacation as soon as he got back.

She took the suitcase out of his hand and placed it on the floor next to him. Then she put her arms around him and squeezed.

"You have a safe trip, Jimmy. Don't you bug Mr. Henry too much, and don't you eat too much ice cream."

"I will not, Mrs. Dorman. I promise."

Then she stepped back and turned to me. She wrapped her arms around me and we hugged. In my ear, she whispered, "You take good care now. Travel safe. Send me a letter."

CHAPTER THIRTY-SEVEN

Ah-Dee-Ose

WHEN JIMMY SAW THE PACKARD, HE LET OUT A GIGGLE. "OH boy, oh boy, oh boy. That is some fancy car. Is that *your* car, Mr. Henry?"

"It is," I said, looking around in the dark. "Hop in. We need to get on the road."

We drove southeast toward Cadillac. I told Jimmy about my life back in Philly. He fiddled with the radio until he found a station that played music until it went off the air at midnight. Then he got sleepy and leaned against the window. Before long, he was snoring.

A few miles outside Cadillac—it must have been half past midnight—I saw the flashers in the rear-view mirror.

"Damn," I said out loud.

Jimmy woke up and looked out the back window.

"Oh oh. Police."

"Shit," I said. I pulled the car to the side of the road.

"Jimmy, this could be it. Now, I need you to do something."

"Okay."

"Don't talk. Don't say anything about the hospital. Just…be calm."

"Okay. No talking."

I reached into the glove box and pulled out a packet where

Dad kept the registration. I put that with my license on the seat between Jimmy and me.

In the side mirror, I saw the flashlight approach. I rolled down the window.

"Evening, officer. Is something wrong?"

He leaned down to look in. The light shined in my face and then on Jimmy.

"May I see your license and your registration?"

"Of course. I'm from out of state." I handed both to him.

"Pennsylvania?"

"Yes, sir. We're on our way home. From a vacation, up north."

He shined the light on Jimmy again.

"You're *both* on vacation?" he asked Jimmy.

Jimmy shielded his eyes with the crotch of his arm.

"Yeah, vacation," he said.

The officer peered in at him, then looked over my license and registration.

"It's my father's car," I said. "He let us use it. You can call him to double check if you need to. He'll..."

"No need," he said. Then he looked at Jimmy again.

Jimmy put his arm down. He looked straight into the light when he next spoke.

"Bway-nos dee-as bas-tar-do. Ah-mee-go. No com-pren-day. Mooy-bee-en. Ah-dee-ose. " Then, like an afterthought, he added, "Seen-yor-ee-ta."

The cop shined his light to the ground as he stepped back and looked at me.

"What did he say?"

"He's my cousin, officer. He's visiting the U. S...from Spain. He...he doesn't speak much English."

"I can see that." He shined his light on Jimmy again. Jimmy's smile traveled back up to him on the beam of light.

I held my breath.

"Ho-la," Jimmy said, and waved.

The officer returned my license and registration. Well, Mr…uh…"

"Mershartt. It's Dutch."

"All right. The problem is that you've got a tail light out. Left side."

I nearly fainted. Jimmy leaned over and into me and looked up at the officer. I put my hand on Jimmy's shoulder and nudged him back to his side.

"You'll have to get that fixed."

"I sure will, sir. First thing in the morning. We're staying the night in Cadillac."

"All right. No ticket, just a warning. There's a service station at the light in Cadillac. Opens early. They can help you."

I wanted to kiss him. "Thank you, officer. First thing in the morning. You can count on that."

"All right then. I'll follow you into town, just to be safe with that light out and all. There's a motel on your right. You can't miss it. They have a night clerk."

"Perfect," I said. "Thanks for your help. We really appreciate it."

I started the engine and looked over at Jimmy. He stared straight ahead, raised his eyebrows and then looked back at me, smiling.

"Mooch-as Graci-oos," he said.

It was late. I was tired. The cop's headlights shone through the rear window. But at that moment of release, in that instant of recognition, no words could capture my realization that Jimmy was much smarter than anyone had ever figured. Smart—and funny. Very funny.

When we got to Cadillac, I pulled into the Lakeside Motel and got a room with two singles. Jimmy came into the room and looked around.

"Is this our vacation place?" he asked.

"Not yet, Jimmy. This is just for the night. Let's get some sleep."

He dropped his suitcase next to the dresser and fell on top of the blankets. In minutes, he was snoring.

We would have the talk in the morning.

We had breakfast in a mom and pop restaurant with a view of Lake Cadillac. Jimmy had a big waffle with vanilla ice cream. I explained that the *vacation* could last for a long time, but only if he wanted it to. I told him that the hospital would never be the same, that he would never be on maintenance again. I tried to remind him why in terms that he would understand—that the rules for working had changed and that patients had to adjust to the new rules. I told him that some people would have a very hard time adjusting to the new rules and that he would probably be even more unhappy than he had been lately.

"I been real unhappy, Mr. Henry. So was Bernadine. That's why she, you know, flew like a swallow."

I told him that I wanted him to come with me to Philadelphia. He would live there by me and he would be able to have a job.

"A job?"

"One that you get paid for."

"Paid?"

"With a uniform."

"A uniform?"

"And tools."

"I'm gonna have my own tools?"

"And your own toolbox."

"The kind I can carry around? The wood kind with a handle?"

"Whatever you want, Jimmy. My dad says he'll make it for you in his workshop."

"Your dad, he's got a workshop?"

"Yes, he does. In fact, he said you can use his workshop all you want. Any time you want. It's right in the garage behind the house where you'll be living, for a while."

"I'm gonna live in a house, Mr. Henry? Like Gram's house?"

"Well, maybe. I don't know what your Gram's house was like, but this is a real nice house, too. My mother and my dad live there. That's where your first job will be. Dad has lots of maintenance work for you to do, and the neighbors do, too. Dad says he'll help you start a business fixing things in the neighborhood."

"Mr. Jimmy Fixerup! Oh, Mr. Henry. This is the best vacation!"

"But it's your choice, Jimmy," I said. "You can choose, right now, to go back to the hospital. I'll take you right back if that's what you want."

His eyes started blinking as if in a nervous twitch. "I want to go with *you*, Mr. Henry. Brothers stick together. I don't like that hospital any more. I miss Bernadine. I like Mrs. Dorman, and I like Francisco. I'm gonna miss Francisco. He's my other best friend. But I don't like that hospital anymore."

"All right, then," I said. "I can't promise you that everything is going to be perfect, but I can promise you that my parents will love you and take good care of you. My family is eager to meet you. In fact, I have a cousin, her name is Ethel—she's very pretty, very smart, and real sweet. I'll introduce you to her and my aunt and uncle, too. They'll all like you."

Jimmy started clapping his hands and stomping his feet on the floor mat.

"Oh boy, oh boy, oh boy!"

"I can promise that your life will be a good life. That I'll always be your brother, even after I get married."

"You gonna marry your sweetheart Clara?"

"I am. Some day soon, I hope."

"Can I come to see you get married?"

"Of course, you can. In fact, you can be my best man."

"Best man?"

"That means you get to stand by me at the wedding ceremony."

"Best man? I'm gonna be the best man? You always been the best man, but now I'm gonna be the best man! Whoopee!"

We had the broken tail light fixed and went on our way.

By early afternoon, we had crossed the Ohio state line west of Toledo. We headed east.

Charge #3: Kidnapping in the First Degree.

Six hours later, we crossed the Pennsylvania state line:

Charge #4: Interstate Flight to Avoid Prosecution.

I looked over at Jimmy as we passed by the "Welcome to Pennsylvania" sign. Jimmy gazed out at the fields.

"You're the *best* best man," he said.

Additional Reading

For readers who may be curious about the history of the hospital generally, the following resources were invaluable to me in my research for this first book in the series:

Decker, William A., M. D. *Northern Michigan Asylum: A History of the Traverse City State Hospital.* Traverse City: Arbutus Press, 2010. This is the most comprehensive history of the state hospital available and the best biographical account of Dr. James Decker Munson, the founder of and first medical superintendent at the Traverse City State Hospital.

Items Ingested by Patients of the Traverse City State Hospital. Photographs of "objects swallowed by one [unnamed] female patient who lived in the State Hospital during the 1940's and 1950's." Available at the Local History Collection, Traverse City Area District Library (Images 0563 and 1560).

Johnson, Heidi. *Angels in the Architecture: A Photographic Elegy to an American Asylum.* Detroit: Wayne State University Press, 2001. Historical photographs, 1885- 2000, provide a visual history of the Traverse City State Hospital.

Steele, Earle and Kristen M. Hains. *Beauty is Therapy: Memories of the Traverse City State Hospital.* Traverse City: Denali and Co., 2001. The story of the state hospital as revealed through letters sent by Earle Steele to his granddaughter, Kristen M. Hains. Mr. Steele's career as gardener, grounds supervisor, and museum curator spanned sixty-six years.

Ross, Hugh A. "Hospitalization of the Voluntary Mental Patient." *Michigan Law Review.* Vol. 53, No. 3 (Jan. 1955), 353-392. Argues the case for legislation governing voluntary admission procedures to state hospitals. I found the discussion of the "Rights of the Mentally Ill Patient" helpful in that chapter in the novel where patient rights are enumerated.

Acknowledgements

FIRST THANKS GO TO MY WIFE AND BEST FRIEND, JUDY VanDeWeghe, who read so many (and so very messy) drafts of this novel; she thoughtfully offered insightful suggestions and encouragement every step of the way.

Much gratitude extends to friends and colleagues who read and critiqued various drafts over the years, who asked probing questions that kept me looking and relooking at what the story might ultimately become, and who gave good advice.

The Special Collections Librarians at the Traverse Area District Library have been very helpful in locating resources and photographs in the historical archives.

Finally, thanks also to the wonderful people at Deeds Publishing for the enthusiasm and professionalism they have shown through the publication process.

About the Author

RICHARD VANDEWEGHE IS PROFESSOR EMERITUS OF ENGLISH
from the University of Colorado, Denver. In his non-fiction book, *Engaged Learning*, he examined learning from both neurological and humanistic perspectives. He lives in Traverse City, Michigan, in what was the Men's Infirmary at the old Traverse City State Hospital. The hospital buildings and grounds are being restored by The Minervini Group in one of the largest historic preservation and redevelopment projects in the country. Tours of the asylum grounds are available daily.

In keeping with Dr. Munson's philosophy of beauty, nature, and work as therapy, the hospital farm has been repurposed as a public park, with a botanic garden, community garden, small farm, and event venue in the restored Cathedral Barn. The Botanic Garden also offers daily tours.

Jimmy Quinn is the first novel in the Traverse City State Hospital Series.

Photo courtesy of Kate Matwychuk

CPSIA information can be obtained
at www.ICGtesting.com
Printed in the USA
BVHW081048020119
536775BV00001B/28/P

9 781947 309296